Sacred Playgrounds

Sacred Playgrounds

Christian Summer Camp in Theological Perspective

Jacob Sorenson

CASCADE *Books* · Eugene, Oregon

SACRED PLAYGROUNDS
Christian Summer Camp in Theological Perspective

Copyright © 2021 Jacob Sorenson. All rights reserved. Except for brief quotations in critical publications or reviews, no part of this book may be reproduced in any manner without prior written permission from the publisher. Write: Permissions, Wipf and Stock Publishers, 199 W. 8th Ave., Suite 3, Eugene, OR 97401.

Cascade Books
An Imprint of Wipf and Stock Publishers
199 W. 8th Ave., Suite 3
Eugene, OR 97401

www.wipfandstock.com

PAPERBACK ISBN: 978-1-5326-9462-2
HARDCOVER ISBN: 978-1-5326-9463-9
EBOOK ISBN: 978-1-5326-9464-6

Cataloguing-in-Publication data:

Names: Sorenson, Jacob, author.

Title: Sacred playgrounds : Christian summer camp in theological perspective / by Jacob Sorenson.

Description: Eugene, OR : Cascade Books, 2021 | Includes bibliographical references and index.

Identifiers: ISBN 978-1-5326-9462-2 (paperback) | ISBN 978-1-5326-9463-9 (hardcover) | ISBN 978-1-5326-9464-6 (ebook)

Subjects: LCSH: Christian camps. | Christian education, Outdoor. | Wilderness survival. | Christian education of young people.

Classification: BV1587 .S67 2021 (print) | BV1587 .S67 (ebook)

06/29/21

Scripture quotations, unless otherwise indicated, are from the New Revised Standard Version of the Bible, copyright © 1989, by the Division of Christian Education of the National Council of Churches of Christ in the United States of America.

To Anna:

My Bible camp sweetheart, faithful partner, and fellow worker in the kingdom of God. I am thankful to be on this journey with you.

And in memory of Jerry Manlove.

Contents

Acknowledgments | ix

Part 1: **Welcome to Camp** | 1
1. An Invitation to Play | 5
2. The Camp Story | 18
3. Toward a New Understanding of Summer Camp | 44

Part 2: **The Fundamentals of Christian Summer Camp** | 63
4. A New Perspective: Camp Is Unplugged from Home | 67
5. Taking the Leap: Camp Is Participatory | 85
6. Faith at the Center: Camp Is Church, Too | 104
7. The Face of the Other: Camp Is Relational | 121
8. On Belay: Camp Is a Safe Space | 139
9. Taking Us Home | 159

Appendix A: Self-Evaluation for Camp Directors and Full-Time Staff | 181

Bibliography | 187

Index | 195

Acknowledgments

This project is a labor of love borne out over years of learning, listening, and interacting with countless people who have supported me through the journey. The stories I share are only a small sample of the wisdom I have gained from the many campers, summer staff members, and directors who walked with me in the mud and the sun. Their voices speak through this project. I want to especially acknowledge Brian and Aric, the Sugar Creek Bible Camp counselors who mentored me in my childhood camping experiences and started me on this path. My colleagues in camping ministry have offered words of wisdom and advice through the years that echo in these pages, and there are those among them whose words could express better than mine the value of this ministry, if only their schedules allowed them to sit still long enough. I owe special thanks to my mentors, Joel Abenth and Dick Iverson, two of the church's most faithful ministers, who repeatedly hired me as a camp staff member, instilled in me the values of camping ministry, and have continued supporting me throughout my work on this project.

Research is not possible without generous people who catch the vision and commit their financial resources. Special thanks to my friends at Lilly Endowment, Inc. for their generous support of The Confirmation Project and the Camp2Congregation Project. Thanks to Siebert Lutheran Foundation, Gronlund-Sayther-Brunkow Consulting Services, and numerous individuals for funding the initial phases of the Effective Camp Research Project. Thank you to the thirty-seven camps that have participated in the Effective Camp Project and Power of Camp Study through 2020. Camp directors and individuals contributed personal money to get the initial research projects off the ground and fund the research at their camps.

I was privileged to participate with a tremendous group of scholars on The Confirmation Project, and their support helped make this project possible. Thank you to Richard Osmer, Katherine Douglass, Kenda Dean, Lisa Kimball, Terri Elton, Reginald Blount, and Gordon Mikoski, who believed that camping ministry deserved a place in scholarly discussions and gave me the opportunity to demonstrate it.

Thank you to the research team that has supported my efforts along the way and has helped gather, compile, and analyze tremendous amounts of data over the past several years. Special thanks to my coworker, Amber Hill Anderson, for her dedication to research on camping ministry and the tremendous contributions she has made to numerous research projects over the years. Rollie Martinson has been a consistent supporter and continues to sharpen my research. My friend and Effective Camp Project cofounder Paul Hill helped me discern the path of scholarship while I was still working at camp, and he has been a steadfast advocate for research on camping ministry, even when others were dismissive.

Thank you to all those who read early chapters of this book and provided feedback that helped sharpen my arguments and writing. In addition to some already named above, these conversation partners include: Andrew Root, Brian Frick, Rich Melheim, Mark Burkhardt, and Rob Ribbe.

Finally, I want to thank my family. They have been incredibly supportive through this long process, and they are the ones who have kept me grounded. Thank you to my parents for always being there to support me, for taking me to church even when I would rather not go, and for sending me to camp. Huge thanks to my brother, Sam Sorenson, who not only taught me the Superman grace when he returned from camp all those years ago, but also read through this entire manuscript and provided invaluable feedback. He is an excellent writer and awesome storyteller who makes my writing better. Thank you to my two amazing boys, Elijah and Nathanael, who have constantly reminded me of the importance of play, brought me back to camp as a camper parent, and have kept me smiling through this journey. I remember the value of the playground because of you. The greatest thanks of all goes to my wife, Anna. She always takes time to read my work, offer valuable feedback, and sharpen my ideas. She keeps working and supporting our family while I play at camps across the country and around the world. She is a wonderful minister, a great scholar, and an amazing partner. Thank you.

Part 1: **Welcome to Camp**

We rounded the first corner of the island and felt the wind buffet the side of the canoe. I chanced a look around and saw the disaster that was befalling our group. We were only a few hundred yards from the beach, but the dozen canoes were scattered in disarray. We were supposed to stay close together. That was the plan: stay close together, stay close to the shore, paddle around the island. It will be fun, they assured us. Ben and I were determined to stay on course and complete the circuit. Our counselor, Brian, sat in the middle of our canoe with a rescue tube across his lap. He was the lifeguard. He never said aloud that we were the best canoeists because he did not want the others to feel bad, but everyone knew that the lifeguard had to be in the fastest canoe.

"Hey, are they supposed to be going that way?" Ben asked.

I looked around and spotted the wayward canoe. It was drifting farther and farther away from shore. The two girls were fumbling awkwardly with their paddles, and they were laughing. Laughing! They clearly did not understand their peril. We were on the Mighty Mississippi River, and the current might draw them far downstream, capsize them, or deposit them in the mythical land known as *Iowa*.

"Let's go get them," Brian said.

Ben and I gave each other a meaningful look. It was up to us. This is where our forty-five minute canoe orientation would pay off. We pulled with all our might, straining our developing eighth-grade muscles to the max, and set an arrow-straight course to the floundering vessel. We both saw the river buoy as we passed it, knowing that we had just crossed into the main channel of the Mississippi River. As we approached the other canoe, Brian calmly gave instructions to the girls. They tried to obey, and they managed to get their canoe turning in circles, laughing the whole time.

"Barge!" we heard someone yell from shore. "BARGE!"

I looked up and saw it rounding the nearest bend in the river, heading downstream straight toward us. Our camp counselors had warned us about river barges. They were enormous, cargo-hauling flat boats, 200 feet long and churning up a huge wake that would capsize canoes and create a tremendous undertow. They could not stop or swerve to avoid you. If we encountered a barge while canoeing, we were to quickly get to shore. Barges were the precise reason we were supposed to stay close to shore in our trip around the island that morning.

Brian acted quickly. He reached out and pulled the girls' canoe toward ours, clamping them together with his powerful man-hands. He looked at me with utmost confidence. "Okay, let's get to shore."

Upstream, into the wind, pulling two canoes with five people, with certain death churning inexorably nearer, Ben and I paddled for shore. We reached a rocky outcropping and disembarked into knee-deep water, exhausted but exhilarated. "Good job, guys," Brian said to us meaningfully, as the giant river barge slipped past at a safe distance.

The girls were no longer laughing. "You saved our lives," they said in awe.

Ben and I looked at each other and nodded. We had just met three days ago and become fast friends. Now, we were brothers. We waded through the water in dramatic slow motion. The rest of our beleaguered group came into view as we rounded a bend in the island, and a cheer broke out. We were heroes.

We never made it around the island that day. After the morning's excitement, our counselors opted for a more relaxed day of games, Bible study, and conversation on the beach. Our evening campfire that night was emotional and powerful. Our four counselors led an interactive worship service that included a skit about Jesus' teachings and some of our favorite songs from the week. During the prayers, one of the girls from the rescued canoe thanked God for keeping her safe that day by sending Ben and me to save her. I went to the tent that night wide awake with thoughts from the day's events. It was our second and final night on the island. In the morning, we would pack up and canoe the short distance to the mainland before being driven back to camp. There, we would rejoin the rest of the camper groups for some unnamed large-group activities.

Ben and I shared a tent with Jon, another eighth-grade boy we had befriended that week. None of us were tired, so we talked. After our harrowing experience on the river, our conversation quickly turned to the topic of death and specifically what happens when you die. The next question came up naturally, as if it were a topic we discussed all the time. The truth is that in thirteen years of church and Sunday school, nobody had ever asked me that question. Ben asked it:

"Do you really believe in God?"

The funny thing is that I have almost no recollection of the conversation beyond that point. What I remember is that we talked about God, faith, and doubt into the wee hours of the morning. There, in a small tent on an island in the middle of the Mississippi River, three cocky eighth-grade boys shared their faith and fears with one another. For the first time in my life, I had an open and honest conversation about who I am in relation to God.

Brian was in the tent next to ours. It occurred to me years later that he must have been listening. He knew that we were awake past curfew. In fact, we were probably keeping other people awake. But he did not tell us to be quiet or speak up to correct our juvenile theology, which was probably well into the realm of heresy. He was our guide that week. He did not orchestrate the damsels in distress that day or call the barge to appear at the precise moment. He merely guided us along the way, giving us space to succeed and helping us interpret our lives' events through theological and biblical lenses.

Looking back more than twenty-five years later, I consider that night's conversation to be a turning point in my life that directed me on a path of discipleship and professional ministry. It was in the middle of my first camp experience. That specific community in that specific context provided space for the Holy Spirit to move in a way that I was able to recognize and articulate. I am not sure how that evening's conversation affected Jon or Ben, neither of whom I have seen since our camp experience ended two days later. I also wondered where the Spirit led Brian after his time at camp. As I was finalizing the manuscript for this book, I finally did something that I had been meaning to do for years: I tracked down Brian and sent him a message. I told him about where the Lord had taken me and thanked him for his role in guiding me all those years ago. He wrote back a few days later, saying that he remembered that week we spent together at Sugar Creek and has used stories from that week as sermon illustrations. Maybe it should not surprise me that he is a pastor now.

Stories can be powerful. They can also be misleading. More than 2 million young people attend Christian camps in the United States each summer, but not everybody has a life-impacting experience like mine. My story does not prove the power of the camp experience, but it changed my life. This book delves deeply into the Christian camp experience to discover why stories like mine are so common and why other camp participants do not have such positive experiences. First, we will welcome you into the camp experience and orient you to what camp is and what it is not. We will venture through generations of tradition, and we will also view camping ministry through a new lens of emerging research. If you are new to camp, I hope and pray that you find a place of welcome through these pages. If you are a camp veteran, I hope the stories here come alongside your own in powerfully evocative ways.

1

An Invitation to Play

Camp Changes Lives

We are here because camp changes lives. This conviction begins, of course, with my personal camp experiences, and I will continually reference these experiences in the pages that follow. I have been deeply impacted as a summer camp participant, a camp counselor, and a camp director. I have also walked alongside campers and staff members during their impactful and even life-changing experiences at camp. I am privileged to share many of these stories in the pages that follow. But we have to rely on more than just anecdotes. There is a wealth of empirical data that we are just beginning to uncover.

The turn to scholarship and research was a difficult one for me to make. Many of my camping colleagues were dumbfounded by my decision to pursue a PhD degree. I was on the front lines of an incredibly vibrant ministry, interacting with hundreds of young people and adults throughout the year and having a direct impact on individuals, families, and congregations. Why was I exchanging people for books, ministry for theology? There were similar reactions from my colleagues in academia, who were surprised at the idea that summer camp could be a legitimate area of scholarly inquiry. In the ensuing years, I have worked to keep a foot in both circles, always coming back to the practical realities and complexities of camp as I continue with scholarly research and writing. The simple reality is that I would much rather have a guitar in hand than a computer, and I would rather be discussing faith and life with seventh-graders than running statistical analyses. So I keep going back to camp. Each time I do, I learn something new. I invite you to join me.

When my research team first began what came to be known as the Effective Camp Project, we did not know what we would find. We had all been impacted by personal camp experiences in various ways, but we had no idea if a scholarly look at summer camp would show that camp made a substantial difference in the lives of the primary participants, their families, and congregations. We were prepared to discover that camp was only particularly impactful for a few or that outcomes did not tend to last. The major finding of the study was overwhelmingly clear: "The Christian summer camp experience directly impacted the participants in empirically recognizable ways, and these impacts extended to their supporting networks."[1] The subsequent studies of thousands of Christian campers at dozens of camps across North America have revealed that camp experiences have statistically significant impacts on multiple measurements of faith formation, along with more general camp outcomes, such as self-confidence. There is also ample evidence that these outcomes do not constitute a simple *camp high* that fades immediately after the euphoria wears off. We have measured significant outcomes that are maintained at least three months after campers return home.[2] Other studies have demonstrated that outcomes remain significant at least six months after camp.[3] There is even empirical evidence that religious camp experiences show significant positive impacts on participants at least *five years later*, especially related to communal religious practices and identification with particular faith communities.[4]

It turns out that our team's remarkable stories of how camp personally impacted us are remarkably common. As I sit here writing, I have access to data from more than 7,000 Christian summer campers, 4,000 camper parents, and 1,000 summer staff members. It is true that not everyone has an incredible, life-changing experience at camp, and we will explore why this is the case in the coming pages. We will also identify the key characteristics that, when in place, give rise to an effective, life-impacting camp experience. As we begin, let us consider a few numbers. More than 97 percent of summer campers and summer staff members have positive experiences at camp (that is, they have *fun*). This means that a small number have somewhat negative experiences, and we will explore how and why this happens.

Fun is one thing, but impact is something different, and the easiest way to get at impact is to ask the parents. In the weeks following camp, more than 90 percent of camper parents we surveyed agreed that camp clearly impacted their child. This is an incredible number and shows the far-reaching benefits of camp experiences, even when impacts are subtle. The impacts identified range from simple things like the child being nicer

1. Sorenson et al., "Effective Camp Research Project," 2.
2. Sorenson, "Fundamental Characteristics."
3. Thurber et al., "Youth Development Outcomes," 241–54.
4. Sorenson, "Summer Camp Experience," 28–29.

to family members or having a more positive outlook on life, to dramatic increases in faith commitment or what some describe as transformation. To get a better sense of how many campers have these more substantial impacts, we see that over a quarter of all parents identify what they call *significant changes* in their child following the camp experience. Drilling down a little deeper into specific impacts, we find that more than two-thirds of Christian summer campers in our surveys show clear growth in faith commitment, along with at least that many showing growth in self-confidence. When it comes to life-changing or transformational experiences akin to my own camp story, our best estimate is that about 5 percent of participants experience this level of impact. For the staff members who serve at camp for the entire summer, the numbers of significant and life-changing impacts are even higher, with consistently over 90 percent of summer staff indicating that the experience had a significant impact on their lives.

These quick numbers give us a better sense of what we are talking about in terms of camp experiences and impacts. Almost everyone has fun, the vast majority are impacted in positive, lasting ways, and as many as one out of every twenty campers has a personally transformative experience. Congregations are impacted by increased participation and engagement of young people, not to mention the thousands of campers and staff members who discover their vocational calling to professional ministry. Families are impacted by having more positive interactions with each other, more frequent faith conversations in the home, and increased family faith practices. The data are overwhelmingly clear that camp changes lives. We will explore how this happens so that camp leaders can make camp better for participants and so that parents, scholars, and church leaders can come alongside, learn from, and supplement these ministries.

Orientation: The Playground

As I try to keep one foot in the camping world and another in the academy, I invite friends from both of these playgrounds to join me. Camp friends, join me in a hike through the halls of learning and academic rigor. Wipe your feet at the door, but please come as you are. Colleagues in academia, join me in a literal field, one of study and of play. You may get your feet dirty, but you are sure to learn something along the way. Like children who have briefly evaded the watchful eyes of our parents, let us play together. And to the parents who are watching over our shoulders, I hope that you find in these pages affirmation of your decision to send your children to summer camp and practical steps for how you might help extend the impacts of the experience for a lifetime.

I am blessed to be a parent, as well. My youngest son always had an uncanny ability to spot a playground. He would be dozing off in the backseat of the car as we drove sixty miles per hour down the highway, and he would suddenly blurt out, "Look, a playground!" It might be a giant jungle gym near the side of the road or a single rusty slide in an overgrown field on the horizon. If it was there, he would find it, and he would want to stop and play. He knew that it was a place set aside for him. It was not one of those boring places to which mom and dad dragged him along. We would not stop at every playground we passed, but when we did, it was always fun to watch him play. He would find some stranger who happened to be there and ask that beautiful question of invitation, "Do you want to play together?" If there was no one else present, he would settle for his older brother or for me, but he has always had a clear understanding of what to do at a playground. It is a place to play with others.

We can think of play as an unstructured, joyful encounter in which relationship is fostered and creativity is encouraged. The unstructured nature of play means that it is open to possibilities; the outcome is not predetermined. This aspect of play makes it an essential element of education and discovery. We will look more closely at educational theory as we go forward and how the concept of play is central to learning. As people play together, they develop a deeper understanding of one another and can learn from each other new possibilities. Watching one child play is joyful. Watching children play together involves new depths of creativity and negotiation as each adds imaginative layers, leading to new discoveries and scenarios. Consider this scene that I witnessed involving a simple puddle on the edge of a playground. One child played there by himself, experimenting with floating leaves, which became sailboats on a small pond as he gently blew them to the other side. A few other children noticed the boy by the puddle and abandoned the expensive playground equipment to join in. Soon, the puddle was a castle moat filled with alligators, which one group had to cross in order to rescue the captives on the other side.

People never lose their longing for a playground. The apparatus simply changes. Consider the way that some adult eyes light up at the sight of a golf course, a concert stage, or an unfurled sail on the open water. Some of my colleagues and I may even get excited at the sight of the stacks in the Princeton library. Others make a laboratory their playground, where their creativity and ingenuity uncover cures for terrible diseases and improved methods to feed the world. Playgrounds look different, but we never outgrow them. Our invitation today is not to climb onto a particular apparatus but rather to find a space where we can play together. At the heart of our longing for a playground is the deep-seated human desire to be in relationship. This is part of what fundamentally makes us human, and it is an outpouring of the divine relationship.

What Is Camp?

Camp is not defined by apparatus. The word "camp" is used colloquially to mean many things. Some people immediately picture A-frame tents and insects crawling across their arms. Others use the word to characterize every youth program that lasts at least an hour. My kids go to the local YMCA every Thursday afternoon for a month, and the organizers call it *Basketball Camp*. Still others conjure images from popular movies like *Meatballs*, *Wet Hot American Summer*, or even *Friday the 13th*. If the oversexed teenagers and masked serial killers did not scare them off, they may have seen the 2006 Oscar-nominated documentary *Jesus Camp*, which portrays a Christian summer camp that is manipulative and theologically problematic, at best. Those who only view camp from afar or through a distorted lens run the risk of conflating the multitude of meanings of the word. Conversely, those who only view camp from deep embeddedness in a specific location run the risk of making their understanding normative. They tend to see camp in terms of the apparatus. The reality is that not all camps have tents or high-ropes courses. Not all camps have campfires and S'mores. Not all camps end with a cry-fest on the last night or an altar call where kids are encouraged to give their lives to Jesus. It is time to leave behind the assumptions and stereotypes.

We need to move past anecdotes in order to accomplish this. Isolated stories are not enough, especially when the word *camp* is so often misunderstood and misused. The American Camp Association (ACA) sets the national standards for camps in the United States, and they have become the leading body for research on camping in recent years. They divide their camping membership into three major streams: private camps (these are both for-profit and non-profit), agency camps, and religiously affiliated camps. Chapter 2 will trace the development of these three streams, as well as the emergence of ACA. ACA publications offer a helpful starting place for a definition of camp, something called "the essential trinity of organized camp: 1) community living; 2) away from home; 3) in an outdoor, recreational setting."[5] I have always found this succinct definition helpful for understanding the camping industry as a whole. ACA has done a

---

5. Thurber et al., "Youth Development Outcomes," 242.

tremendous job in recent years of promoting research on the outcomes of camp experiences. Their findings are important as we consider the benefits and characteristics of Christian camping because Christian camps prioritize many of the same things as secular camps, including the essential trinity of organized camp. But in Christian camping, we add another Trinity to the mix, and it is through the lens of faith in the Triune God that we interpret the camp experience.

We can turn to Christian camping expert Lloyd Mattson for a more distinctly Christian perspective on camping ministry. He writes, "Christian camping is a group experience for an extended time in an outdoor setting under trained leadership with spiritual objectives."[6] This is a very appropriate, if a bit technical, description of camping ministry based on some of the key characteristics, and this book will certainly affirm Mattson's definition. We will also lift up some different emphases based on the perspectives of those who are most directly impacted by camping ministry.

There has been comparatively little research focused specifically on Christian camping, but this is beginning to change. We have the chance to look deeply at some of the recent scholarship on the characteristics and benefits of Christian camping ministries. We do not seek a positivist or deterministic approach that will tell us the one thing that camp is. Neither do we seek to prove that camp is more effective or de facto better than other forms of ministry. Our journey will help us come to a working definition of Christian camping and an understanding of some of the forces at work in the camp model. I propose the following definition:

Camp is a set-apart space that facilitates relational encounter between the self, the other, and God.

I say that camp is a *space* because it has physical boundaries. It is not a concept or an idea but rather a unique physical location. These boundaries mean that it is *set apart* from the places that are recognizably not camp. The set-apartness facilitates an awareness of similarities and contrasts with what is left behind. *Relational encounter* is essential to the camp experience. I say *encounter* because these relationships are not mediated by technology, and they do not involve passing interaction, like two people waving from a distance or brushing past one another on the sidewalk. They involve physical presence and being brought up short by the other. I use the word *facilitates* because the encounters are not forced. Rather, the set-apart space intentionally provides opportunities for relational encounter. The space is not the cause but rather the occasion. These relational encounters are threefold. They necessarily include the *other*. Camps are

---

6. Mattson, *Christian Camping Today*, 16.

places where real people interact and run up against the reality of other unique human beings. This relational encounter with the other facilitates a deeper encounter with the *self*. As we will see in the coming pages, the self only exists in relationship to others. The set-apart space of camp also facilitates relational encounter with *God* through the concrete presence of the living Christ and the creative movement of the Holy Spirit. This happens in multiple ways but most clearly through person-to-person encounter. God in Christ is present in the midst of these encounters. The use of Christian practices and exposure to the natural world also facilitate an awareness of God's presence in the set-apart space of camp, and this increased awareness is often experienced as encounter.

Notice that we are not defining camp by its program or specific setting. There is a spirited debate among camping professionals as to what qualifies as camp. Most of the controversy centers on how much a camp uses the outdoors. Even Richard Louv's bestselling *Last Child in the Woods*, which desperately seeks to get children outdoors, mostly critiques camps as not focused enough on nature.[7] Most camps are excellent spaces for people to interact with the natural world, but reducing our understanding of camp to this aspect will get us lost in the weeds.[8] There are some purists who essentially believe that any permanent structure marks the difference between a camp and a resort. They may allow these approximations to be called camps, but they want to include an asterisk. Others are willing to embrace cabins as long as they are rustic enough. They might allow electricity and even indoor plumbing but draw the line at air conditioning. These folks have evidently never been to Texas in July! Two camps might be situated on beautiful lakefronts, but one will claim the superior experience because that lake only allows canoes and sailboats, while the other has powerboat traffic. We need to get past these rivalries. There is a consensus that the outdoors are an important component of camp, but there is wide variability in the duration and quality of the outdoor experiences. The above definition is expansive enough to include inner-city camps and mountain wilderness excursions under the same proverbial canopy. There is an assumption that the set-apart space includes interaction with God's creation. We can say that this interaction involves somewhat more than a potted plant but is not the unspoiled wilderness of Shangri-La.

Programmatic differences are more germane to our discussion. The set-apart spaces that we are calling camps offer remarkably different

---

7. Louv, *Last Child in the Woods*, 228.

8. The American Camp Association (ACA) responded to Louv's critique with a survey of member camps, which found, "83 percent of the camps had programs primarily staged in the outdoors" (James and Henderson, "Camps and Nature Report," 3).

experiences. Day camps do not include overnight experiences, while residential (or *sleep away*) camps do. Some camps offer family camp programs, when young people experience the set-apart space with parents or grandparents. Some camps offer retreat experiences, which can be generally defined as including one or two overnights. Three or more consecutive overnights can then be called residential camp experiences. Our definition of camp does not seek to exclude day camps, family camps, and retreats, but our primary focus will center on the residential summer camp experiences. There are historical reasons for this focus that we will explore in the next chapter, but by way of introduction we can say that residential summer camp is the core experience behind the above definition of camp. While many camps offer multi-week programs and some even have sessions lasting the entire summer, the core Christian summer camp experience is one week long.[9] There are an estimated 12,000 camps in the United States alone, and 62 percent of these are residential.[10]

Other programs are understood as analogous experiences or historical offshoots of residential summer camp. Family camps, day camps, and retreats deserve separate and intentional consideration. Some camps also operate as conference centers. They share historical roots with residential summer camp, but conferences are here understood as qualitatively different from camps and retreats because they tend to focus more on meetings and large-group presentations than on relational encounter. This conference model has influenced the tendency for large-group gatherings at camps that follow a *centralized* camping model. Other camps place a much stronger emphasis on the small group, which is often referred to as a *decentralized* model. We will explore these two models, including the benefits and drawbacks of each, in the pages that follow.

Our camp orientation is almost complete, but we must acknowledge that this definition of camp reveals a theological starting point. This project has a clear preference for camps that are intentional about engagement in Christian practices. We focus, therefore, on Christian summer camps and their analogous ministries. We will discover that even Christian summer camps differ a great deal in their programs, priorities, and fundamental definitions of the camp experience. Some Evangelical camps emphasize conversion experiences, while some camps in Mainline traditions shy away from religious experience altogether. Neither extreme is helpful. The

---

9. In a 2018 survey of more than 300 Mainline Protestant camp directors, 98 percent indicated that their camp offered week-long sessions, while 23 percent offered single-day programs and only 16 percent offered multi-week sessions (Sorenson, "Outdoor Ministries Connection," 9).

10. Meier and Henderson, *Camp Counseling*, 12.

distinctions between Mainline Protestantism and American Evangelicalism are frequently blurred in the intensely relational and often ecumenical camp experience. I hope that the working definition and theological priorities are inclusive enough that all feel welcome to play. We learn more together, and Christ is present where we gather in his name. May this playground be one of those spaces.

Relationship as a Theological Starting Point

The invitation to play is an invitation to relationship. We can consider this our theological starting point because God is the being revealed to us in relationship. Karl Barth has helped theologians since the early twentieth century reclaim the primacy of the doctrine of the Trinity, especially as the Cappadocian fathers articulated it: *perichoresis*, or mutual indwelling. Relationship is the starting point for our understanding of God because this is how God acts in the world. Barth writes, "God seeks and creates fellowship between Himself and us, and therefore He loves us. But He is this loving God without us as Father, Son, and Holy Spirit, in the freedom of the Lord, who has His life from Himself."[11] We can affirm that God exists as an eternal relationship and has no ontological need of creation or humankind. This is a profound and mind-boggling insight, but Barth sees no purpose in trying to describe God in relational isolation. The simple fact is that God has acted. We have no knowledge of a cloistered, cut-off God, but rather a relational God who has reached out in love to creation. We can say that God is relationship, God seeks relationship, and God creates relationship.

Jürgen Moltmann is one of the giants of twentieth-century theology who is indebted to Barth and his insights, though he helps us move beyond Barth in many ways. He provides a helpful metaphor to understand the Triune God reaching out in relationship to creation. He writes, "The creation is God's play."[12] There is no need for the created world to exist. The created world is an outpouring of God's divine love and exists as an expression of God's joy. Creation is God's playground. This is not to say that creation exists for pleasure or that God is toying with creation. Creation exists as a place of relational encounter. God is moving and working in this temporal space as the one who seeks relationship with the creation, and God inspires creation itself to relationship. Humanity is drawn to God as the source of relationship. Moltmann, therefore, considers theology itself to be a form of play. Limiting theology to a theory of a practice is insufficient. He writes,

11. Barth, *Church Dogmatics* II/1, 257.
12. Moltmann, *Theology of Play*, 17.

"Christian theology is also an abundant rejoicing in God and the *free play* of thoughts, words, images, and songs with the grace of God."[13] Humanity is invited to be in relationship with God. Our God is not distant and cut off but rather personal and inviting: "Do you want to play together?"

Our theological starting point suggests a dynamic connection between relationships and play. Play is both the outpouring of relationship and the means by which we nurture relationship. This leads us to two understandings of playground. Our relationships with each other and with God are expressed in terms of play, so the place where we interact in relationship can be considered a playground. There are also specific places where we go in order to play and interact with others. It is to this second understanding of playground that we can categorize camp. Camps are set apart as places of encounter, as places of play. Camps are sacred playgrounds.

Camp Rules: A Note on Interdisciplinarity

The research and discussion throughout this book will draw from multiple fields of study, including psychology, sociology, and neuroscience, to name a few. Many of my colleagues in the Christian camping world have a certain level of disdain for secular sciences, believing that the gospel message is above all worldly wisdom. This is one reason why there is so little empirical research available about Christian camping. The line of thinking stretches back to an early church father named Tertullian, who famously asked, "What has Athens to do with Jerusalem or the academy with the church?" However, there is solid biblical support for using the logic of the world to share the gospel. While debating the philosophers of Athens in Acts 17, Paul adopts their rhetorical style and presents Christ's resurrection as empirical evidence of the gospel message. The field of practical theology continues this tradition by putting theology in dialogue with other disciplines. Whenever we do this, it is important to name some of our biases and lay out some guidelines, similar to how a camp community might form a group covenant or camp rules. As at camp, respect for the other and a desire for relational encounter should guide our interaction. God has broken into the world in the person of Jesus Christ, and this revelation reorders our entire understanding of existence.

James Loder has articulated a helpful way of engaging in dialogue with secular fields that he calls a "Christomorphic approach."[14] He understands the human sciences to go through a process of transformation in

---

13. Moltmann, *Theology of Play*, 27 (italics original).
14. Loder, *Logic of the Spirit*, 40–41.

dialogue with theology. This is not to do damage to the perspectives or to use them for selfish purposes but rather to deny the assumption that any field can speak of anything that is not related to God. Loder puts this more poetically, "The Creator Spirit . . . will negate any presuppositional negation of theological reality."[15] Not only can we reject Tertullian by engaging the human sciences, Loder argues that dialogue between fields is essential because this dynamic interplay is a living out of the relational wholeness of Jesus Christ, who is inseparably God and human. Loder uses the Chalcedonian understanding of Christology as a framework for understanding his methodology. His insights demand intentional listening to the perspectives of the human sciences because without them we have an incomplete understanding of the human spirit. Denying their perspectives would be, for Loder, denial of the humanity of Jesus Christ. Our faith leads us into deep relationship with a variety of disciplines in order that we might better understand God's activity in the world. He argues that the discipline of theology has priority over the other disciplines, as Christ's divine nature has ontological priority over his humanity.

Loder tends to give too much credit to theologians, particularly those in the Western tradition. Dwight Hopkins is one of many who offers a critical voice that brings us up short. He points out that the dominant voices of theology "have had the resources to promote their voice, their experiences, and their thinkers as normative or as *the* tradition."[16] He lifts up valuable theological voices that are often silenced or marginalized, notably black, womanist, feminist, mujerista, Latino, Asian American, and Native American voices. Even as we agree with Loder that theological categories have de facto priority over the human sciences, we must acknowledge that our understanding of the human sciences is needed to critique the field of theology itself. Theology is always embedded in the practical, so we must repeatedly call into question whether our theological categories are mere human contrivances. In fact, a Christomorphic understanding compels us to do just that, lest we give the human priority over the divine.

Theology and the human sciences are united in relational unity that together point to God who has come in the flesh. The human sciences are transformed by Christ's active presence in the world, through whom we are able to understand how God is at work. That is to say, the human sciences help us develop a more informed theology, which helps us better understand that the human sciences themselves are grounded theologically. We enter with various disciplinary fields into this playground seeking a shared

---

15. Loder, *Logic of the Spirit*, 41.
16. Hopkins, *Being Human*, 15 (italics original).

understanding, but this understanding is always oriented toward the Triune God who has reached out in loving relationship to the world in the person of Jesus Christ and has made our interaction itself possible.

A Rough Schedule for Our Journey

Participants come to camp with a mixture of excitement and anxiety. They often want to know right from the beginning what they are getting into so they have time to prepare themselves. The child who has a deathly fear of heights wants to know when the group is scheduled for the high ropes so she has time to consider whether or not this will be the year she climbs to the top. The one who absolutely loves animals wants to know when he will get the chance to ride a horse or visit the farm animals. You, the reader, likely want to know what activities we are in for in our journey together through the coming pages. You may decide to opt out of certain pages, knowing that all camp activities are, after all, *challenge by choice*. Others have already skipped this section, like the camper who tunes out the schedule review, because they either like being surprised or are in a hurry to get going. There will certainly be some surprises and unexpected encounters in the pages to come, but it is still helpful to have a rough idea of where we are going.

Our journey will follow a schedule that is reminiscent of the camp experience itself. We have begun here in chapter 1 with brief introductions and an orientation to the rules for our time together. Chapters 2 and 3 will take us on a tour of the camp landscape. Like any good tour, we will hear some camp history and some fascinating stories of what people say about camp. Chapter 2 is an overview of the history and heritage of Christian camping ministry. It is not only intriguing to hear about where camp comes from, but this history also gives us insight into the present realities of camping ministry. We will pay special attention to the dominant models of Christian camping ministry that have been present from the very beginning: the crisis conversion model and the Christian nurture model that facilitates intentional connection with congregational ministries. We will also gain insight into the genesis of centralized and decentralized models of camping ministry. The history provides us great insight into why camp is often dismissed in the scholarly literature. Chapter 3 will examine camp's treatment among scholars and make a case for camp as a locus of practical theology. Our review of the literature will also make clear that we must take a deep empirical approach in this project, since there has been so little scholarship on camping ministry.

Chapters 4–8 immerse us in the camp experience by considering the five fundamental characteristics of Christian camping. These five chapters are in no set order, since the five characteristics have no set order or direction of influence. Rather, they interact relationally and together give rise to what we define as the Christian camp experience. These characteristics are grounded in theological convictions and extensive empirical research. They include: camp is church, camp is relational, camp is a safe space, camp is a place to unplug, and camp is participatory.

Chapter 9 brings our experience to a close by proposing a theological understanding of Christian summer camp. We will consider camp as a theological playground that functions alongside other experiences and relationships to facilitate spiritual growth and transformation. We will close by being sent out to our home environments, where we will seek, like the camp participants, to integrate what we have learned into our lives and unique contexts. We will explore some pragmatic steps to continue our process of learning and engagement, situating camp in the larger ecology of Christian ministry.

I invite you to delve deeper with me. Our theological and theoretical parents may have never thought this possible or even desirable, but here we are in relational encounter. Do you want to play together?

2

The Camp Story

My first day as a camp director met with near disaster. I was moving into my new office at Cross Roads Outdoor Ministries in New Jersey, and I noticed a black plastic bag in the middle of the bookshelf. I took it down and opened it, discovering a charred log that smeared soot all over my hands. Confused and exasperated, I carried the mess at arm's length, intending to return it to the forsaken ash heap from whence it came.

"Stop!" exclaimed one of my staff members. "You can't throw away *the log*!"

I listened intently as she explained that a charred remnant of each campfire was saved and added to the next one, connecting each camp group, in continuous succession, to decades of other faithful campers. The dirty log in the black plastic bag was from the last campfire of the previous summer. Months later, I watched as it was solemnly added to the first campfire of summer staff training.

Camps are virtually dripping with history. Christian camps claim a shared history connected to a biblical narrative of wilderness wanderings, and many are quick to evoke Jesus' model of ministry in the outdoors with his small group of disciples. Some camps draw connections to desert fathers like Saint Anthony and religious leaders like Saint Francis, tracing an arc of camping ministry from the garden of Eden to the present day. Each camp also has a unique history connected to specific individuals, whose pioneering efforts are legendary in that particular place. Each site has its holy places or artifacts that are evocative of those who have come before and passed on the faith, like the log at Cross Roads. But not many know the shared history of organized camping, which emerged as a distinctly North American phenomenon before spreading throughout the world.

Setting the Stage: Nineteenth-Century Antecedents to the Summer Camp Movement

Organized youth camping has its origins in late-nineteenth-century New England. The camping movement gathered momentum along with a myriad of cultural forces and not because of individual genius. It is a great metaphor for camp that, in effect, it has no founder because camp is essentially a communal enterprise. In one of the definitive histories of summer camp, Leslie Paris describes camp as a "hybrid" arena, where multiple forces interact in unique ways to produce something entirely new.[1] Among the cultural and counter-cultural forces that gave rise to the organized camp movement were urbanization, the back-to-nature and fresh air movements, the youth movements, the camp meetings, Chautauquas, and the rise of compulsory education.

The origins of organized camping must be seen in the context of the industrial revolution and the rapid urbanization of the nineteenth century. Henry David Thoreau exemplified the early back-to-nature movement in his influential *Walden* (1854). John Muir, John Burroughs, and other conservationists took up the cause of preserving the American wilderness. In the meantime, an idealized picture of the American West permeated the imaginations of city dwellers, exemplified in Buffalo Bill's Wild West Show that opened in New York in 1883, just as the nascent camping movement was beginning. There was an increasing fear, especially among upper-class white New Englanders, that city living was not only detrimental to health, but also to humanity and the American spirit that longed for adventure and wilderness. The upper classes sought leisure in outdoor settings, and charity groups provided opportunities for lower-class children to escape urban life for short stays in the countryside. These exoduses of poor urban children, largely initiated by Protestant church leaders in the 1870s, came to be known as the *fresh air movement*.

The youth movement took shape at the same time and in response to the same perceived problems as the back-to-nature and fresh air movements. Concerned Christians, many of them ministers, saw children living in deplorable urban conditions. The Young Men's Christian Association (YMCA) and the Sunday school movement were both attempts to care for urban young people. They emerged in the midst of the industrial revolution in England and quickly spread to the United States. A concerted effort and evangelistic fervor among churches in Philadelphia in 1830 led to a surge in the number

---

1. Paris, *Children's Nature*, 9.

of Sunday schools in the frontier areas of the Ohio and Mississippi valleys.[2] The YMCA, along with its counterpart YWCA (Young Women's Christian Association), spread with similar fervor across the country in the 1850s and following. By the beginning of the Civil War, specialized youth work had spread throughout the country. The YMCA and YWCA focused their efforts on Christian care of young people in urban settings, while the Sunday school spread rapidly in both urban and rural areas.

The religious fervor that precipitated the early youth work movements was a product of the most immediate antecedents of Christian summer camping: the camp meetings. Camp meetings originated in the outdoor revivals of the Second Great Awakening, with the movement gaining considerable momentum at the turn of the nineteenth century, exemplified most famously in the well-publicized 1801 revival in Cane Ridge, Kentucky. They held in common some of the basic components of Christian camping: community, set-apart locations, and the outdoors. Unlike summer camp, the attendees gathering on the open prairies for revival and emotional conversion experiences were mostly adults. Camp meetings transcended denominational lines, though they were most closely associated with the Methodist and Baptist traditions. These set-apart locations used the natural beauty of the outdoors to convey a sense of holiness and liminality to provide safe space for social interactions and displays of the Holy Spirit that would be considered disgraceful or indecent in everyday life. Historian Andrew Rieser notes, "The camp meeting, with its typical leafy enclosure, formed an interior space where guests could reflect on the divine presence in Nature, apprehend God's immanence, monitor their internal states of grace, and focus without distraction on the journey to salvation."[3] The faithful would return to the same grounds year after year, giving the camp meetings an important sense of permanence, which kept the movement going for decades. The grounds themselves became hallowed places where people had been converted or had recommitted their lives to Christ. Powerful religious experiences tied to a specific outdoor space remain key to the Christian summer camp movement, in which young people return in hopes of reliving a powerful experience or rekindling their faith. Many Christian camps trace their site history to nineteenth-century camp meetings.

Philanthropist Lewis Miller and Methodist pastor John Heyl Vincent founded the Chautauqua Institution in 1874 on a former camp meeting site in *the burned-over district* of western New York. Chautauqua was designed

---

2. Senter notes, "Over half of the eight to ten thousand new communities in the Mississippi Valley were provided with Sunday schools in a two-year period" (Senter, *When God Shows Up*, 107).

3. Rieser, *Chautauqua Moment*, 32.

to train Sunday school teachers. It exemplified the Protestant desire to retain a distinct identity and also shape the destiny of the nation, especially as a dramatic influx of immigrants in the 1870s and 1880s threatened the dominance of Mainline Protestants in New England and the Mid-Atlantic states. The movement successfully blended the set-apart outdoor spirituality of the camp meeting with Christian education. The model was widely publicized, and similar programs quickly sprang up at sites across the country, so that by the 1880s and 1890s, seventy or more Chautauqua assemblies existed and were visited by more than a half million people annually.[4] These early Chautauquas were ecumenical, but they were decidedly Protestant. The movement was characterized by a strong anti-urbanism and an idealized notion of nature, though the pristine natural settings were largely manufactured and manicured. It was a chance to temporarily suspend real life and be welcomed into a set-apart, sacred realm. The adults that attended Chautauqua assemblies were Christian educators who would not only bring the learned Protestant ideals and ethics to Sunday school classes but would also expand the outdoor ministry and education model of Chautauqua to outdoor camping programs focused specifically on young people.

Chautauqua was part of a larger educational movement that was sweeping the nation in the decades following the Civil War. Compulsory education was increasingly common, and public-funded secondary education gradually followed. Chautauqua also exemplified the increasing public attention to leisure and recreation. Many primary schools had a summer term for much of the nineteenth century. An early camping experiment that is often credited as the first summer camp was actually a summer term class held in an outdoor setting. This was Frederick William Gunn's and Abigail Gunn's Gunnery School for Boys. The Gunns took the boys on a two-week camping excursion in Connecticut in 1861, and this continued periodically until 1879. It is a significant precursor to organized camping because it was well publicized and led to emulation of programs. The major distinction is that the Gunnery Camp was part of the school program, whereas summer camping emerged as the extended summer vacation gained popularity. Increased interest in leisure, recreation, and a retreat from city life were essential to school camps like the Gunnery Camp and the Chautauqua movement. Rieser notes, "The Chautauqua leisure model gave clerical sanction to the summer vacation and helped make it a defining ritual of middle-class life."[5] The middle-class demand for leisure resulted in an explosion of the vacation industry and a rapid elimination of the summer school term.

---

4. Rieser, *Chautauqua Moment*, 51.
5. Rieser, *Chautauqua Moment*, 48.

Freeing up the months of July and August in the youth schedule, while the rising middle class was still expected to work during the summer months, opened the space for the summer camp experiment.

While compulsory education increased and secondary education became more common in the closing decades of the nineteenth century, the youth movement gained considerable momentum and produced numerous organizations and opportunities for young people to engage in healthy community activities. The most influential of these was Christian Endeavor, founded by Francis Clark in 1881. Youth ministry historian Mark Senter marks this as a major transition in approaches to specialized youth ministry from "the period of associations" (such as the YMCA and Sunday school) to "the period of youth societies."[6] The activities of Christian Endeavor were widely publicized and adopted in congregations across the country. Clark designed the regular gatherings to be youth-led. The stated objective of Christian Endeavor was, "To promote an earnest Christian life among its members, to increase their mutual acquaintance, and to make them more useful in the service of God."[7] Clark's description of Christian Endeavor societies as "a half-way house to the church" highlights their role in providing safe space for young people to interact with each other for the purpose of connecting them more fully to the church community.[8] Christian Endeavor was part of the *Christian nurture* movement popularized by Horrace Bushnell, who argued against the necessity of dramatic conversion experiences: "The child should grow up a Christian, and never know himself as being otherwise."[9] This model of Christian education sharply critiqued the revivalist model popular in camp meetings, and this disagreement would cause early diversity in the camping movement that is still evident today in camps emphasizing the last night conversion experience compared with camps seeking intentional integration with homes and congregational ministries.

Congregations in all of the major Protestant denominations soon had vibrant Christian Endeavor societies. Denominational leaders who were concerned to keep the particularity of their denomination intact formed youth societies that adopted the model of Christian Endeavor but were specialized to denominational bodies. The Episcopal Church founded the Brotherhood of St. Andrew in 1883 and its counterpart, Daughters of the King, in 1885. Soon to follow were the United Presbyterian Youth Fellowship (1889), Epworth League (Methodist Church, 1889), Baptist

---

6. Senter, *When God Shows Up*, 95, 147.
7. Clark, *Children and the Church*, 40.
8. Clark, *Children and the Church*, 52.
9. Bushnell, *Christian Nurture*, 10.

Young People's Union of America (1891), Walther League (Lutheran Church Missouri Synod, 1893), and Luther League (1895). Senter notes, "Denominational control and loyalty seemed safer than the nondenominational approach of Christian Endeavor."[10] The rise of the summer camping movement occurred at the same time as the formation of these youth societies and should be seen as part of this broader movement toward specialized ministry with young people.

The First Camps: Conversion or Christian Nurture

Urbanization, the rise of the middle class, the back-to-nature movement, the youth work movement, the ubiquity of compulsory education, and the leisure movement leading to the elimination of the summer term coincided perfectly in New England in the 1880s to give rise to the summer camp movement. The most influential of the early camps was Ernest Balch's Camp Chocorua, founded in 1881, the same year as Christian Endeavor. Balch's camp was widely publicized and emulated, making it an early prototype, but it is erroneous to credit him with founding the movement simply because he left a historical record. The Reverend George Hinckley of East Hartford, Connecticut, took a group of boys from his congregation for week-long camps in Rhode Island in 1880 and 1881. The record of these outings survive because of Hinckley's fame in later founding the Good Will Farm for Boys in Maine, a camp that has been serving underprivileged children since 1889. The Detroit YMCA publicized successful multi-day camping ventures in the summers of 1882–84, the success of which led directly to the founding of the first week-long YMCA summer camp in New York in 1885 by Sumner Dudley. Incarnation Center, the longest-operating Christian summer camp, was founded in 1886 in Upstate New York by the Reverend Arthur Brooks. These early summer camps were founded independently in a very short span of time, demonstrating that the summer camp movement can best be described in terms of emergence. These camps are part of the written history because their records survive, and they give hints of an early movement that may have included many pastors who experimented with organized summer camping like Hinckley and Brooks.

The early camps are remarkable not only in that they were founded independently of one another but also because they exemplify the major branches of the organized camping movement that we see today: private,

---

10. Senter, *When God Shows Up*, 181.

agency, and religiously affiliated. These different branches held in common, at the outset, a focus on faith formation and Christian education of young people, though this would shift in the years following World War I. They differed in their programmatic strategies, and these differences would determine the history of the organized camping movement.

Balch's Camp Chocorua served as the prototype for subsequent *private* camps in terms of wealthy Protestant clientele, programs spanning the entire summer, and the need for effective publicity. Balch was the son of an Episcopal minister and dropped out of Dartmouth to found Camp Chocorua. He first arrived at Squam Lake in New Hampshire with a romanticized view of it as untouched wilderness, though it was a popular vacation destination. He began setting up plans for his camp on a small island as if he had discovered it. He soon found out that someone else already owned the island, so he promptly purchased it! Camp Chocorua operated for nine summers, allowing Balch the opportunity to hone his camping model. Christian life and teaching were essential to all aspects of the camp program, with daily Bible study, worship, and regular group prayer. Balch was very intentional in focusing on community living, outdoor skills, recreation, and democratic decision-making. The rustic chapel that the boys built is still open for Sunday worship services during the summer, accessible only by boat. I had the opportunity to kayak out to the island one beautiful summer day, where I walked in the footsteps of those first campers and prayed in the chapel they built.

The Chocorua experiment was publicized among the New England Protestant elite, and through these channels it spawned similar private camp ventures, among them Camp Asquam (1885) and Camp Algonquin (1886), both founded on the same lake as Chocorua. The centrality of Christian education and faith formation to the program of these early private camps can be attributed in large part to the target clientele. Christian education and faith practices were essential pieces of the dominant culture in New England, so they featured prominently at camp. City living was seen as dangerous physically and spiritually, so camp was a safe place for upper-class males to conform to the white Protestant ideal. Paris notes, "Educated, native-born, and often quite young, the men who founded the first camps were idealists committed to countering the seeming enfeeblement, depletion, and degeneration of middle- and upper-class American boys."[11] Early camp history is often characterized in terms of upper-class white male idealism because of the influence of these early private camps on the literature and on New England's elite. It is important to recognize that this represents one branch

---

11. Paris, *Children's Nature*, 37.

of organized camping, the smallest branch in terms of camper numbers. It has a disproportionate effect on camp history because it served the elite, therefore receiving the most publicity and greater resources for marketing, the materials from which now constitute the bulk of the historical record. The private camp movement was so small that as late as 1896, when Hanford Henderson founded Camp Marienfeld on the upper Delaware River, he thought that he had started the movement.[12]

Dudley's YMCA camp (named Camp Dudley after his death) is the prototypical *agency* camp that was quickly replicated by other YMCAs and later by the YWCA, the Camp Fire Girls, and other agencies focused on youth work. These agency camps featured one or two-week camping sessions that served the burgeoning middle class, and even the working class. Whereas Balch charged 175 dollars for the full ten-week summer at Camp Chocorua, the early agency camps charged only four or five dollars per week.[13] Early agency camps resembled private camps in their gender exclusivity and centrality of Christian teaching. Private camps tended to incorporate Christian instruction as part of a well-rounded experience and path to responsible citizenry, while YMCA camps focused on proclamation and conversion. One to two hours per day were devoted to Bible study, and worship was central to the program. Dudley himself noted in the YMCA publication *The Watchman*, "Pleasure seeking does not necessitate any relaxation of Christian study and work."[14] A writer in another YMCA publication, *Association Men*, wrote in 1905, "The major aim of a boys' camp . . . should be to lead boys to Jesus Christ."[15] Agency camps had no particular connection to denominational bodies, so Christian teachings were not directly reinforced by congregational leaders. Camp served as an isolated Christian experience for groups of young boys that they were left to incorporate into their own faith stories upon returning home. Agency camps are seldom places of crisis conversion today. They moved away from this emphasis in the inter-war years, though the American Evangelical camping movement quickly picked up the conversion torch.

The third branch of early camping was markedly different in its approach to Christian education, and it is also the most difficult to trace because the early pioneers of *religiously affiliated* camps did not found lasting camping organizations or network with other camping leaders to the same extent as private and agency camp leaders. Their goals were not to found

---

12. Paris, *Children's Nature*, 39.
13. Paris, *Children's Nature*, 37–40.
14. Hopkins, *History of the Y.M.C.A.*, 205.
15. Quoted in Hopkins, *History of the Y.M.C.A.*, 469.

camping businesses or promote an ideal as much as they were to connect relationally with groups of young people in their care. Pastor Hinckley took groups of boys for a week of camp in 1880 and 1881 because he wanted to get to know his Sunday school students better and to share his love of the outdoors with them. Programmatically, his camping ventures looked remarkably similar to Camp Dudley and Camp Chocorua in terms of Bible study, outdoor recreation (with an emphasis on aquatics), singing, and worship. The key difference was that he returned home with his campers and interacted with them continually through his congregational ministry. Pastor Brooks, likewise, reached out to young people in his own community when he began what was to become Incarnation Center in 1886. Brooks had a passion and a calling to serve the urban poor, particularly recent immigrants. His early camping ventures can be seen as part of the fresh air movement, as well as an outreach designed to serve poor communities and to engage them in the ongoing life of his congregation.

Another key difference that sets the early religiously affiliated camps apart is the inclusion of diverse camper groups. Early private camps and agency camps were gender segregated, with predominantly native-born white campers. Hinckley's first camp venture was all boys, but three of them were Chinese. Brooks led a mixed group of white Protestant campers from his congregation and recent immigrants from the Lower East Side of Manhattan. Equally significant, Brooks's first group of twenty-five campers in 1886 was coeducational. This is intriguing, considering that the vast majority of agency and private camps founded before 1900 were exclusively male.[16] Luther Halsey Gulick, who later founded the Campfire Girls, is credited with founding the first camping experience for girls in 1890, even though Pastor Brooks was already taking young girls to camp for several years.[17] It makes sense that an Episcopal congregation like Pastor Brooks's would be among the first to offer coeducational camping experiences, since the Christian Endeavor offshoot *Daughters of the King* was already established by the time he led his first camping outing. Congregations were offering increased opportunities for young people to gather in age-specific ministry ventures, and summer camping ministry was a natural extension that allowed ministry leaders to deepen relationships with their young congregants in set-apart locations for extended periods of time as part of their Christian nurture.

16. Paris, *Children's Nature*, 46–47
17. Meier and Henderson, *Camp Counseling*, 14.

Early Expansion and Muscular Christianity

The first two decades of organized camping, from 1880 to 1900, showed modest expansion as early successes were replicated. The more visible arms of the movement attached themselves to the ideals of *muscular Christianity*, which portrayed the idyllic Christian man as tough and virtuous, having moral authority to lead the household and the other civilizations of the world. Early private camps, such as Chocorua and Asquam, can rightly be characterized as attempts to get white males out of the squalor of city living and domestic feminization to pursue the more manly pursuits of wilderness, self-reliance, and (male) Christian values. This connection to muscular Christianity dominated the literature because of the influence of private camps and YMCA camps, leading some to be skeptical of the whole movement. However, the idea was absent or even rejected in many of the congregational camping ventures and the charity camps, which can be better associated with the fresh air movement and the social gospel.

Private camps were largely confined to New England, with approximately twenty-five camps operating by 1900 and serving approximately 1,000 campers each summer.[18] Agency camps expanded more quickly because of the communication and idea sharing of the YMCA. Paris notes, "By the turn of the twentieth century, hundreds of organizational camps served many thousands of boys, far more than the number who attended private camps."[19] One hundred sixty-seven of these were YMCA camps, serving an estimated 5,000 boys per summer by 1901.[20] There is evidence that religiously affiliated camps continued to expand in popularity during this period. The first Catholic camp was founded in 1892, and the first Jewish camp followed in 1902.[21] The Reverend George Gray of Chicago began taking young people from his congregation to the shores of a lake in Saugatuck, Michigan, in 1899, and this site would later become Presbyterian Camps. Camp meeting grounds and Chautauquas also continued operations during this period, with some used as camping grounds for families and others for congregational youth outings of the burgeoning Christian Endeavor groups. Epworth League outings began in 1888 on the Dimock Grove camp meeting site in northeastern Pennsylvania and are credited with saving the grounds from closure.[22] Dooly Campground in Georgia,

---

18. Paris, *Children's Nature*, 39.
19. Paris, *Children's Nature*, 40.
20. Paris, *Children's Nature*, 42; Hopkins, *History of the Y.M.C.A.*, 469.
21. Paris, *Children's Nature*, 58; Sales and Saxe, "How Goodly Are Thy Tents," 24.
22. Bugbee, *He Holds the Stars in His Hands*, 76.

Crystal Springs Camp in Michigan, and Kavanagh Life Enrichment Center in Kentucky are three Methodist sites founded between 1860 and 1875, as the popularity of the camp meeting was in its twilight. They existed at the crossroads of traditional revivalist camp meetings, Chautauquas, and summer youth conferences.

The conference setting focused on ministry with youth in the outdoor setting, but it differed from the summer camp model in its focus on large-group presentations. The Winona Lake Bible Conference in Indiana is an important example. It was founded in 1895 as a large-group camping and conference center aimed primarily at adults, so it was known as a Chautauqua. It held its first outdoor youth conference in 1908, giving birth to Camp Kosciusko, which is recognized as the first Presbyterian camp.[23] Another example is Lake Geneva in Wisconsin, where a conference of the International Sunday School Association in 1912 expanded in subsequent years to include camp conferences and other events for youth. The Lake Geneva conference, which Lutheran camp historian Mark Burkhardt identifies as "the first American camping program to receive the broad based support of institutional churches," was an important precursor to youth camps operated with the support of denominational bodies.[24]

The first two decades of the twentieth century saw some important organizational changes in the camping movement. Edgar M. Robinson, an early YMCA camp director, became international secretary of the YMCA in 1901, and he immediately began advocating for increased work with boys younger than eighteen. This included a dramatic expansion of YMCA camps, the number of which nearly doubled by 1905.[25] Robinson also gave tremendous support to the fledgling Boy Scouts of America, founded in 1910, and encouraged an expansion of their programs into camping. Paris notes, "By 1920, almost 45 percent of all Boy Scouts, or over 160,000 boys, spent at least a week at camp in the summertime."[26] The founding of the Campfire Girls in 1910 prompted an expansion of girls' camps.

This tremendous growth in camping was facilitated, in part, by G. Stanley Hall's influential *Adolescence*, first published in 1904. Hall's *recapitulation theory* gave credence to sending young people to camp so that they could enact their more primitive phase of life, which Hall tied to human evolution. Hall's theory fit particularly well with the ideals of white male superiority and inevitable dominance over races deemed more

---

23. Brubaker, "History of Camp Kosciusko," 19.
24. Burkhardt, "History of Lutheran Church Camping," 16.
25. Paris, *Children's Nature*, 42.
26. Paris, *Children's Nature*, 45.

primitive, so YMCA camps, Boy Scout camps, and private camps doubled down on their version of muscular Christianity. Because of these influences, athletic competition and reward systems became popular at camp during this period, and many camps still retain these systems. This is particularly true among secular camps, which are the primary successors of the early private and agency camps.

Exclusivity at private camps meant gender and racial segregation. Many of the early camps, like the Chautauquas of the same period, were enclaves of whiteness, and the notions of muscular Christianity validated this separation as beneficial for society. Camps co-opted American Indian traditions and perpetuated notions of the inferiority of African-Americans. Seton's Woodcraft Indians, founded in 1901, sought to romanticize Native American culture, but Van Slyck points out that these and similar efforts also led to perpetuation of stereotypes and "naturalizing the white conquest of North America."[27] Some camps continued to have campers live in teepees or wear headdresses into the twenty-first century. Also problematic in early camps was the tradition of *blackface* dramas, which caricatured African-Americans. Paris notes that desegregation of camping was slow and that blackface dramas continued at some camps into the 1950s.[28]

Early religiously affiliated camps, largely overlooked in the accounts of Paris and Van Slyck, offered important exceptions to the norms of segregation. Hinckley and Brooks both operated intercultural and interracial camping experiences, and one of the earliest Lutheran camps at Lake Pepin, Wisconsin, in 1920, was multiracial.[29] The history of organized camping in America, however, is dominated by white children and white camp leaders. Influential members of the American Camp Association delayed adoption of an official statement recommending racial integration until 1966, at which point "a large number of private independent camps in North Carolina and Texas did not renew their membership or accreditation the following year."[30] Summer camp became an integral part of the history of white America, but the early exclusion of black Americans caused a tremendous racial divide in camping that is still evident in the twenty-first century. In the midst of these racial disparities in the nationwide camping movement, most religiously affiliated camps continued serving young people from different ethnic backgrounds and socioeconomic statuses.

27. Van Slyck, *Manufactured Wilderness*, 170.
28. Paris, *Children's Nature*, 269.
29. Burkhardt, "History of Lutheran Church Camping," 26–27.
30. Ball, "How the American Camp Association Has Evolved," 37.

The increase in popularity in the early twentieth century meant a degree of permanence to the camping movement that led to the first camp directors associations, first for boys' camps in 1910 and then for girls' camps in 1916. These associations combined the private camps and agency camps into a more unified whole, while the religiously affiliated camping experiments were left largely to their own devices. The associations soon merged in 1924 into what was to become the American Camp Association (ACA). The sites also took on greater degrees of permanence. Most were transient in the early days of camping. Camp Dudley, for example, moved twice before finally settling at Lake Champlain, New York, in 1891, though the camp rented the property until it was purchased in 1908. Van Slyck notes that the early camps usually had very few, if any, permanent structures. Campers usually stayed in tents, often mimicking military encampments (another feature of the muscular Christian movement) until the more established camps began constructing cabins in the 1910s and 1920s.[31]

The experiments of Hinckley, Brooks, Gray, and other ministers demonstrate that camping was part of some congregational ministries in the early years of the movement, but these experiences were isolated, focusing on intentional, ongoing relationships with congregation members. Ferguson and Burch note, "Church-related and denominational camps grew at a much slower rate due to the fact that many private and agency camps were led by Christians and had a religious and moral nature."[32] Congregations had Christian Endeavor or analogous youth associations that focused on ministry with young people, and they largely left the camping movement to the youth professionals in agencies like the YMCA or Girl Scouts, whose ministries could strongly support the ministries of the congregation. The two exceptions were: 1) individual ministers who recognized the value of attending camp with their congregants; and 2) large youth conferences at camp meeting grounds. As the dominant camping movement shifted away from Christian education and faith formation following World War I, individual congregations and entire denominational bodies began investing more heavily in camp.

---

31. Van Slyck, *Manufactured Wilderness*, 14–15.
32. Ferguson and Burch, "Religious Camps," 50.

The Interwar Years: Camping Comes of Age as Progressive Education

The growth in camp participation was dramatic in the interwar years. Camp attendance reached 1 million campers per summer in the 1920s and doubled to 2 million per summer in the 1930s.[33] This growth can be attributed in part to the successful marketing of the camp experience among professional educators and the publicity in popular magazines, but several cultural factors are equally significant. The surge in the national economy following the First World War fueled a rising middle class that had the funds to attend summer camp, and it also allowed camping entrepreneurs to purchase property in order to begin new camping ventures, with war surplus army tents often serving as camp buildings. The interwar years saw a tremendous increase in high school attendance, which is closely related to an increase in summer camp participation. Thomas Hine notes, "In 1920 students made up 28 percent of youth fourteen to twenty; by 1930 the figure was 47 percent."[34] On the eve of World War II, two-thirds of American teenagers were enrolled in high school.

The sign that the camping movement had come of age was a speech in 1922 by former Harvard University president Charles Eliot, in which he proclaimed, "The organized summer camp is the most important step in education that America has given the world."[35] Educators in prestigious institutions across the country extolled the benefits of summer camp, which was tied to the *progressive education* movement of John Dewey and others. Proponents of progressive education critiqued pedagogies that focused on rote learning, emphasizing experiential learning and critical thinking, combined with social interaction. Lloyd Burgess Sharp was a student of Dewey's, and he distinguished himself as the first person to earn a PhD with an emphasis on camping education in 1929.[36] He was a strong proponent of the educational value of the small-group camp experience, and he heavily influenced Protestant camping to embrace the small-group model over the conference model, leading to what is now known as *decentralized* camping. The period saw the first major publications about the educational benefits of summer camp, among them the influential *Organized Camping and Progressive Education* (1935), in which Carlos Ward explains, "The Camping Movement has been making a transition from recreational and

---

33. Paris, *Children's Nature*, 62–63.
34. Hine, *Rise and Fall of the American Teenager*, 198.
35. Paris, *Children's Nature*, 238.
36. Meier and Henderson, *Camp Counseling*, 17.

physical educational types of program to the more comprehensive objectives of personality enrichment."[37] The expansion of camping as a legitimate educational outlet was concentrated in agencies that, as Senter describes, "emphasized wholesome activities designed to build character in boys and girls, such as Boy and Girl Scouts, Camp Fire Girls, 4-H Clubs, and Boys Clubs of America."[38] Senter argues that the expansion of these agencies led to the decline of youth societies like Christian Endeavor. He signals this as a major transition in Protestant youth ministry, and this transition led directly to an increase in denominational camp ventures.

The trend in organized camping away from Christian evangelism and Christian education is most evident in the industry-leading YMCA camps. Hopkins notes that explicit Christian teachings at YMCA camps were increasingly called into question in the late 1920s and into the 1930s, with group work and "creative freedom" dominating the literature and changing the nature of the movement.[39] As Paris describes it, "Although camp leaders continued to praise the goal of 'character' development . . . most did so in far less explicitly religious terms than had their late-nineteenth and early-twentieth-century predecessors, deemphasizing the link between muscles and morals."[40] Most camps of the 1920s and 1930s cannot be described as anti-religious. Rather, specific religious teachings were deemphasized. YMCA camps and scouting camps did not stop having worship services, but campers were increasingly given a choice of whether or not to participate.

Agency and private camps could no longer be counted on to provide experiences of Christian nurture that supplemented the ministries of the congregation, so religious groups moved beyond the isolated congregational approaches exemplified by Hinckley, Brooks, and Gray to establish larger summer camp organizations. The first Lutheran camping organizations were founded during this time as outreaches to the urban poor by chapters of the Lutheran Inner Mission Society: Camp Wa-ba-ne-ki in Pennsylvania (1919), Lake Pepin in Wisconsin (1920), and Camp Wilbur Herrlich in New York (1922). Note the difference in emphasis, as private camps focused on wealthy or middle-class families, while Christian organizations continued to view camping as a way to serve the poor and marginalized. It was often the passion and determination of individual pastors that made early camps successful. Methodist Pastor Mark Freeman not only drove some of the first youth groups to Camp Twinlow (Idaho) in the 1930s and led the programs,

---

37. Ward, *Organized Camping*, 146.
38. Senter, *When God Shows Up*, 183.
39. Hopkins, *History of the Y.M.C.A.*, 552.
40. Paris, *Children's Nature*, 235.

but he also single-handedly dug over a hundred feet of the first well and devoted his time to saving the camp from financial ruin.[41] Pastor Frank Richter is credited with the early success of Camp Wa-ba-ne-ki through his tireless work as "nurse, father, pastor, athletic director, chef, and chief entertainer."[42] Many camps grant these early pioneers near-legendary status, though they are virtually unknown outside the circle of that particular camp.

Aside from the dedication and small-group focus of pastors like Richter and Freeman, the primary mode of denominationally sponsored Christian camping remained the Bible conference. No fewer than twenty new Methodist camps and conference centers were established in the interwar years, while the Presbyterians expanded their youth conferences during this period at places like Camp Kosciusko and Montreat Conference Center in North Carolina, where the large auditorium was completed in 1922. Early Luther League camps at Long Lake in Illinois (1920) and Fortune Lake in Michigan (1930) followed a hybrid version of the conference model that included small-group time, the model that has evolved into *centralized* camping. The conference model emphasized large-group gatherings and dynamic speakers that harkened back to the conversion events of the camp meetings, but conferences also included intentional connections to congregational ministries. Christian Endeavor, Epworth League, or Luther League groups often attended conferences together and shared in the experience with pastors from their home congregations. Many youth conferences were relatively small events, with a few dozen youth in attendance, though the numbers grew steadily as they increased in popularity through the 1920s and 1930s. This expansion undermined the ability of congregational leaders to connect with their youth at the events, and it led church leaders to move away from the conference approach toward the small-group camping ministry advocated by L. B. Sharp.

Senter characterizes the period of youth ministry beginning in the early 1930s as "the Period of the Relational Outreach," which was dominated by congregational youth fellowships and para-church organizations designed to engage young people outside of the congregation.[43] The camp model became one of the primary ways in which the relational focus of this period was lived out. The youth conference model, the direct successor of camp meetings and Chautauqua assemblies, transitioned to the familiar small-group model focused on relationships that was pioneered in the 1880s. Ferguson and Burch date the official transition to a 1938 meeting of the International

---

41. Freeman, "Short History."
42. Burkhardt, "History of Lutheran Church Camping," 24.
43. Senter, *When God Shows Up*, 189–91.

Council of Religious Education, when educators "became concerned about the inappropriateness of the Bible conference model for children under twelve."[44] The council, no doubt influenced by the increasing numbers of denominational camp ventures, advocated a small-group model of camping that featured Bible study, outdoor recreation, and crafts. By this time, each of the major Protestant denominations already had multiple well-established summer camps operating across the country, with the Episcopalian camp founded by Pastor Brooks already celebrating its fiftieth anniversary of co-educational, congregation-based camping ministry.

Post-World War II and the Explosion of Summer Camping

The years following World War II saw a dramatic expansion of Christian summer camping in America. Denominational leaders in the major Protestant traditions were convinced of the potential of the summer camp experience for Christian education, and they designated tremendous resources to summer camp programs. Evangelical groups, most notably Young Life, identified the summer camp model as fertile ground for conversion and religious experience. Church membership and attendance increased during this period, which enabled numerous building projects of churches, camps, and conference centers. High school, including the extended summer break, had become a nearly ubiquitous experience across the nation, and the population surge of the Baby Boom generation produced a tremendous increase in the number of potential summer campers. These forces, combined with the established success of the summer camp movement in the interwar years, led to a virtual explosion of Christian summer camping.

There was a noticeable distinction between the agency and private camps that constituted the mainstream camping movement and explicitly religious camps by the close of World War II. This was due to the secularization tendencies of the interwar years. ACA was a well-established leader in the camping movement by this time, and the organization sought to represent the camping movement as a whole, but many camping organizations resisted membership. Leadership of wealthy private camps and well-established agency camps dominated ACA in the interwar years, leading Ward to characterize it as "a sort of aristocracy of camping."[45] The elitist attitude of private camping is exemplified in their dismissal of the fresh air

---

44. Ferguson and Burch, "Religious Camps," 51.
45. Ward, *Organized Camping*, 146.

camps "as *fun and games* as opposed to *camping as education*."[46] Eells notes that ACA struggled with internal rifts over particular models of camping (e.g., centralized v. decentralized), the governance of the organization, and what constituted camping programs that were educationally sound. She describes "a rather tenuous relationship" between ACA leadership and religious camp leaders in the 1940s and 1950s, with ACA membership expressing "the lack of good standards and acceptable practices in many church camps."[47] Christian camps often shied away from association with the broader movement in order to distinguish their emphasis on Christian education. Many Christian camps were also coeducational and interracial, while most private camps continued gender exclusivity and racial segregation. Christian camps began forming their own associations in 1949, and these associations eventually merged to become the Christian Camp and Conference Association (CCCA). The formation of a special Camp and Conference Committee during the first year of the National Council of Churches in 1950 signaled that the Christian camping movement had broad ecumenical support at the national level.

Some camps retained the camp conference model, but the majority of new camps adopted the small-group model advocated by L. B. Sharp. A spike in post-secondary education, facilitated by the G.I. Bill of 1944, contributed to the expansion of the small-group model. College students were available to fill the ranks of summer camp staff members, relieving older adults from the responsibility of attending camp for an entire week. Using college students as camp staff members dates back to the first summers at Camp Chocorua and Camp Asquam, where the term "councilor" was first applied to the young members of the Asquam Camp Council in 1894.[48] Only the wealthier private camps could afford to employ students from the prestigious colleges in the early days of camping, which is why most of the early religiously affiliated camps were operated by the pioneering spirit and dedication of local pastors. The 1940s and 1950s witnessed an expansion of the model of camping in which college-age staff members guided and stayed overnight with small, single-gendered unit groups, which interacted with other unit groups in a larger camp environment. The week at camp continued to include instructional time with pastors or church leaders, but the primary responsibility of caring for the campers was passed to the camp counselors, who increasingly utilized a Christian education curriculum designed for the camp environment. This transition may have distanced the

---

46. Eells, *History of Organized Camping*, 43 (italics original).
47. Eells, *History of Organized Camping*, 66.
48. Paris, *Children's Nature*, 36.

camp experience from congregational ministries in some cases, but it also opened the camp experience to many more young people, whose pastor or church leader no longer had to take them to camp.

Mainline camping flourished. No fewer than a hundred camping organizations were founded in the Methodist traditions alone from the end of World War II through the 1960s.[49] Episcopalians, Presbyterians, and Lutherans witnessed similar growth. These camps were founded in every state and in diverse locations. Lake camps remained popular, and other camps were founded in remote wilderness areas to emphasize the set-apart nature of camp (e.g., Wilderness Canoe Base in the Boundary Waters of Northern Minnesota, 1957) or near major metropolitan areas to provide easy getaways (e.g., Heartland Presbyterian Center just outside of Kansas City, 1956). Some of the first camps in the 1880s were clustered around resort lakes, such as Squam Lake, and the denominational camps followed suit in their rapid expansion. Lake Okoboji, in the so-called Great Lakes of Iowa, is a prime example. The first denominational camps on the lake were camp conference centers typical of the interwar period begun by the Methodists (1915) and the American Lutheran Church (1924). As youth camping became the dominant model, these camps adapted their programming, and other youth camps sprang up for the Lutheran Church, Missouri Synod (1940), Presbyterians (1954), and the Lutheran Church in America (1960). The picturesque Flathead Lake in Montana was another center of denominational camp expansion, with the Presbyterians founding a youth conference center in 1930, followed by youth camps for the Lutherans (1943), Methodists (1947), and Episcopalians (1947).

A significant portion of the denominational camp expansion happened at the expense of private and agency camps, for which the progressive educational mandate of the 1920s and 1930s had begun to wane. An early New Hampshire private camp was founded as Camp Ossipee in 1902, sold to another private owner in 1938 to become Camp Canaan, and after serious financial struggles, was purchased by the Augustana Synod of the Lutheran Church in 1960 to become Camp Calumet.[50] The cases of Flathead Lake and Lake Okoboji demonstrate a degree of denominational rivalry in establishing camps, but there were also significant cases of ecumenical cooperation. Camp of the Cross, North Dakota, was founded in 1954 as a cooperative effort of four different Lutheran bodies: Augustana Synod, Evangelical Lutheran Church, American Lutheran Church, and Missouri

---

49. Information provided to the writer in 2015 by the Camp and Retreat Ministries division of the United Methodist Church.

50. Dacey, "History of Calumet."

Synod.[51] Cooperative camp ventures were significant points of interdenominational connection that were part of the movement toward unity that led to the formation of the Lutheran Church in America in 1962 and eventually the Evangelical Lutheran Church in America in 1988.

The success of new Evangelical summer camps paralleled the expansion of Mainline camping during this period. The Christian education goals of the Mainline camps focused on Christian nurture and looked very different from early agency camps that focused on using the emotionally charged camp environment as a vehicle for conversion. With the agency camps shifting away from conversion toward character building, a new generation of Evangelical camps was mobilized. The Christian agency most known for its camps in this period was Young Life, with Jim Rayburn founding the first near Colorado Springs in 1945. Camp was recognized as an "effective delivery system" of the gospel message.[52] Successful conversion stories were widely publicized, and the Evangelical camping movement spread rapidly. Senter writes concerning Young Life's influence, "Camp began playing a key role in the evangelization of nonchurched young people."[53] Young Life camps served nearly 17,000 young people each summer by the 1970s.[54] Evangelical groups and Baptist church fellowships founded numerous other camps during this period. The Young Life camp model focused on small groups and relationship building, while other mid-century Evangelical camps featured large-group rallies, emotional altar calls, and dynamic preachers. Some featured the notable Evangelical voices of the day, such as Billy Graham, in the same way that the camp meetings featured Charles Finney and the early YMCA camps featured Billy Sunday. While Mainline camps formed associations within their denominations, the disparate Evangelical camping ventures were instrumental in the formation of the CCCA.

Christian educators, following the lead of the progressive education proponents in the preceding decades, embraced the camping model in the 1950s and 1960s, giving the movement greater momentum. Courses on Christian camping became common at undergraduate and graduate levels in places like Fuller Theological Seminary and Winona Lake School of Theology. The difference of educational approach between Mainline camps and Evangelical camps is clear in the literature. Writing on behalf of the CCCA and other Evangelical groups (such as the Baptist General Conference), Todd and Todd wrote in 1963, "Evangelical camps are

---

51. Yernberg, *Camping Movement*, 1:80.
52. Senter, *When God Shows Up*, 220.
53. Senter, *When God Shows Up*, 84.
54. Senter, *When God Shows Up*, 285.

frankly evangelistic in nature. Their supreme and conscious aim is to see each camper won to Christ in a definite, personal, religious experience whether it be in a public service, in a private counseling session, or alone in a quiet woods."[55] Another camping manual that was written on behalf of the Committee on Camps and Conferences of the National Council of Churches argued, "The purpose of church camping is the same as that of the church: that all persons may respond to God in Jesus Christ, grow in daily fellowship with him, and meet all of life's relationships as children of God."[56] These different views of Christian education at camp can be seen as the continuation of the longstanding disagreement about emphasizing camp's potential for emotional conversion versus emphasizing Christian nurture. Alongside these two streams of Christian education at camp has been a third stream that makes use of religion as a cultural and moral force for character building. We can see this approach in the early private camps, including Chocorua, continuing through the present-day interest in nurturing the spirituality of young people.

Camping from the 1970s to the Present

The Baby Boomers were rapidly aging out of camp by the close of the 1960s, and camps of all types began to feel the strain. An economic recession in the early 1970s compounded the pressure, and camps across the country began to close. Paris notes, "As many as twenty-five hundred camps nationwide, or about one in five, went out of business from the 1970s through the 1990s."[57] The expensive New England private camps took the biggest hit, with Maine losing a third of its camps in the 1970s alone, while the YMCA closed nearly half of its camps nationwide.[58] The rapid expansion of denominational camps came to an abrupt halt during this period, but many of their existing camps survived or even thrived.

The financial success of Christian camping in the 1950s and 1960s, together with official recognition by church bodies and Christian educators, buttressed many camps for the difficult years of the 1970s and 1980s. Many camps had transitioned from volunteer staff members to employing full-time directors, and these dedicated individuals fought for the viability of their sites. In addition, denominational sanction of camping ministry was well-established, so full-time advocates at the denominational level pressed the

55. Todd and Todd, *Camping for Christian Youth*, 34.
56. Davis, *Church Camping*, 12.
57. Paris, *Children's Nature*, 273.
58. Paris, *Children's Nature*, 273.

case for their ministries. One key example was Jerry Manlove, who helped professionalize camping ministry in the American Lutheran Church (ALC) during his tenure as National Outdoor Ministries Director from 1969 to 1979. Manlove was heavily influenced by his experiences in the professional network of YMCA camping. When I spoke with him about his early days in camping, he told me that he became a strong advocate of the decentralized, small-group camping model after personal conversations with L. B. Sharp. He advocated for professional education of camp executive directors in marketing, theology, and other key areas. He also led a campaign to expand camping ministries beyond the summer youth camp to include year-round retreat ministries, family camps, and other programs that directly supported the ministries of congregations. Manlove had a tremendous network of supporting colleagues that helped make Lutheran camping a particularly successful case, including his counterpart Paul Howells in the Lutheran Church in America. Yernberg notes that during the 1970s, economically lean years for the camping industry as a whole, "it was estimated that over 32 million was raised by camp directors for ALC camp facilities."[59]

Camps in other denominations survived through a similar stream of ongoing support, though their programs followed different paths of development, and some camps struggled. One camp advocate described the struggles in his 1972 dissertation, "Churches are running out of money. Declining resources have necessitated a variety of cut-backs in programming, with one of the most frequently eliminated items being camping."[60] The period as a whole can be seen as a time of consolidation, as denominational camps developed professional groups of camp directors, who maintained their successful summer camp ministries and began expanding to year-round operations in response to financial pressures.

Christian educators had embraced the camping model in the 1950s and 1960s, contributing curricula, training manuals, and articles, but the support waned in the 1970s. This change is most dramatic in the literature. The substantial bibliography of 1950s and 1960s materials nearly dries up in the ensuing decades. It is difficult to account for this change, but there appears to be an increased skepticism among professional educators about the educational value of a week-long summer camp experience. Importantly, this change coincided with the professionalization of the Christian camp director, which may have put some distance between camps and theologians, since many directors were not seminary-educated ministers. It is plausible that mainline pastors and theologians in the neo-Orthodox

59. Yernberg, *Camping Movement*, 1:35.
60. Miller, "Lutheran Camping," 2.

stream of thought grew wary of a tendency in camping ministry toward natural theology or a general notion of spirituality.

The progressive education love affair with camp had largely ended by 1950, and Christian educators followed suit as support for camp waned in the major academic institutions. Ozier notes, "Despite tremendous momentum during the first half of this century by leaders in education and camping, little reference to camping's educational importance appeared after 1950."[61] Miller, writing in 1972, indicates that the "pendulum has swung" too far in the direction of process rather than content, necessitating camps to reclaim a Christ-centered approach.[62] His insights indicate that educators increasingly viewed camp as a method (or, perhaps, a gimmick) that was theologically shallow and lacking in the ongoing relationships required of Christian nurture. Evangelical camping groups continued to emphasize the value of camp for the emotional conversion experience, and this emphasis became associated with Christian camping as a whole, making Mainline educators who were suspicious of religious experience increasingly wary of the camp model. The professionalization of camp directors, while instrumental in the expansion of camping ministries, contributed to the notion that camp was separate from the life of the congregation. Pastors increasingly sent the young people to camp rather than accompanying them. Camps that were established as extensions of congregational ministries became associated with the *parachurch* organizations. This divide placed the burden of justifying the value of camping ministry on the camp professionals, a change that has tremendous consequences for Christian camping in the twenty-first century. One of the most important movements I am advocating in this book is a reemphasis on the partnership between camp and congregation.

Expansion of the national economy in the 1990s fueled a boom in organized camping. Specialty camps that focused on things like sports, music, and religion flourished. The established denominational camps saw dramatic increases in camper numbers, with many peaking in the early years of the twenty-first century at double the numbers they were serving in the 1980s. The financial success enabled enormous building projects, many in excess of a million dollars, as camps upgraded year-round retreat facilities to host adult groups that were not keen on rustic accommodations. These projects sparked spirited philosophical debates about rustic camping versus resort-like facilities, though it is instructive to note that quests to return camp to some rustic ideal are almost as old as the movement itself.[63]

---

61. Ozier, "Camp as Educator," 26.
62. Miller, "Lutheran Camping," 49–52.
63. "The purists among the early founders felt that real camping was fast

Evangelical camps also saw considerable growth. Young Life camps, after a stagnation of growth in the 1980s, more than doubled their enrollment to more than 40,000 campers by the turn of the century. The Fellowship of Christian Athletes (FCA), most known for its presence on high school campuses, also ran camps offering the dual specialty of sports and Christian evangelism. Their modest camper numbers of just under 7,000 in 1988 more than doubled to over 16,000 campers in 1998, and then more than doubled again to 42,000 at 240 camps by 2007.[64]

The Great Recession of 2008–09 hit Christian camps particularly hard. The ACA's annual survey showed a decline in camper numbers across the board during the recession, but the subsequent rebound in 2010 and following was markedly slower among religiously affiliated camps.[65] This can be attributed, in part, to changing religious views in the American public, as people increasingly professed no religious affiliation. Connection to denominations sustained camps through the difficult years of the 1970s and 1980s, but this connection increasingly became a hindrance to growth in the early twenty-first century. Camps that relied on Sunday schools and confirmation groups to provide the bulk of their summer campers saw enrollment decline as church membership declined. Camps that were closely attached or even owned by denominational bodies were the most vulnerable. In the years following the Great Recession, dozens of denominational camps were closed or liquidated by their synods or conferences in order to support other struggling ministries that were deemed more valuable. You recall our earlier mention of Presbyterian Camps in Saugatuck, Michigan, founded originally by Pastor Gray in 1899. The presbytery that owned this camp sold the property, in part, to cover a lawsuit levied against it. I spoke to former campers and parents who expressed the heartache caused by this decision. Other Mainline camps drifted away from their denominational connections toward a broad ecumenism or deemphasized specific Christian teachings in favor of a general notion of spirituality in hopes of attracting a wider clientele.

The ACA, meanwhile, reestablished itself as the nationwide leader in camping by reimagining its vision and turning toward scholarship designed to benefit the entire industry. These moves are reminiscent of the successful alignment of the camping movement with progressive education in the 1920s, and the dramatic increase of camping literature since the

---

disappearing, for by 1910 camping had become institutionalized" (Eells, *History of Organized Camping*, 57).

64. Senter, *When God Shows Up*, 286–87.
65. Bennett, "Camper Enrollment," 34.

turn of the century is analogous to that period. The current educational movement with which camping finds traction is known as *positive youth development* (PYD). The movement focuses on outcomes of education that extend beyond academics to such things as self-esteem, leadership, and spirituality. Meier and Henderson note, "In the first decade of the 21st century, the value of camps relative to positive youth development as well as human development has become a prominent focus. An emphasis on purposeful or intentional programming to attain desired outcomes in campers is widely accepted."[66]

Camp directors have proven enormously successful in marketing their own camp programs over the years, but they have struggled to demonstrate the value of Christian camping among Christian educators and scholars. Consequently, clergy members and educators who have had positive camp experiences are camp advocates, while those who have had negative experiences or have not been to camp are oftentimes skeptical of camp's value. Clergy members and educators who were trained in the 1950s and 1960s, when denominational camping was booming and Christian educators publicly endorsed the camp model, have been replaced in recent years. The new generation may have only heard of camp's benefits from a camp director's impassioned speech that sounds like a marketing ploy. Those who believe in the value of Christian camping may entrust their congregants to the camping professionals. Other pastors and youth ministers choose to follow the oldest model of church camping, dating back at least to Hinckley, Brooks, and Gray, by taking the young people or families of their congregation on an extended outdoor experience in hopes of building deeper relationships with each other, God, and creation. But leaders who are skeptical of the benefits of camping ministry have proven willing to liquidate camp properties, which are often very valuable.

In spite of these challenges, there was a steady resurgence of Christian camping following the Great Recession. While some camps were forced to close or consolidate, many were thriving, with progressive increases in summer camper numbers throughout the 2010s.[67] Even as Mainline church attendance continued to decline and Sunday school numbers dropped, summer camp enrollment was increasing, indicating a hunger for this ministry and its unique characteristics. Mainline camping leadership also began a new wave of ecumenical cooperation during this period, forming

---

66. Meier and Henderson, *Camp Counseling*, 16.

67. My research team at Sacred Playgrounds conducted surveys of Christian camp directors in Mainline camping associations connected with the group Outdoor Ministries Connection in 2014, 2016, and 2018, documenting these increasing numbers across seven denominations (Sorenson, "Outdoor Ministries Connection").

the group known as Outdoor Ministries Connection in 2014. Their efforts culminated in the Great Gathering of outdoor ministries professionals at Lake Junaluska in fall 2019, a gathering that facilitated numerous cross-denominational efforts and projects. While CCCA had a long-established annual conference of outdoor ministry leaders, mostly from Evangelical traditions, such a large gathering of professionals from Mainline camping traditions was unprecedented and has the potential to signal a new chapter in cooperation across Christian camping ministry.

It is important to know this history as we consider how Christian camps might respond to changing economic and religious times. Especially in the wake of the COVID-19 pandemic of 2020, many camps were forced to close temporarily and rethink how they do ministry. Some camps continue in the educational stream of evangelism and conversion. Others continue to rely on local congregational ministries to provide camp participants, even as this pool of participants continues to evaporate. Still others have softened their Christian message and adopted a more general notion of spirituality as part of a well-rounded upbringing. The choices that camping organizations make are critical because camping ministry has an important role to play in the revitalization of the Christian church not only as extensions of congregations, but also as primary entry points for lifelong faith formation and ministries that can prophetically move the church in new directions. It is not a matter of choosing between the dueling models of conversion or Christian nurture. Effective camps must be places for both. In order to reorient the understanding of camp's value among church professionals, we must explore why so many scholars have become dismissive and develop an understanding of how camping ministries are most effective in the twenty-first century church.

3

Toward a New Understanding of Summer Camp

My first full-time ministry job was director of youth ministries at a Lutheran church in the suburbs of Philadelphia. I was fresh out of seminary and hungry to apply my book learning to the practice of ministry among young people and families that I quickly grew to love. I remember diving into the literature for tips and tricks on youth ministry, quickly discovering that I could fill an entire bookcase with titles on the subject, ranging from very practical ideas for games or challenge activities to deeply theological works. As I read through these, I was consistently surprised to see how most well-known youth ministry authors treated camp. They either dismissed it as largely unimportant or used camp as a negative example. This was deeply troubling to me, though camp experiences remained an essential part of the youth ministries in my congregation. When I later transitioned to a ministry role at summer camp, I searched for books on camping ministry to fill my shelves. Surely, there would be a variety of resources available for this important ministry! I searched in vain. The lone resource I was able to cling to was a beautifully written book by Lutheran camping legend Jerry Manlove called *A Common Book of Camping*. The book was self-published and spiral-bound, available only in Lutheran circles. Where was the research on camp? Where were the theological treatments of this essential ministry?

Camp is a place of stories. These stories are powerful marketing tools, and camp directors have, for decades, been using their most potent stories to convince people of the value of camp. The reality is that throughout its history, organized camping has seldom enjoyed an institutional mandate like those which have existed for classroom learning and Christian education (e.g., Sunday school and confirmation training). Young people are required to attend school and, in many cases, receive formal religious instruction at churches, but camp is optional. Consequently, camp directors have been compelled to justify camp's existence to potential clients and supporters. Compelling stories of life-changing experiences provide that justification and help directors make *the case for camp*. The result is that the bulk of camp literature is based on anecdotal evidence for the value of camp, and this evidence is based on the exceptional cases of life-changing experiences. My friend and fellow camp researcher, Rob Ribbe, notes, "For too long, camp leaders have run their ministries with wonderful hearts, compelling vision, and undying effort, but with little qualitative and quantitative understanding of how camp experiences actually change lives."[1] Consequences for a reliance on anecdotal evidence are clear: camp itself is devalued and considered dispensable, contributing to the string of camp closures in recent years.

Camp as Locus of Practical Theology

In his classic *Brief Outline*, Freidrich Schleiermacher described practical theology as the crown of his theological tree, but he envisioned the field as an application of the theology generated in the other fields of philosophical and historical theology.[2] Theologians over the past century have sought to redefine Schleiermacher's notion of practical theology. Don Browning followed the work of Hiltner and others in reordering theory and praxis, redefining the entire field of theology in his influential *A Fundamental Practical Theology*. Browning argues that theory cannot be separated from practice and that theology itself develops from "theory-laden practices."[3] Practical theologians differ in their interdisciplinary approaches, but there is widespread agreement that practice informs theology. The practices and experiences once regarded as application of theory actually influence and redefine a person's understanding of God.

Ribbe has described camp as "an experiential laboratory."[4] While I agree with his assessment of camp as a place where experience constructs knowledge, I prefer the term *theological playground* because I think it implies a less formulaic environment, more akin to the playful work of the creator God in the world. Camp is a place with the potential to shape and sharpen theological perspectives. Scholarship is beginning to attend to ways in which the Christian camping experience affects participants' faith and understandings of God. This perspective is based on the notion that Christian practice and experience shape theology, leading to what

1. Ribbe, "Redefining Camp Ministry," 159.
2. Schleiermacher, *Brief Outline*.
3. Browning, *Fundamental Practical Theology*, 7.
4. Ribbe, "Redefining Camp Ministry," 144.

Browning calls "more critically held theory-laden practices."[5] Studies that operate from a *theory-to-practice* model are more concerned with efficacy of instruction based on preconceived (or divinely revealed) theories, while studies on faith formation assume that practice shapes meaning itself, including theological understanding.

Christian summer camp is a locus of practical theology. The *fun and games* of camp turn out to be generative theological praxes that take seriously the activity of Christ in the world through the power of the Holy Spirit. As practical theologians, and youth ministry scholars in particular, continue to make the case that their field is not mere application but rather the very foundation of theological understanding, they would do well to recognize Christian camping ministry as a place where the activity of practical theology is already underway. Practical theologians can learn a great deal from observing the theological playground of camp, and they can offer valuable insights to improve camp practices and thereby impact faith formation in the church. A look at the literature reminds us that we have a long way to go to convince scholars to take a serious look at camp.

How Camp Fell Out of Favor

The 1920s and 1930s saw the first doctoral dissertations about the educational benefits of camp, most notably from Columbia University students who studied with the major proponents of progressive education. Dimock and Hendry's 1929 study of Camp Amhek begins with the hopeful words, "The summer camp as an educational agency has unusual possibilities. . . . The camp is a new venture and willing, at least at the best, to make a fresh attack upon the problem of education."[6] L. B. Sharp, Carlos Ward, and others added to the literature that latched onto camp as a new educational enterprise with exciting possibilities to counter traditional, top-down educational models focused on rote learning. We considered some of their perspectives in the previous chapter. Scholarly attention on organized camping dried up in the 1940s, and it would not see a resurgence to equal the progressive education period until the turn of the century. In the interim, Christian educators began publishing about camping ministry as Christian camps thrived in the 1950s and 1960s.[7] These Christian camping writers relied heavily on the work of Dimock, Sharp, and Ward, essentially

---

5. Browning, *Fundamental Practical Theology*, 7.

6. Kilpatrick, "Foreword," vii.

7. Notable examples include: Bowman, *Spiritual Values in Camping*; Todd and Todd, *Camping for Christian Youth*; and Davis, *Church Camping*.

extending their progressive education arguments to include Christian education, faith formation, and conversion. For a time, camp was recognized as an essential piece of Christian education. Ensign and Ensign asserted in the 1950s, "Church camping is an integral part of the total program of Christian education in our churches, and camping contributes unique learning opportunities that cannot be duplicated in the church or church school."[8] As noted in the previous chapter, camping lost its privileged place in Christian education literature through the 1970s and 1980s.

Christian camping ministry has fallen from favor in academia with the rise of youth ministry as a professional field. The 1980s brought the beginning of what Senter describes as the "professionalization of youth ministry."[9] Conventions and academic conferences on youth ministry began across the country, and academic institutions began conferring doctoral degrees with emphases in youth ministry. The 1990s and following witnessed a corresponding explosion of youth ministry literature. The curious thing is that camp is almost entirely absent from the youth ministry literature from this period. Part of asserting the relevance of their theological discipline has meant that youth ministry writers must contend with the constant stream of manuals on silly skits, songs, and games that flood the market of youth ministry. Senter elaborates, "Perhaps the most frequently repeated criticism of Protestant youth ministries at the beginning of the twenty-first century was the accusation that they were merely fun and games."[10] Camp has proven to be an easy target for caricature, so it is often used as the antithesis of what youth ministry strives to be.

Youth ministry scholars use camp anecdotes to illustrate particular points, but camp is seldom examined as a ministry in its own right. Chap Clark shares the story of "Darrin," a youth group member "who became an overnight leader" after a significant camp experience but who quickly "left the faith behind" in college.[11] Clark's anecdote illustrates the type of faith that seems so vibrant but does not *stick* long-term. Mark Yaconelli shares a camp story in which he and his son buck the trend of the activity-saturated camp environment by walking slowly while the other kids "bolted toward the dining hall."[12] Yaconelli shares positive anecdotes from several spirituality retreats that he personally led in camp settings, but his brief summer camp stories serve primarily as contrasts to his vision of *contemplative youth ministry*.

8. Ensign and Ensign, *Camping Together as Christians*, 62.
9. Senter, *When God Shows Up*, 292.
10. Senter, *When God Shows Up*, 307.
11. Powell and Clark, *Sticky Faith*, 31–32.
12. Yaconelli, *Contemplative Youth Ministry*, 199.

Besides anecdotes, youth ministry writers describe camp as another youth group event, comparable to ski outings and lock-ins. It is oftentimes used as an example of an activity that overtaxes harried youth workers.[13]

Camp is most often used as a negative example of ministry that is emotionally charged but not lasting. The use of the emotionally charged camp experience as a vehicle for conversion dates to the earliest days of camping in the 1880s, but as the previous chapter notes, there is another stream of camping that deemphasizes conversion in favor of Christian nurture. Duffy Robbins highlights the problems of youth ministries that focus too much on "warm fuzzies" by sharing an anecdote about a camp leader who leads an activity in order to get the kids to cry.[14] David Kinnaman includes camps as part of the "mass production of disciples" approach to ministry that is impersonal, shallow, and focused on "more-is-better."[15] Kinnaman adds a brief anecdote about a young person who grew in her faith as a result of a camp experience, using this as evidence that "God can, of course, meet with anyone anywhere," implying that faith formation at camp is the exception to the rule.[16] Robbins reduces camp to a creative gimmick: "If we're building students whose faith is dependent primarily on a weekly skit, a creative Bible study, or a summer camp that is 'the best week of your life,' then we're building Christians whose faith simply won't sustain them beyond the high school years."[17] Setran and Kiesling warn that the intense religious experiences of "Christian camps, youth group retreats, conferences, mission trips, and service projects" might spark growth in faith, but "reliance on such experiences can be a barrier to emerging adult spiritual formation."[18] The argument is that the intensity of the summer camp experience sets an unrealistic standard for faith formation that is unsustainable in the home environment, making everyday Christianity and weekly church services seem blasé. These youth ministry writers are not examining camp as a ministry but rather as an idea that they apply to every form of camping ministry. They neglect the camp model, dominant among Mainline Protestant camps and present in most Evangelical camps I have worked with, that focuses on intentional partnerships with families and congregations.

---

13. Yaconelli, *Contemplative Youth Ministry*, 52; Devries, *Sustainable Youth Ministry*, 185.

14. Robbins, *Building a Youth Ministry*, 24.

15. Kinnaman, *You Lost Me*, 120–21.

16. Kinnaman, *You Lost Me*, 126–27.

17. Robbins, *Building a Youth Ministry*, 85.

18. Setran and Kiesling, *Spiritual Formation*, 43.

One of the most revealing references to camp in youth ministry literature is Mark Devries's characterization of the *camp counselor youth worker*. He does not define what he means by the term, as though he assumes everybody will understand the reference. He contrasts the "camp counselor youth worker" with the "sustainable leader," presumably referring to the relatively short duration of the camp experience in comparison to years of ministry in a youth group.[19] "Regular communication takes time," he says, "the kind of time a camp-counselor youth worker will not spend."[20] His major point seems to be that camp counselors are focused on individual relationships with young people, so the *camp counselor youth worker* builds a ministry centered around the person of the youth worker rather than building a team of leaders. He contends, "The result of growing a youth ministry through a camp counselor is the implosion of the youth ministry (and often the youth minister)."[21] Devries's language is telling in its dismissiveness of the role of camp counselor and the use of camp as a contrast to professional (or *sustainable*) youth ministry.

My own doctoral advisor and friend, Andrew Root, uses camp in a similar way. Following Bonhoeffer, Root argues against the practice of idealizing the Christian community because it alienates people from the realities and messiness of actual community, where Christ is found in ministry to the Other. He argues, "Youth ministry, then, has no task of locking young people down into some idea of faith. Rather, youth ministry seeks only to open free spaces where young people are affirmed and loved as persons, and through person-to-person encounter are asked to listen for the call of the living Christ."[22] As a camp advocate, I see clear echoes of the typical camp experience in this description! However, Root then goes on to say that camp, which is often held up as an ideal community, does not deal with the messiness of life but rather serves as a retreat from it. In arguing against reducing the church to an idea, Root reduces camp to an idea: a "self-enclosed" space that "exists for its short time by forgetting the messy realities of our day-to-day lives."[23]

Karen-Marie Yust offers one of the first peer-reviewed articles on Christian camping ministry to appear since youth ministry's emergence as an academic discipline. She summarizes the findings of the Indiana Camp Ministries Enhancement Program, a study of twenty-three diverse

19. Devries, *Sustainable Youth Ministry*, 140.
20. Devries, *Sustainable Youth Ministry*, 154.
21. Devries, *Sustainable Youth Ministry*, 143.
22. Root, *Bonhoeffer as Youth Worker*, 181.
23. Root, *Bonhoeffer as Youth Worker*, 197.

Christian camps in Indiana. Yust calls into question what she describes as the "conventional wisdom among camp directors that the experience of attending church camp is, for many people, one of the most significant factors in their overall spiritual formation as Christians."[24] She offers sharp critiques to the programs and methods of the camps she studies, dismissing them as largely "indistinguishable from similar camps in non-Christian settings."[25] She critiques the poor quality of the religious instruction and notes that what little religious programming she observed "is more tolerated than embraced."[26] She dismisses the findings of camp surveys that indicate significant gains in camper spirituality, asserting that they are based on unreliable end-of-week surveys that come too closely after the final night's climactic religious experience, which she also critiques as manipulative. The fun and games of camp, Yust argues, take precedence over religious instruction and faith formation. Her scathing critique ultimately concludes that camp is not much more than "an extension of their youth culture into another arena, where activities are comfortably similar to what one might do at school or home, but with a spiritual gloss."[27] Yust's article offers formal articulation of the reasons why camp is overlooked or dismissed in the majority of youth ministry literature.

The strange thing is that I have met and spoken with many of these youth ministry scholars. Though they do not write favorably about camp, most of them are camp supporters and will affirm the benefits of camp when I ask them. I have heard some speak at camping ministry conferences and offer stories of how they or their children were impacted by camp experiences. Somehow, there remains this disconnect in their writing that has tremendous consequences on professional ministers' perceptions of the value of camping ministry.

My colleague Kenda Creasy Dean has offered one of the only scholarly voices that is overtly supportive of camping ministry. Her turn to intentional theological reflection in the field of youth ministry includes summer camp, which she connects with eschatology. She presents camp as a "liminal space," arguing that in the traditionally climactic ending of the camp week "the heavenly life-as-it-should-be briefly merges with the life of a teenager, and young people glimpse, momentarily but significantly, the inbreaking of God."[28] It is significant to note that she is compelled to acknowledge traditional concerns about the camp experience, insisting multiple times

---

24. Yust, "Creating an Idyllic World," 178.
25. Yust, "Creating an Idyllic World," 180.
26. Yust, "Creating an Idyllic World," 183.
27. Yust, "Creating an Idyllic World," 187.
28. Root and Dean, *Theological Turn*, 172.

that it is not necessarily manipulative. It is also significant that, like other youth ministry writers, she refers to a specific model of camping ministry (with the climactic ending) as representative of the whole. Elsewhere, Dean argues, "Religious camps have impressive records of helping young people become more intentional about devotion, more secure in their faith identities, and therefore more confident and explicit in telling the God-story of their tradition."[29] She describes camp as a "faith immersion" experience that functions to improve fluency in the language and practices of a faith tradition.[30] We will return to this metaphor in chapter 6.

Amanda Drury echoes Dean's notion of camp as an immersion in faith language and practices. She contends, "A teenager might pick up on more religious language and imagery in a week away at church camp as opposed to one hour's worth of exposure once a week for the entire year at church."[31] Drury is one of many practical theologians calling for a serious examination of experience in faith formation, and her project focuses on the need for testimony. She notes the gradual excising of testimony from Christian worship and practice, locating "the testimony's final resting spot around the campfire on the last night of camp."[32] Some youth ministry scholars would cite this informal setting of testimony as one of the theological dangers of the camp experience, but Drury and Dean are among those calling for a reconsideration of camp as a locus of practical theology.

Youth Ministry Research

Research firms like Barna Group and Search Institute, along with academic institutions, have led the dramatic increase in youth ministry research since the 1990s. These studies focus on family life, congregations, and even short-term mission trips, but camp is excluded from nearly every study. Roehlkepartain makes no mention of camping ministry in his extensive description of the faith lives and commitments of Lutheran youth that is based on a review of multiple Search Institute studies.[33] The Exemplary Youth Ministry study includes seven denominations with strong camping traditions, but does not directly address the role of camping ministries partnering with and strengthening the exemplary congregations that are identified. The study highlights the significance of "youth retreats,"

29. Dean, *Almost Christian*, 154.
30. Dean, *Almost Christian*, 154–55.
31. Drury, *Saying Is Believing*, 50.
32. Drury, *Saying Is Believing*, 82.
33. Roehlkepartain, "Loose Bonds," 93–114.

"mission trips," and other "common youth ministry practices" without including camping ministry.[34]

There are tantalizing references to camping ministry in a handful of small youth ministry studies, but the data are quickly passed over or largely peripheral to the larger study. One study of youth attending Seventh-day Adventist schools examines the effects of youth ministry involvement on faith maturity. The study focuses on youth group and mission trips without mentioning camp a single time until the conclusion, when the writers ironically state that "Christian camping ministry featured as an important element" and that it "should not be overlooked as an important part of youth ministry."[35] In another study, "camp counselor" registered as an influential mentor relationship in spiritual formation among Christian adolescents, though the particulars of the camper-counselor relationship were not examined.[36] Another small study of Christian youth in New England found that "summer camp" was one of several key experiences that respondents indicate have "a lot of influence on their faith."[37] The 2013 "Hemorrhaging Faith" study identifies the Christian summer camp experience as one of many factors in young people's long-term engagement in faith communities, and a significant number of Canadian young people who stayed engaged in church said that their faith "came alive" at camp.[38] These studies show a peripheral but important inclusion of camp in youth ministry scholarship.

It is notable that these studies are mainly focused on Evangelical Christian communities and that camp is often included for its role in providing intense religious experiences, the very *mountaintop experiences* that Yust, Robbins, and others critique. Camp has a role in Evangelical youth ministry studies because of its perceived usefulness for conversion experiences. Fleming and Cannister emphasize camp's role in facilitating "the life-changing event of first accepting Christ," noting that 17.9 percent of their respondents "made a personal commitment to follow Christ at summer camp," along with "16.3 percent at a retreat."[39] One study sought to analyze the effects of spiritual transformation on adolescent virtue development. The researchers selected participants at a Young Life camp as the research subjects, postulating that the conversion event common on the last day of camp would function as a spiritual transformation. They were able to draw

34. Martinson et al., *Spirit and Culture*, 133.
35. Gane and Kijai, "Relationship," 62.
36. Lanker and Issler, "Relationship," 99.
37. Fleming and Cannister, "Assessing the Spiritual Formation," 76.
38. Penner et al., "Hemorrhaging Faith," 99.
39. Fleming and Cannister, "Assessing the Spiritual Formation," 80–81.

connections between spiritual transformation and virtue development, but they were confused by mixed results from examining the youth who experienced a conversion or recommitment to Christ. "Somewhat unexpectedly, change in spirituality and spiritual strivings was unrelated to reports of commitment or recommitment to God at camp in our sample."[40] The researchers stumbled across evidence that the conversion events so common at some (but not all!) Evangelical summer camps, and critiqued by many scholars, frequently offer a sort of camp high that quickly fades. As we will explore, this is particularly common when camps are not connected to congregational ministries, leaving young people with intensely emotional experiences that are difficult to interpret on their own. Theological skepticism about the significance of such conversion experiences in the camp setting, which are so dramatically caricatured in the 2006 documentary *Jesus Camp*, cause some youth ministry scholars and Christian educators to discount the relevance of the camp experience or to reduce all of camping ministry to short-term, emotionally charged experiences that contrast with *sustainable* or *professional* youth ministry.

National Study of Youth and Religion

The National Study of Youth and Religion (NSYR) is arguably the most significant youth ministry study of the early twenty-first century, leading to many scholarly publications in multiple fields. The first wave of the study (2003) gathered a nationally representative sample of American teenagers and, among scores of questions, asked how many times the teen had been a camper at a religious summer camp with religious teachings and songs in its program. The results show that fully 39 percent of American teenagers at the turn of the twenty-first century had attended a religious summer camp at least once, including more than half of Mainline Protestant and conservative Protestant teenagers.[41] These numbers, which are higher than the numbers of teenagers participating in mission/service trips and comparable to the numbers attending retreats, demonstrate that it is a glaring omission to exclude camp from youth ministry studies. Smith does not explore the camp variable in depth but rather concludes, "The effects of such involvements remain to be explored."[42] The five-year follow-up study of the NSYR (2008) does not address the camp variable at all, though camp is mentioned in the anecdotal

---

40. Schnitker et al., "Virtue Development," 33.
41. Smith and Denton, *Soul Searching*, 53.
42. Smith and Denton, *Soul Searching*, 54.

accounts without further assessment.[43] However, like many other youth ministry studies, it assesses the effects of mission trips on faith formation, finding them "not independently important."[44]

In one of my first forays into quantitative research, I was able to do secondary analysis of the NSYR data to measure the long-term effects of the religious summer camp experience. Essentially, we can compare the young people who attended religious camp as teenagers with those who did not attend to see if there were any differences after five years. The findings are fascinating. On the one hand, there were no statistically significant independent effects on measures of individual spirituality like belief in God, personal prayer, and perceived importance of faith after five years. However, on measures of communal spirituality, "a significant positive effect is clearly evident in the five-year follow-up, even when controlling for seventeen different variables."[45] These measures of communal spirituality included college campus ministry participation, participation in religious small groups, and frequency of religious service attendance. This was a revelation! Not only do we see evidence of long-term impacts of the camp experience, but we also get an idea of what those specific impacts are. Long-term impacts are not related to the content of camp lessons but, rather, to ongoing connection to Christian community. Many pastors and youth ministers are concerned with what they perceive to be bad theology espoused by some of the young college-age counselors in the camp setting. The long-term findings from the NSYR suggest that belief statements and theology are not the things that last from the camp experience. What lasts is engagement with Christian community and, as we shall explore, understanding that faith is important for daily life. Another concern in recent years among youth ministry scholars is the attrition rate of young people leaving their faith behind in later years, joining the ranks of the irreligious, the so-called *nones*. In the NSYR data, those who attended religious summer camp were over three times more likely to remain religious five years later than their peers who never attended camp. These findings present a strong argument for camp's lasting impact on faith formation. This is part of a turn to research in the broader field of summer camping, begun with ACA's "Directions" study in 2005, and it begins to bridge the gap between youth ministry scholarship and camp scholarship.

---

43. "Amanda" reflects on experiences as a camp counselor at a religious camp (Smith, *Souls in Transition*, 26–32).

44. Smith, *Souls in Transition*, 218.

45. Sorenson, "Summer Camp Experience," 28.

Camp Research

The American Camp Association (ACA) sought to reestablish itself as the leader of youth camping beginning in the late 1990s, casting a renewed vision aiming to reach the rather ambitious goal of 20 million campers per summer by 2020 (which was sadly made impossible by the COVID-19 pandemic that year). Among the priorities identified to attain this goal was a turn to outcomes-based research and scholarship. The "Directions" study, published in 2005, set a new standard for research in the field. It involved more than 5,000 campers and their parents from eighty camps in a mixed-methods assessment of camp's impact on ten developmental outcomes. The centerpiece of the study was a quantitative assessment that measured the developmental outcomes before camp, immediately after camp, and six months later. Campers showed statistically significant growth on all ten outcomes, and much of the growth persisted through the six-month follow-up.[46] The study spawned numerous scholarly articles, multiple camp assessment tools, and many subsequent studies. One of the measured outcomes was "spirituality," so the study lent itself to secondary analysis of the religiously affiliated camps that participated in the study (about a quarter of the total, with the rest private and agency camps). Henderson et al. note that campers at camps that are intentional about religious/spiritual programming show much higher spiritual development postcamp and also retain some of this growth in the six-month follow-up, whereas campers at other camps do not.[47] Camp research, following the lead of the "Directions" study, has demonstrated the importance of intentional goals and programming in order to attain desired outcomes. Another study concludes, "Positive outcomes do not just occur because children attend camp; these desired outcomes must be planned, measured, and then incorporated into future program planning efforts."[48] These studies offer solid evidence that camps focused on faith-centered programming can offer faith-based outcomes, in addition to those outcomes present at camps of all types.

In the years since the "Directions" study, ACA has presided over an explosion of camp research, including regular articles in their publication, *Camping* magazine, peer-reviewed articles, dissertations, and major research projects focused on the outcomes of camp experiences. They also began hosting a research forum at their annual conference, inviting professors and graduate students to present new research on camp. A host

---

46. Thurber et al., "Youth Development Outcomes," 241–54.
47. Henderson et al., "Questions Raised," 179–95.
48. Garst et al., "Youth Development," 83.

of scholars has persuasively and repeatedly affirmed that summer camps are remarkably successful in achieving desired outcomes related to leadership ability, social skills, self-confidence, independence, and many others. Research has become a strategic priority of ACA, as camp directors have begun to understand the importance of research in telling their stories in new ways. ACA director of research Laurie Browne notes, "Doing research in camps is not easy, but something our industry needs to support our work into the 21st century."[49]

Spirituality and Religion in Camp Literature

One of the difficulties of the ACA studies is that *spirituality* is a difficult term to define. Friends and colleagues who were part of the panel developing the "Directions" study indicated that they advocated the inclusion of questions specifically related to faith formation but were overruled. The final questionnaire had only four survey items to assess spirituality, and the questions were designed so that they would not be offensive to secular camps (e.g., "Nature helps me feel closer to God").[50] The spirituality questions were also the only items in the survey to be made optional. As Henderson and Bialeschki point out, "Camp experiences offer the potential for spiritual development, but often in an implicit and tangential way."[51] The tension between religiously affiliated camps and the mainstream camping movement, which led to the formation of CCCA as a separate organization, has continued to the present day. Fewer than half of Christian camps are accredited through ACA, in large part because there is a strong perception that religious viewpoints are not taken seriously.

Spirituality as a generic affective construct is markedly different from *faith formation* and *Christian education*. Ferguson argues that "the interconnection between religion and spirituality must be untangled" in order to properly understand camp's role in nurturing spirituality. She defines spirituality as "the intrinsic capacity of the human for self-transcendence and recognizes that each human is rooted in something larger than just the self—perhaps even the holy."[52] While this definition of spirituality tries to encompass religious believers, it is inadequate to capture the stated outcomes of religiously affiliated camps, whether they are focused on conversion experiences or nurturing ongoing faith formation. Paul Heintzman and his colleague

49. Browne, "Research 360," para. 1.
50. Henderson et al., "Development and Application," 15.
51. Henderson and Bialeschki, "Spiritual Development," 108.
52. Ferguson, "Camps and Spirituality," 50.

uncovered this truth in a small qualitative study of Canadian YMCA camp participants in which they let the participants themselves define spirituality. They concluded that camp nurtures a general sense of spirituality in four ways: "the camp's natural and non-urban setting," "experiencing time alone," "social experiences," and "positive feelings experienced at camp."[53] However, they note that one religiously committed participant did not perceive growth in spirituality because "he related his spirituality with his religion, which was not cultivated at camp."[54] These studies demonstrate the difficulties of disentangling religious beliefs from spirituality, particularly in quantitative measurements. Many of the findings from studies on summer camp point to the activity of God in the world, including such things as strengthening relationships and developing affinity for the natural world, but the general attempts at measuring spirituality are insufficient.

Jewish Camping

Jewish camping is the most well-researched branch of religious camping, and it demonstrates the importance of overt religious instruction as opposed to general spirituality. Summer camp is well integrated into the religious education of Jewish young people, and research has helped to improve the quality of Jewish camping and to provide a rationale for the importance of summer camp. Sales and Saxe, in their exemplary study of Jewish camps throughout the country, found that one of camp's primary roles is that of a Jewish socializing experience. As members of a minority religion, Jewish young people are pressured to assimilate their religion with societal norms, but camps provide them with experiences of immersion in Jewish community that serve to help them live more fully into their Jewish identities. They poetically note, "When Judaism is in the air, as it is at many camps, children take it in as effortlessly as breathing."[55] They note the power of relationships in the camp experience and the tremendous influence of the summer staff members, even though they found that many of them lacked more than surface knowledge of Judaism. They also discovered among some camps a degree of "compartmentalization" of religious studies and fun activities that Yust notes is so common at the Christian camps she studied in Indiana. They reject this approach, instead extolling the educational benefits of camps that practice an integration in which Jewish learning is "infused into

---

53. Sweatman and Heintzman, "Perceived Impact," 25–28.
54. Sweatman and Heintzman, "Perceived Impact," 30.
55. Sales and Saxe, *"How Goodly Are Thy Tents,"* 77.

many different activities."[56] The experience of Jewish camp participants living and breathing their religious identity is a key element of camping ministry that is applicable to Christian camping, which affirms the movement of the divine Spirit, or breath (*ruach*), over the waters of creation (Gen 1:2) and in the flesh of humanity (Gen 2:7).

The Confirmation Project

The Confirmation Project was the first major youth ministry study to intentionally consider camping ministry's contribution to Christian education and faith formation. This inclusion can be seen as part of a broader move in practical theology to consider religious experience, and it was also the result of the increased scholarly attention garnered by the ACA studies. These movements aligned with the release of findings from a study on confirmation work in Europe, on which the Confirmation Project was based.

The centerpiece of the European study was a two-wave quantitative study of the effectiveness of confirmation work in seven countries. The study found that, on average, there was very little change in religious commitment or education over the course of confirmation instruction. (Those of us who have spent countless hours in confirmation ministries groan collectively.) However, there was a glimmer of hope. Two countries in the study—Finland and Sweden—showed significantly higher growth than the other five in several of the religious commitment and program satisfaction variables. The key difference that set the Finnish and Swedish confirmation programs apart from the others was that the majority of their confirmation training took place at camp.

I traveled to Finland as part of the American research team to observe their camping programs, and our group got to attend a Finnish confirmation camp. I discovered on this trip that nearly everyone in Finland (90 percent of the total population!) attends confirmation camp at age fifteen. In fact, a higher percentage of young people attend confirmation camp than the percentage of the Finnish population that is Lutheran, indicating that some young people attend simply because everyone else is doing it. On the plane ride to Helsinki, I sat next to a middle-aged man who fondly recalled his camp experience more than thirty years previously. On the flight home, I sat next to a woman in her twenties who loved her own camp experience so much that she returned for two subsequent years as a young confirmed volunteer (known as an *isonen*).

---

56. Sales and Saxe, *"How Goodly Are Thy Tents,"* 60.

What was remarkable to me when I arrived was how similar the camp experience looked and felt to what I was accustomed to in the United States. I felt like I could have been at any Lutheran camp in the upper Midwest. The camp was eight days long. There were games, silly skits, kayaking on the lake, and grace sung before meals. Bible study and Christian education were creatively woven into the programming. The real tragedy in Finland is that the camp experience is difficult to connect to the congregation because hardly anyone finds value in church attendance or personal religious practices. None of the campers I spoke with went to church with any frequency, and it was laughable to most of them that they would engage congregational ministry after camp was over. "Church is for old people and women with babies," one boy told me pointedly. Faith was valuable to them in only certain times of life, such as marriage, death, or personal tragedy. Young people in Finland regard the church as a sort of *spiritual storehouse* that provides access for contents that are valuable, but for occasional use only.[57] However, the camp experience demonstrated great potential for transformation in the lives of these young people, along with the volunteers that were serving at camp. My conclusion was, "The camp model may, in effect, be offering two keys. One is the key to access the spiritual storehouse. The other is the key to change the church."[58]

In many ways, it was a haunting experience for me because I could see in vivid clarity what might happen in the United States if congregational engagement continues to decline. In Finland, camp is recognized and promoted across the country as a vibrant and even transformative ministry. There are church professionals and scholars that help support camp financially and improve the ministries. My colleague Kati Niemelä has extensively researched camp in Finland, demonstrating that while the *camp high* so evident in postcamp surveys fades gradually over time it is also maintained to some degree, long-term, a finding similar to what we observed in the NSYR data. She notes, "Over the course of five years attitudes sank from what they were at the end of confirmation training, but were still more positive than at the beginning of training."[59] Camp was, in fact, transformative in the lives of these young people, but there were few structures besides camp to sustain faith. Even the young woman I sat next to on the plane was only able to sustain her faith throughout high school because she continued volunteering at camp as an *Isonen*. In the United States, we seem to have the opposite

57. You can read more about the findings of the qualitative study I did on the Finnish confirmation camp experience in Sorenson, "Transforming the Spiritual Storehouse," 179–80.

58. Sorenson, "Transforming the Spiritual Storehouse," 188.

59. Niemelä, *Does Confirmation Training Really Matter?*, 94.

problem. We still have bright lights of congregational vitality, even in the midst of overall decline, but camping ministry lacks the institutional and scholarly recognition that it enjoys in Finland. The task before us is to envision camping ministry as an integral part of a faith-forming ecology, one that can provide new vitality to congregational ministries and transform practice in ways that bear witness to the inbreaking of God in the world. This view of camp's role in offering something substantive and transformative to the life and ministry of the church is vastly different from the literature that reduces camp to *fun and games*, emotional manipulation, or, at best, a brief spiritual high. Camping ministry is moving past the status of anecdote to consideration as a valuable field of inquiry in its own right.

Four Types of Christian Camps

Our review of the literature and the field of camping ministry makes clear that Christian summer camp is a diverse industry. Besides programmatic differences and the ongoing tension between conversion and Christian nurture, there are at least four distinct types of Christian summer camps that have emerged.[60] These camps do not always have the same goals. It appears that many of the scholars who are dismissive of camp are actually critiquing certain camp models.

Type 1: Nominal Camps

Yust and others have shed light on a subset of Christian camping that is almost indistinguishable from secular camps, aside from a spiritual gloss or occasional Christian practices. This first type can be summarized as *nominally Christian* camps in that they have historical connections to Christian groups or denominations but have adopted an approach that has little to do with faith formation. Historically, the YMCA camps were the first to trend in this direction, though there are now some denominationally affiliated camps that would place themselves in the nominal category. Some of these camps prioritize a general notion of spirituality over overt Christian teachings. This is the least common type of Christian camp, accounting for less than 10 percent of Mainline camps and less than 5 percent of Evangelical camps. We will not extensively address this camp

---

60. This typology first emerged as part of the Confirmation Project research and is detailed quantitatively in my dissertation (Sorenson, "Theological Playground," 157–61).

type because it is uncommon among Christian camps and robustly studied through ACA and other organizations that focus on the nonreligious outcomes of summer camp.

Type 2: Compartmentalized Camps

This subset of camps is difficult to cleanly categorize because it is characterized by a moderate connection to Christian faith and teachings. In general, these camps are only loosely connected to congregational ministries. Faith may be an important element, but it is not at the center of camp programming and goals. As opposed to the faith-centered characteristic that we will cover in chapter 6, these camps might be considered faith *adjacent*. What these camps often look like in practice is a compartmentalized ministry, where faith-based programs like worship and Bible study happen separately from more traditional camp programming. Games and activities are seldom connected intentionally to faith reflection. When I speak with camp counselors at compartmentalized camps, I often find that they do not consider themselves Christians, and they might even take their daily break while their campers have a time of Christian education with a visiting clergy member or specialty staff member. As many as a quarter of Christian camps operate compartmentalized programs, and camps tend to fluctuate in and out of this category based on the intentionality and commitment of camp leadership.

Type 3: Disconnected Camps

These camps operate faith-centered, often highly impactful ministries without a strong connection to congregations. They can be seen as islands of faith with only a few routes leading to partnership ministries. We can see this model clearly in our example from Finland, though it looks slightly different in the United States. The prototypical disconnected camp might offer a highly emotional religious experience without intentionally connecting the campers to ministries that can help them interpret the experience and incorporate their new understandings in ongoing lives of discipleship. This type of camp is also common among denominational camps that find themselves disconnected from denominational teachings. The disconnect is sometimes intentional, as with camps that see themselves as more conservative or progressive than their affiliated congregations, though it sometimes occurs through simple neglect of historical partnerships. Another common pathway to a disconnected camp is when congregational ministers downplay the impacts or importance of camping ministry, thereby reducing their support from what has the potential to be an important partnership ministry. Over time, this disconnect can lead some camps to deemphasize their faith-centered programs as they reach out to clientele that may be less receptive to overt Christian teachings. Because of this, disconnected camps occasionally trend toward a more compartmentalized ministry, something that can further distance them from their congregational partners. Disconnected camps comprise roughly a quarter of Christian camps.

Type 4: Integrated Camps

Integrated camps have both a strong emphasis on faith formation and a strong connection to congregational ministries. This remains the most common camp type, comprising nearly half of all Christian camps. While my research team has measured fluctuation among the other camp types, integrated camps tend to stay in this category over time. My hunch is that this is because they have developed durable partnerships that help the camp maintain its identity. Congregations and their leaders rely on camping ministries as part of an integrated ecology of faith formation, and they have a stake in keeping these ministries both faith-centered and connected to the congregation. The research we will continue to explore reveals the clear benefits of the integrated camp model. We have identified some of the historical reasons that some Christian camps have moved away from it, but our task now is to explore how and why camps can reclaim an integrated approach so they are established as integral parts of the ecology of faith formation.

What we require is a deep understanding of the logic of Christian camp. We will explore the fundamentals of Christian camping in part 2, drawing from personal stories, empirical research, and associated literature to discover how and why camp works. We will focus especially on integrated camps because these are the ministries where the five fundamentals of Christian camping are most consistently found. Disconnected camps can also have all of the fundamentals, though they tend to be less effective in nurturing outcomes that last long-term because they are less likely to be reinforced in the weeks and months following camp. It is evident, therefore, that camps and their congregational partners should work toward a more integrated approach to ministry.

Part 2: **The Fundamentals of Christian Summer Camp**

"All clear?"

The voice rang out to my right, and I was jolted out of my reverie. It was a beautiful day at camp Lutherlyn in western Pennsylvania. The near constant rain from the past few days had mercifully stopped, and the sun was peeking in diagonal beams through the canopy of hardwoods. The babble of a nearby creek and a gentle breeze through the leaves were the only sounds until the cry broke the spell. I was sitting alone in a large outdoor amphitheater, with seating for over 300. It was settled into a hillside and arranged like a large sanctuary, with a stone altar and rough-cut wooden cross at the front. Over a hundred summer camp participants were scattered throughout the camp, participating in afternoon activities while the sun shone. This week was confirmation camp at Lutherlyn, when pastors from area congregations accompanied young people to camp for a week of camp activities interspersed with Christian education.

I was at Lutherlyn as part of The Confirmation Project, a nationwide study on confirmation ministry in five Protestant denominations and one of two major research projects I was involved with that summer. The second was a small study that our team called the Effective Camp Research Project. Try as I might to stagger these projects to limit time away from my family and my PhD studies, the site visits for both ended up being in the same summer. The upshot was that I was deeply immersed in a variety of camp experiences that summer, at the same time that I was reading deep scholarly works for my PhD program and in consistent conversation with some of the best scholars in the country. I went on five four-day site visits that summer, travelling to Pennsylvania, Texas, California, Illinois, and Wisconsin to camps in four different denominations. My colleagues on the Effective Camp Research Project visited two additional sites. At each site, we observed the programs, participated in the activities and worship services, and interviewed camp directors, summer staff, visiting church leaders, and campers.

As I sat in the outdoor sanctuary at Lutherlyn, I was deep in thought and prayer, wondering how I might characterize the camp experience. That is when the shout rang out. An answering shout came from far to my left: "All clear!" Then I heard the unmistakable "z-zz-zzz-Z-ZZ-ZZZ" of a zipline. The young girl appeared through the trees on my right, a look somewhere between pure joy and sheer terror on her face. She zipped right past the rough-cut wooden cross and out of sight to my left. I smiled. In all of the grand theological language available to me, I could not do much better at describing camp than *a zipline through a sanctuary*.

Of course, as our research team got together and pored over the transcripts, field notes, and survey data from camper parents and the campers themselves, we came up with something more systematic. We identified five characteristics that were clearly fundamental to the Christian camp experience.[1] We will unpack each of these characteristics in turn over the next five chapters. These characteristics have no set order or direction of influence, and they do not cause the change that we so often identify at camp. Rather, the five fundamental characteristics together give rise to the camp experience and open the space for change to happen, alongside the movement of the Holy Spirit. When one characteristic broke down, the camp experience itself broke down and, in the words of several participants, no longer felt like camp. The characteristics we identified are: unplugged from home, participatory, faith-centered, relational, and safe space.

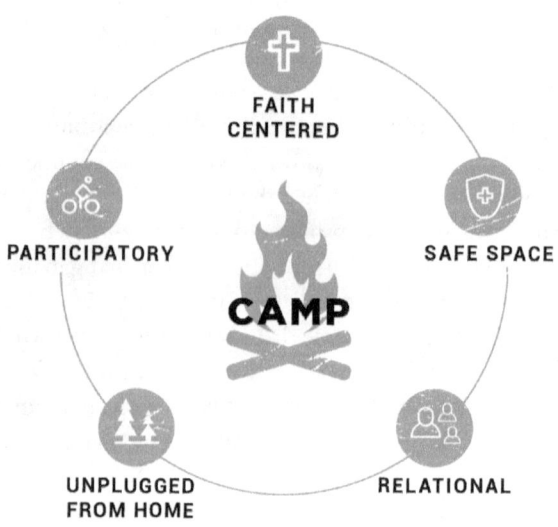

The five fundamental characteristics of Christian summer camp

1. Sorenson et al., "Effective Camp Research Project."

The funny thing is, we could have just summed it up as *a zipline through a sanctuary*. Camp is *unplugged from home* in that campers are physically removed from their home lives and from their familiar *habitus*, or way of life, particularly their connection to technological devices. The zipline at Lutherlyn begins from a platform more than 40 feet in the air, physically separated from what is familiar (the ground!) and affording a fresh perspective on the world around. The *participatory* nature of camp is on full display in the zipline, as all of the senses are engaged in experiential learning and camper agency, hallmarks of the camp experience. The zipline at Lutherlyn passes right through the sanctuary, an experiential trip through the *faith-centered* nature of camp, where campers are immersed in faith practices and language throughout the experience. At first glance, the zipline is a solitary element, but that ignores the staff members at each end of the zipline ensuring camper safety, the others who supported the camper on the climb to the platform, and all of the cabinmates who encouraged the camper on the journey. While each camper has their own unique experience, whether on the zipline or at camp, both of these are highly *relational* experiences. The final characteristic, camp is a *safe space*, is on full display on the zipline, one of the most dangerous activities common at many camps. The campers are kept physically safe with a series of belay systems and redundant equipment checks, and they are kept emotionally safe as they are encouraged but not forced each step of the journey.

As we explore each of these five fundamental characteristics in depth, we will see a clearer picture of how the camp experience functions as a sacred playground and opens the space for lasting change in the lives of participants. Along the way, we will dialogue with key thinkers and incorporate theological concepts alongside stories and research data from camps across the country. Since that highly immersive summer of site visits, my research team has surveyed and spoken with thousands of campers, parents, and summer staff members. These data will offer depth, confirmation, and clarity to the observations that follow.

4

A New Perspective: Camp Is Unplugged from Home

Stargazing is one of my favorite camp activities, something I remember vividly from my very first camp experience, when my counselor, Brian, took our group on a night hike and had us make up our own constellations (I can still find the wheelchair we identified!). I love helping young campers discover the wonder of the night sky. When I was a camp program director, a donor gifted the camp a forty-eight-inch reflecting telescope, and he showed me how to use it. I never tired of the awe and wonder of the young campers who looked at the rings of Saturn or the moons of Jupiter for the first time. I always strove to get campers away from light pollution and let them look up. Usually, I would help them find the North Star and draw connections with Jesus, who serves as the focal point of our faith, around which the rest of our lives revolve. But I would also just let them look in silence. More often than not, the role of the facilitator is to keep silent and make space for the experience.

My youngest son came home from his most recent summer camp experience talking about one night that his group camped out. He was in a tent with two other boys, and he explained that there was a hole in one side of their rather worn-out tent. One boy was joking around by sticking his head outside the hole, and he was brought up short. "Wow, look at the stars!" he said. The other two boys partially unzipped the bottom of the tent door and slipped their heads out to have a look. "Wow!" they said in awe. The Milky Way stretched luminously across the sky, and they marveled at the sight of more stars than they had ever seen. My son identified for his friends a few of the constellations that he remembered from our times stargazing. Then they started making up constellations of their own, laughing together at what they identified drawn across the night sky. They fell asleep that way: three preteen boys with their heads hanging out of a tattered A-frame tent.

We start with being unplugged from home not because it is the most important (remember, there is no set order) but because it is probably the most recognizable characteristic of camp. This characteristic has several meanings. The most obvious is the absence of technology, but even more prominent than this is the idea of disconnecting from everyday life. Camp participants often have a strong sense that they are *away*, and this opens them to new experiences and consideration of new possibilities. The feeling is visceral for many campers, some of whom experience a high degree of homesickness and even shed tears as they talk about missing members of their families. Whenever she led groups on backpacking trips in the Rocky Mountains, my wife, Anna, would explain to the group leaders, "Out of our comfort zones is where we grow." The novelty of the camp setting helps young people find their growing edge.

Other campers express relief of being in a relaxing environment away from stressful or conflict-ridden home lives. One group of boys I met with at Camp All Saints spoke of having relief from their violent home neighborhoods in Dallas, and other campers expressed how nice it was to be away from the *drama* of school. Many campers describe the feeling in terms of being safe, a characteristic we will cover more thoroughly in chapter 8. They spoke of feeling safe to be themselves and safe to express their beliefs freely, something that many considered unsafe at school or at home, where they thought they might be *judged*. "It feels like another world," one camper summed it up to me.[1]

Returning to our analogy of a *zipline through a sanctuary*, we are speaking here about the view from the platform. When campers participate in a high-ropes element like a zipline, they climb to a platform that is high off the ground (in the case of Lutherlyn, more than 40 feet). There is oftentimes a sense of disequilibrium when they are up this high. Even those who do not think of themselves as scared of heights tend to grip the safety rope pretty tightly or cling to a support pole. There is a palpable sense of adventure when a person is up this high, and this is combined with a new perspective that is not possible when their feet are on solid ground. They have a birds-eye view of the surrounding area of camp and, looking down, they can see their friends looking back up at them, shouting words of encouragement. "I feel like people don't really end up getting away from everything that they're comfortable with," one young camper told me. "Once you actually get away from your life, you can see a whole different angle, and it can be a lot more fun and exciting."[2] One of the greatest

1. Camp Lutherlyn Girls.
2. Lutherdale Girls.

benefits of the camp experience is providing this chance to see life from a different perspective. This new perspective and the act of stepping outside their comfort zones prime the campers for growth.

Away from Home: Camp as Pilgrimage

Camp is a journey to and from. Stephen Venable and Donald Joy describe this movement of camp as, "First, we are uprooted from our normal, everyday lives" and then "Second, we are re-rooted in a place where we can grow in grace and faith."[3] Participants leave their homes for a set period of time and embark on a spiritual journey, which helps offer a new perspective on their life back home. In these ways, camp is closely related to the practice of Christian pilgrimage. Brett Webb-Mitchell writes, "Key to all pilgrimages is both a *reason* for leaving and a place of departure, the genesis of the journey, *and* the destination point."[4] Summer campers give a variety of reasons for why they come to camp. Some are forced or compelled to be there by parents who either want them to have a growing experience or simply want some respite for themselves (or both). Some are interested in making new friends or are invited by a friend to come. The ongoing Effective Camp Project research has demonstrated, however, that the two most important reasons for campers to come to camp are that they want to have fun and that they want to grow in their faith or learn more about God. This latter reason often surprises parents and ministry professionals, who tend to think that young people are more interested in friends or new experiences than faith. The campers indicate otherwise. Most campers are very aware that they are coming to a Christian camp, and they have the expectation that the experience will be spiritually fulfilling or renewing in some way.

The destination of a summer camp pilgrimage is most often a specific camp property that has a deep history of religious experience. We explored some of these histories in chapter 2. Most camps hold as much religious meaning to participants as the most sacred pilgrimage sites do for their pilgrims, like the Catedral de Santiago de Compostela, or the Church of the Holy Sepulchre. Like these places, camps are dripping with history and religious significance. I still get chills every time I return to my home camp and cross the creek over the narrow bridge that serves as the only entrance. I have heard people recounting miracles that have occurred at their camp property, religious conversions that have taken place, and famous faith leaders who have preached there. Campers travel to these holy places and

---

3. Venable and Joy, *How to Use Camping Experiences*, 9–10.
4. Webb-Mitchell, *Practicing Pilgrimage*, 20 (italics original).

are open to the possibility of change in their lives or a unique encounter with the holy. This structure of the camp experience creates a liminal space. Webb-Mitchell explains, "In a liminal state, a person is on the threshold of change, being in between a phase of life, from the old to the new."[5] Webb-Mitchell goes on to describe some of the key characteristics of pilgrimage, including the value of community, the role of education, the performance of regular rituals or Christian practices, and the ability to get outside in God's creation. All of these are hallmarks of the camp experience. It is certainly not a stretch to name the Christian summer camp experience a pilgrimage designed for young people.

The Gifts of God's Creation

Let's consider the outdoor environment of camp, which Webb-Mitchell highlights as a key component of pilgrimage. The outdoor environment does not create the feeling of being away, whether at camp or on pilgrimage, but it clearly adds to it. Gazing at the clear night sky, lying in the wet grass, or hiking through the woods are novel experiences for many participants that can both relax them and serve to heighten awareness. Camp participants are able to use the feelings of freedom and disorientation to gain new perspective on their lives away from camp. More and more, it seems, I hear comments from people who say something like, "Camping for me is staying in the Motel 6." Even more common is the claim, "I am not an outdoors person." Theologically and anthropologically, of course, this is a ridiculous statement. We are created from the dust of the earth and destined to return there (Gen 3:19), and the human species has evolved to thrive as part of the Earth's ecosystem. We are designed to be outdoor people, and there is a growing body of research uncovering the adverse effects on physical and psychological health linked to separation from nature. In her book *The Nature Fix*, Florence Williams makes the case that connection to nature is necessary for basic human health, drawing heavily from the fields of neuroscience and psychology. The perceived need to be removed from the outdoors is unnatural, though it is increasingly common, particularly in Western society. Williams notes wistfully, "We once had a familiar relationship with nature; we knew it on a first-name basis. But now we need professionals to help us reacquaint ourselves with the woods."[6]

Outdoor ministry is one of these professional fields that functions to reconnect people with nature. This has been part of camp's appeal since it

---

5. Webb-Mitchell, *Practicing Pilgrimage*, 21.
6. Williams, *Nature Fix*, 159.

began in the 1880s during the Industrial Revolution, when people were increasingly alarmed at the squalor of city living. Cities are much cleaner than at the height of the Industrial Revolution, and they generally go to great lengths to plant trees and provide open green space. The challenge now is getting people outside in the first place. This is especially true with children. In his book *Last Child in the Woods*, Richard Louv traces the shift of childhood free play to indoor settings, noting that outdoor experiences that were once commonplace, like exploring the woods alone or climbing a tree, are portrayed as scary or dangerous. He also contends that a highly intellectual understanding of the outdoors has replaced a simple sense of awe and wonder. He notes that when these are combined with the availability of numerous engaging video games and Internet options, many children dismiss outdoor experiences as boring. He coins the term *nature deficit disorder*, arguing along with Williams and others that chronic separation from the natural world has detrimental effects on physical health, mental well-being, and social interaction.[7]

Interaction with creation is also essential for a healthy relationship with God and understanding of humanity's place in the world. Theologians trained in the Western traditions are often wary or dismissive of outdoor ministries because of the tendency toward natural theology. There is concern among many theologians (usually influenced by Karl Barth) that a general revelation present in all of creation might supersede the special revelation of God in Jesus Christ. Moltmann helps us move past this unease with a highly developed pneumatology that acknowledges the presence of God's Spirit in all of created life. The Spirit is the divine *ruach* that hovers over the waters of creation (Gen 1:2) and gives breath to all life (Gen 2:7). Moltmann is bold enough to say, "Every experience of a creation of the Spirit is also an experience of the Spirit itself."[8] Moltmann does not confuse these experiences with the definitive revelation of Christ, but he affirms that a Trinitarian understanding of God must acknowledge the creative movement of the Spirit in the world.[9]

Camping ministry professionals are often accused of being pantheists (or at least, along with Moltmann, panentheists), and I know at least a few that would proudly claim this as a badge of honor. Lutheran camping theologian Jerry Manlove notes that he was surprised when systematic

---

7. Louv, *Last Child in the Woods*.

8. Moltmann, *Spirit of Life*, 35.

9. On his Trinitarian understanding of revelation, Moltmann writes, "We can see who God 'the Father of Jesus Christ' is, solely from Jesus' experiences of God, and from people's experiences of the Spirit when they live in fellowship with Jesus" (Moltmann, *Spirit of Life*, 101).

theologians labeled him in such a way. He muses that the commonly used term "Bible camp" carries connotations of boot camp and oftentimes seems more interested in indoctrination or conversion to a particular denomination. He writes, "I think 'outdoor ministries' is a better description of church camping. It implies that learning about the outdoors and our place in creation are important parts of one's faith journey."[10] Camp is a place where Christian thinkers understand and acknowledge that God is present and at work in the created world, a truth attested in Scripture and many non-Western theological traditions.[11] Creation joins us in offering praise to God (Ps 98), celebrates alongside us (Isa 55:12), and groans with eager longing for the redemption of the world (Rom 8:19–23). The primary biblical locus of theophany is the wilderness. Consider the explicit role of the outdoors in God encounters for people like Jacob (Gen 28), Moses (Exod 3), Elijah (2 Kgs 19), Ezekiel (Ezek 1), John the Baptist (Mark 1), and the disciples (Matt 17). We should not be surprised that people feel greater connection to God and are more aware of encounters with the holy when they are outdoors, particularly in wilderness locations. Campers in the Effective Camp Project left camp significantly more likely to agree that "being in nature helps me feel closer to God" compared with the first day of camp.[12] As we continue to see, the campers' experiences of God were much more complex than finding God in creation, but the outdoor context contributed to their encounters with the holy.

Moltmann points out that part of this attunement to the holy involves separation from technology. He writes, "In the mass cities, human beings encounter only their own products," arguing that this leads to a narcissistic and "anthropocentric view of the world."[13] Connection with nature, on the other hand, opens humanity to the experience of awe and wonder. Theologians may quibble about the experiences of God's Spirit in the created world, but they can come together in the understanding that we only glimpse the majesty of God doxologically. The wonders of the created world, from the majestic sunset and mysteries of distant star systems to the intricate workings of tiny insects and microbial life, draw us to seek out and praise the

---

10. Manlove and Kettl, *Common Book of Camping*, 118–19.

11. I am especially captivated by the Native American understanding of creation, which understands life as intertwined, with humans codependent with and part of the same family as animals and plant life. For an illuminating exploration of Native American Christian theology, see Kidwell et al., *Native American Theology*.

12. On the last day of camp, 76 percent of campers agreed with this statement, compared with 68 percent on the first day of camp. The change was statistically significant: $t5692=17.328$, $p<.001$.

13. Moltmann, *Spirit of Life*, 31.

one who creates and sustains all life, the one revealed in the person of Jesus Christ and present in all of creation.

The Cycle of Dwelling

If camp did nothing but expose children to the natural world for extended periods of time, it would have great value, but there is much more to the experience of being unplugged from home. Campers are removed from what we will call their cycle of dwelling. F. LeRon Shults and Steven Sandage offer a helpful model of this. They contend that human spirituality cycles between spiritual dwelling and spiritual seeking.[14] Spiritual dwelling is characterized by feelings of familiarity, comfort, and safety, oftentimes in the context of a spiritual community that normalizes practices and rituals. Transformation is possible when someone is taken out of their cycle of spiritual dwelling and into a period of seeking, something that happens intentionally both at summer camp and on pilgrimage. They note that this often happens because of a rupture or crisis in a person's life that causes them to question or doubt their current understanding. This might include the death of a loved one, a significant life passage like the birth of a child, or a kind of spiritual awakening. With guidance during their period of seeking, they can enter a new cycle of spiritual dwelling with more deeply held or complex understandings of the holy. They dub this process of alternating cycles *the crucible of spiritual transformation.*[15]

This model is helpful for us to understand the transforming potential of the camp experience, which leads campers rather intentionally through a period of increased openness to new ideas, which is analogous to a time of spiritual seeking. Each camper has a normal cycle of life that includes such things as home life, school, online presence, and some level of church engagement. There might be additional elements, such as a second home, if their parents are separated and share custody. Whatever their unique circumstances, they develop a sort of equilibrium in this cycle. There is a rhythm to the routine, and they often take the integrity of this routine for granted. They feel a certain degree of safety and comfort in this cycle, though they may also experience a degree of boredom or complacency.

My children are involved in so many activities that it seems like I am always carting them somewhere. In addition to school and homework, they have sports practices, music lessons, and a growing number of social engagements. We do our best to carve out time to visit family members or go

14. They borrow these terms from Wuthnow, *After Heaven.*
15. Shults and Sandage, *Transforming Spirituality,* 31–36.

on an outing together, but sometimes that seems like just another thing to put on the schedule. Now as teenagers, it is increasingly difficult to get them up in the morning and out the door for school, much less excited about doing something like going for a walk in the woods, fishing, or a day trip somewhere. If we are able to stay at home, they usually seek diversion in one of many electronic devices. They are firmly embedded in their routine and have even come to depend on it.

This dependence on routine seems even more pronounced with young children, though only because they vocalize in different ways. They are liable to throw a tantrum if one little thing changes. When my kids were infants, I began singing to them every night, and I sang the exact same songs in the exact same order for years. I remember occasionally trying to cheat with one of my sons if we had gone a little bit past bedtime and I was tired. I would try to sing just one song, and I would justify it by saying it was late and this would allow us to get to sleep a little sooner. However, by skipping one or two of his songs, I threw off his routine so much that he would throw a fit for ten or fifteen minutes before calming down. I should have just taken one more minute to sing the other two songs. Children at camp are away from these familiar comforts, and the normal response to this unsettling environment is homesickness.

In my years of working at camp, I have seen homesick campers of all ages, from elementary age all the way through senior high. Children miss the comforts of their own beds, their pets, the smells of their bedroom, and their nightlights. Some of the wonders of God's creation that they are exposed to are scary to them, whether spiders or the sounds of owls hooting at night. When I worked at Cross Roads in New Jersey, groups of inner-city kids would actually be frightened by how *quiet* it was, particularly the lack of traffic noise. Unlike a family vacation away from home, kids at camp do not have their parents or other family members to comfort them. This unfamiliar environment, and even the homesickness itself, helps to open the possibility for growth. In his book *Homesick and Happy*, child psychologist Michael Thompson notes that nearly every camper experiences homesickness to some extent, even those who do not show outward symptoms. He regards homesickness as a positive sign that campers are engaging in the important task of differentiating from their parents, a task he argues is increasingly stifled in the interest of keeping children safe.[16] This differentiation is essential for identity formation. It is difficult for camp counselors and leadership staff to see homesickness as anything but an annoyance or a challenge to overcome. Parents are sometimes so worried about homesickness that they

---

16. Thompson, *Homesick and Happy*, 71.

will not send their children to camp, even though camp is one of the safest places for them to learn how to be in different, perhaps scary, environments. It is important to remember that homesickness is very natural and even a sign of the positive benefits of camp.

Children are not the only ones who rely on routine. As we age, our cycles of dwelling become more complex, but we never lose the need for a secure base, a place to call home. When our routines are disrupted and our emotional equilibrium is thrown off, we may not throw a tantrum, but we can sure get ornery. Think of long business trips or even vacations you have taken. At the end of these long trips, we sometimes just need to be home, back in a place that is familiar, back with the things we left behind. We get homesick. But we also recognize the need to get away. Sometimes, we describe our routines in negative terms, like *running the rat race* or *stuck in a rut*. Getting away offers both rest and perspective. Sometimes, we can only get an honest look at our lives from a distance. Our children need these same benefits, but it is so much more important for children and adolescents because they are in important stages of identity formation. They are trying to figure out who they are, and many are in the process of assessing whether the faith they have grown up in is something they want to commit to. In many ways, they are in a natural stage of life for spiritual seeking. Camp provides a safe, intentional space for this seeking.

When we talk about unplugging from home, we mean getting away from the routine by going somewhere that is physically different and doing things that we are not accustomed to doing. Unplugging from home, combined with the unsettling environment of camp, does a couple things to the psyche. First, it raises anxiety and awareness. This is a very human response when we encounter something new. Campers enter a state of hyperawareness at camp, sensitive to new sounds, new smells, and new experiences. We can think of this as the opposite of boredom. They are rapidly processing things that they would not normally notice, like details in the outdoors and every little thing their counselor does and says. In the faith-centered environment of camp, they are also hyperaware of God's activity in the world. This can sometimes lead to impressions that God is more present at camp than elsewhere in the world. Intentional conversations and interpretation of the experience can help campers understand that God is present in all aspects of their lives. Getting away can make them more aware of God's activity in their lives at home.

Secondly, this separation from the normal routine is freeing. It opens campers up to new possibilities. Every camper is different and comes from a unique context. They oftentimes get stuck in a particular way of thinking about themselves and the world. Their mindset becomes set or "fixed," as

Carol Dweck puts it.[17] Maybe they are the smart one in school or the athletic one. Maybe they get picked on and see themselves as inferior. Maybe they are the younger brother who always has to wait until they are older or the older sister who is always supposed to be the responsible one. The new possibilities of camp allow them time and space to shed these identities that have often been imposed upon them so that they can explore the question: Who am I really? This can be incredibly freeing and open campers to new ideas of who they are. It can open them to a "growth mindset" that Dweck characterizes as entering a new world. She writes, "In one world—the world of fixed traits—success is about proving you're smart or talented. Validating yourself. In the other—the world of changing qualities—it's about stretching yourself to learn something new. Developing yourself."[18] This is the world of possibilities where a person has agency, their opinions matter, and they are free to envision what they are becoming.

There are measurable benefits of being unplugged from home in growth related to independence and sense of self. Young people gain an understanding of life away from their parents. They accomplish things *on their own*, so to speak. This gives them confidence in their own abilities, and it prepares them for success in life as they develop towards adulthood. In focus groups, campers consistently describe the pressure they feel at school and home to fit in or conform to other people's expectations of who they are. For these young people, camp becomes a place of self-discovery. As one camper put it succinctly, "You learn to be yourself."[19] In the Effective Camp Project, looking back on their experience two to three months after camp, 83 percent of campers agreed, "Camp helped me grow in my independence." Independence is also one of the key areas of growth identified in the "Directions" study and subsequent ACA research.[20] Campers leave camp with an increased understanding that they can accomplish things on their own and that they enjoy going outside their comfort zones, and these impacts last months after camp is over.

Unplugged from Technology

When we say "unplugged," we primarily mean separation from the home environment and normality of the daily routine, but we also mean literally unplugging from our devices. Camp is one of the last places in existence

17. Dweck, *Mindset*, 6.
18. Dweck, *Mindset*, 15.
19. Camp Wapo Girls.
20. Thurber et al., "Youth Development Outcomes," 241–54.

where young people set aside their mobile devices for more than a few hours at a time. The smart phone hit the markets in 2007 and has made daily technology use nearly ubiquitous among American teens, regardless of race and socioeconomic class. A 2018 Pew Research study found that 95 percent of teens owned a cell phone, and nearly half (45 percent) acknowledged being online "almost constantly."[21] This number keeps rising and is almost certainly higher as you read this. Many summer campers have never experienced two days in a row without exposure to screened devices. This is a gift that camp can give them.

In the many focus groups I have done with campers across the country, lack of technology always comes up as one of the factors that makes camp different from home. The thing that surprised me at first but now I have come to expect is that most campers speak positively about this separation from technology. One camper explained, "If you look around you in the city, you'll see a bunch of people walking really fast, talking on their phone. You don't really see people just stopping and looking around at the world, and camp has given us a chance to do that."[22] Campers will readily admit that if they were at home, they would be on their phones, tablets, or gaming systems. But they see the value of having a respite, and they appreciate simple things like people looking them in the eyes. "Being gone from technology kind of clears your brain," one Lutherlyn camper noted.[23] Multiple studies confirm that this camper is dead-on.

Social media apps and mobile games are designed to create habitual users. They work the same way as slot machines in Las Vegas. They periodically provide mini-rewards in the form of social media likes (introduced by Facebook in 2009) or game achievements that make the user feel good or accomplished. There is an infusion of dopamine in the brain, and the user is compelled to engage the app just a little longer. At the time of this writing, Snapchat is the most popular social media app among teenagers (this will undoubtedly change in the next few years). It keeps young people coming back in order to maintain their all-important streak of consecutive days. This brilliant marketing strategy actually factors in to some young people's decision about attending camp, since in doing so they risk breaking their Snapchat streak.[24] Camp directors and parents have stories of campers who

21. Anderson and Jiang, "Teens, Social Media & Technology," para. 2.
22. Lutherdale Girls.
23. Camp Lutherlyn Girls.
24. My wife, Anna, who is a Lutheran pastor, has noted in recent years that this factor is the number one reason that her confirmation students give for not wanting to attend confirmation camp in the summer.

give their phone to someone else while they are at camp for the sole purpose of keeping up their streak.

Scholars have long disagreed whether or not to classify reliance on technology as an addiction worthy of inclusion in the Diagnostic and Statistical Manual of Mental Disorders (DSM), though there is widespread agreement that habitual use can be problematic, at the very least.[25] Some scholars, such as MIT professor Sherry Turkle, have raised alarm bells about the increased reliance on technology and the consequences such reliance has on human interaction, cognitive functioning, and self-perception.[26] Others acknowledge that increased reliance on technology is more nuanced and complicated. Danah Boyd contended in her study of teenage social media use, "Most teens aren't addicted to social media; if anything, they're addicted to each other."[27] Boyd's argument is that young people have always sought social interaction in whatever networked public has been available to them. Social media is simply the current space of choice, as well as the space most readily available to them with the closure of public spaces and the fear that many parents have of sending their children out on their own. While Boyd is certainly correct, there is growing evidence that online interaction is qualitatively different from in-person interaction.

Jean Twenge, who has assigned the current cohort of teenagers the moniker "iGen," carefully documents how the dramatic increase in time teens spend online has meant less time spent reading, doing homework, getting together with friends, going to parties, and every other face-to-face activity measured in the nationwide surveys she uses. At its best, social media use supplements and even enhances face-to-face relationships, as Boyd suggests, but this is not the whole story. Increased social media use and time spent online generally are linked to increased signs of depression and lower social skills. Twenge summarizes, "Just as for happiness, the results are clear: screen activities are linked to more loneliness, and nonscreen activities are linked to less loneliness."[28]

Whether or not reliance on technology should be classified as an addiction is a discussion for my colleagues in the psychology community to continue debating. While it may not be fair to classify technology use as all bad or all good, it is clear that reliance on technological devices has adverse effects on individuals and communities. Parents are trying to navigate these challenges and establish healthy patterns for their children,

---

25. See, for example, the discussion in Griffiths, "Adolescent Social Networking."
26. See Turkle, *Alone Together*.
27. Boyd, *It's Complicated*, 80.
28. Twenge, *iGen*, 80.

though the airwaves are flooded with ever-changing and often contradictory recommendations about children and screen time. They do not want their children addicted to technology or unable to negotiate face-to-face social interactions, but they also do not want to take away their cell phones indefinitely or cut them off from technology. The reality is that we cannot turn back the clock to a time when our society did not have social media or cell phones. What we *can* do is provide alternative spaces that are unplugged from technology. With the ubiquity of cell phone use among teenagers and the compelling evidence that overreliance on screened technology has adverse effects on teenage social skills and neurological development, the unplugged space of camp has become even more valuable than in previous generations.

Camp provides an important respite from the constant lure of social media and cell phone usage. While the scholarly community disagrees about whether or not to classify reliance on technology as an addiction, this is the language that many young people use. One camper explained, "I think I have a little bit of an addiction to my technology. But here, I don't want to use it, because I get to do so many other things."[29] The vast majority of campers that we have surveyed over the years (over 90 percent) say that they did not have difficulty being away from their technological devices while at camp. The reason is that they are engaged in fun, participatory activities with their peers in a face-to-face setting that is qualitatively better than online interaction. It is well-documented that this face-to-face interaction at camp improves social skills, but we also have evidence that a substantial portion of campers go home with less reliance on technology, at least for a time. About a quarter of parents we surveyed noticed in the weeks following camp that their children were spending less time on electronic devices.

Camp directors and counselors often notice a period of transition during a week of camp, particularly for teenage campers who are accustomed to having a mobile device at hand. The first two or three days of camp become a period that many describe as detox, where campers have difficulty interacting with their peers. Those who have been in camping ministry for a couple decades or more affirm that this is more than just the normal period of awkwardness and breaking the ice when meeting new people, and they report that it has gotten more challenging as mobile technology has become more ubiquitous. This is particularly true with campers over the age of twelve. Many campers are disoriented by their separation from technology, which is one reason multi-day camps are so important. Taking a single day off from technology use (or even a weekend retreat)

---

29. Lutherdale Boys.

is not enough to see the benefits, but when campers become involved in a daily routine that does not include screened technology, they are able to see the value of being unplugged and become more comfortable with social interaction. As we will explore in chapter 7, these social interactions have important neurological implications, as well.

What is strange is that many camps are tempted to include screens in their programming and even allow cell phones at camp. They recount stories of parents hiding cell phones in their children's luggage and the difficulties of getting summer camp staff to put down their phones as evidence that camp might be better off adopting some policy of limited cell phone usage. While there might be some unique cases in which I would consider this a reasonable accommodation, I otherwise push back strongly. Our society needs unplugged spaces, and camp may be the only one left that offers week-long experiences. Moreover, parents see the value in having their children unplugged from technology. The small number that hides a cell phone in the luggage does not really want their children to have access to a cell phone. It is about the parents wanting access to their children. They are accustomed to having constant updates about their children and always knowing where they are. They want to know that their children are safe, and the cell phone gives them peace of mind. We will discuss this more when we talk about safe space in chapter 8, but for now, it is enough to be clear that parents see the value in having their children unplugged from devices and away from screens. In our surveys of nearly 2,000 camper parents, an astonishing 99 percent agreed that camp is a place to unplug from technology. When asked directly about cell phone usage, parents overwhelmingly disagreed (over 90 percent) that children should be allowed to have cell phones at camp.

My argument is that camps should not be trying to find new ways to incorporate screened technology into their programs. They should be doing the opposite. The absence of technology is one of the main aspects of camp that highlights the difference from home. Camps can enhance this characteristic of camp by assessing where they use plugged-in technology and what purpose this serves. This does not mean that I am universally opposed to cabin lights and flush toilets, but the more we can get campers away from even these technological amenities, the more they will have the chance to look up at the stars, hear the night sounds, and feel the breeze on their skin. So if the camp has cabin lights and indoor bathrooms, I hope they are taking the campers on night hikes and campouts. I have been to several camps that show videos or even full-length movies. I think this is a huge mistake and blatantly lazy programming. We want campers interacting with each other and with nature. They can and will interact with screens in every other arena of their life. Camp is designed to be different from home so that the campers have the opportunity to step away from their normal cycle of dwelling and be open to new possibilities and growth.

A more suitable use of technology is to leverage video, photo, and online media to capture key moments and experiences at camp for the campers to view and interact with when they return home. A video or photo montage can help them remember the experience and tell the story of camp to their family, friends, and congregation. Online media can also help them stay connected with new friends they made at camp, offering a powerful tool for sustaining meaningful relationships long-term. Since we already know that campers will reconnect with their devices when they return home, we can use this impetus to keep them connected to the place and people that showed them how to disconnect.

Habitus

French philosopher Pierre Bourdieu offers a helpful contribution to our understanding of camp as unplugged from home. He describes a person's way of being and communicating in the world as something called *habitus*. This is a way of knowing that goes beyond the brain to a *bodily wisdom* that includes precognitive processes and shapes individuals' dispositions. In Bourdieu's words, "The conditionings associated with a particular class of conditions of existence produce *habitus*, systems of durable, transposable dispositions, structured structures predisposed to function as structuring structures."[30] A habitus is not innate instinct but rather is learned over time through experience and tradition, and it seldom includes cognitive reflection. Rather, the body itself recognizes patterns in certain cultural situations that trigger responses based on previous experiences. These responses are often communicative, such as facial expressions, posture, or fidgeting, but they are also associated with learned skills. Habitus affects how a person responds in a given situation, and each new experience adds to the bodily wisdom of the habitus, meaning that this wisdom is adaptable through a process that Bourdieu calls "regulated improvisation."[31] A novel situation, such as a camp experience, can therefore call for an improvised habitus that the body will remember in future situations.

A key example in the camp environment is worship. Participants come to camp with a certain bodily understanding of a worship service. In many congregations, this often includes sitting still in a temperature-controlled indoor space, which has lighting that is either artificial or filtered through

---

30. Bourdieu, *Logic of Practice*, 53.
31. Bourdieu, *Language and Symbolic Power*, 37.

stained glass. Protestant worship services, in both Mainline and Evangelical circles, tend to involve passive listening as someone else reads Scripture and offers a spoken message. Young people's bodily understanding of worship may be that it is nonparticipatory and even boring. Their bodily understanding may need reevaluation when a camp worship involves movement or dancing in an outdoor worship area that is lit by direct sunlight or a flickering campfire. Campers are able to recognize the experience as worship, so it is associated with their habitus in the congregational setting. Through the process of regulated improvisation, they are able to reassess their role in a worship service and, perhaps most importantly, the perceived *value* of worship. This is one reason why young people who have been to camp increase in their church attendance and their understanding of the importance of participating in the life of a church community.

This is also why it is important for camp to be an *integrated* ministry, as opposed to disconnected, as we discussed in the previous chapter. Integrated camps can better partner with congregations to ensure that key elements are present both at camp and during congregational worship. This may be as simple as incorporating favorite camp songs into regular worship in the congregation or incorporating common liturgical prayers into worship at camp. The young person who is accustomed to being disengaged during the congregational worship service jumps up as the familiar camp song begins. She looks across the worship space and catches the eye of her friend who was at camp this past summer, too. They smile at each other and simultaneously start doing the familiar hand motions, momentarily connected to their camp experience across time and space.

This notion of habitus helps us understand the value of the characteristic *unplugged from home*. Each participant brings a certain habitus based on personal experience in a home environment or congregation. In very real ways, participants bring *home* with them. There is a cultural way of being in each camp environment, and the novelty offers opportunities to improvise and even learn new forms of habitus. If we accept Bourdieu's understanding that the new learning is incorporated into the habitus, then participants bring the new understanding (both cognitive and precognitive) with them to home and church. Participants bring home to camp and then camp to home. As we noted earlier, their experiences of camp become incorporated into a now-reevaluated cycle of dwelling in the home environment. The physical separation from home and the novel experiences of camp, including the increasingly important absence of technology, are essential elements of the camp experience that open space for camper growth.

The lasting impacts or life-changing impacts of camp do not happen during the week of camp itself. They happen at the transition between camp and home. Webb-Mitchell writes, "The changes in one's life may not be grasped until after one returns home from a journey, not during the actual pilgrimage itself."[32] Bourdieu makes clear that reintegration into the life at home precipitates refined structuring of the campers' way of being (*habitus*) in both cognitive and precognitive ways. That is, campers in some ways are able to mentally process how the camp experience has impacted them but, in other ways, these impacts are simply incorporated into their bodily way of being. For example, about half of camper parents notice in the weeks following camp that their child is nicer or more pleasant to other family members. While in some cases the campers may be consciously telling themselves to be nicer, it is more likely that their way of being in the camp environment has simply affected the way that they are accustomed to interacting with others in a precognitive way. Whether these and other impacts continue or not are dependent on their continued way of being in their home environments. The increased agency and interest that they feel in church worship services, for example, may continue if they are reinforced after they return home. However, if they do not attend church in the months following camp or their experience in worship is not affirming of their camp experience, their habitus of being in worship is likely to revert to precamp experiences. We do not want campers to see worship at camp as awesome and worship at church as boring. We do not want them to see camp as a place where they do evening devotions and home as somewhere they do not. We want to empower them to take these experiences home.

This understanding makes the transition to the home environment incredibly important. Campers need help reintegrating. Camps are alternative, set-apart spaces. They are constantly receiving and sending. The experiences that camps provide should always have an eye toward what campers will be returning to. They can do this by equipping campers with tools that they can take home, such as mealtime prayers they can teach to their families, activities they can teach to their friends, and songs they can sing in their home congregations. It is okay for worship, Bible study, and other activities to look and feel different, but they must also be recognizable to the campers, including key elements that will trigger their bodily wisdom and help them bridge the gap of camp and home. I remember singing the song "Amazing Grace" at camp when I was a young camper. I had sung the song many times in my home congregation, but it took on new meaning for me at camp. After the song, the worship leader used a simple liturgical greeting: "The Lord be with you." I responded with the words, "And also with you" without even thinking. They were the words we used in my home congregation before

---

32. Webb-Mitchell, *Practicing Pilgrimage*, 72–73.

times of prayer. I remember realizing in that moment that my trusted camp counselors worshiped in congregations like mine, and my home church experience took on new value for me. Weeks after I returned home, we sang "Amazing Grace" in my home congregation, and I was immediately reconnected to my camp experience. These are examples of simple but powerful touchpoints that integrated camps can provide to tap into the power of habitus. Of course, liturgy and music are not the only ways. Camp Judson in Western Pennsylvania works to bridge the gap between camp and congregation by having their counselors do a written review of each camper's faith progress during the week of camp and sending this information to their home congregation so that pastors and youth ministers can build on the personal faith development of each camp participant. This practice of intentionally equipping ministry leaders acknowledges their importance in helping camp outcomes become lasting.

Parents and church professionals can be essential partners in the transition home by helping campers process their experiences and discovering how they hope to live their lives in their new cycle of dwelling. As I think of this transition from camp to home, I am drawn back to the zipline. Those of you who have ridden a zipline know that when the experience is over, the rider slowly comes to a stop and is generally left hanging there by their rather uncomfortable safety harness. At most high-ropes courses, they hang there until someone brings a ladder and helps them climb back to solid ground. Our task as parents, camp directors, and church leaders is considering ways that we can help the campers off the zipline of camp to the solid ground of their continued walk with Christ. We will continue exploring ways to accomplish this in the coming pages. It is essential that we do not leave them dangling on the end of the line.

5

Taking the Leap: Camp Is Participatory

Julia opens her eyes and stares into the blackness, her pupils dilating to the size of shooter marbles. She has to pee. Her counselor Elizabeth had given them a step-by-step lesson on how to do this, and they had all giggled hysterically at the idea. Now she is both excited and terrified to try it. The damp smell and cool air remind her that she is not at home. She makes her way nervously across the wooden floorboards of the platform tent, between the beds of her sleeping tentmates, and opens the tent flap. The light of a million stars greets her. She almost loses her balance looking up, but she is brought back to earth as her bare feet tingle on the dew-laden grass. She can hear the music of bugs and frogs and feel the light breeze on her bare skin. The hoot of an owl momentarily startles her, but then she smiles as her mind latches onto a line from a song they sang the day before, "All God's Critters Got a Place in the Choir." She finishes quickly and gets back inside the tent and in her sleeping bag without waking anyone up. She is exhilarated, and she cannot wait until morning so that she can tell her friends that she did it.

I sat in my office at the end of the week, chuckling as I read Elizabeth's camper evaluations. Each week, at least two or three of the girls in her tent wrote the same thing for what they enjoyed most about their week at camp: "peeing in nature." She was the lead counselor for a village of four platform tents located a little ways from the nearest bathhouse. In order to go to use the toilet, a camper would have to wake up a tentmate so that she did not walk alone. Elizabeth's simple solution to this became an adventure for each new group of campers and one that became a momentous occasion for them. Most had never peed anywhere but in a toilet or in a diaper. Elizabeth was teaching them a new skill that gave them personal agency. It felt a little silly and a little rebellious to these ten-year-old girls. This made it an empowering experience to pee in the grass for the first time.

The research is screaming at us from nearly every academic field. We nod approvingly, feeling that we are wiser. And then we go on doing exactly the same thing. We sit at our desks in front of computer screens (I chuckle wryly as I type these words). We demand more automation in our homes and our modes of transportation. We ask our children to learn by sitting still and taking in information presented to them, while we measure learning by the bubbles they fill in on a test paper. As the world becomes more automated, our camps are pressured to follow suit. Julia's experience of peeing in nature is increasingly rare, even in the camp environment. As I said in the previous chapter, I am not universally opposed to indoor plumbing and cabin lights, but it is clear that we sacrifice some tremendous opportunities of summer camp when we provide all of the modern luxuries campers are accustomed to at home. Not only do modern luxuries dull the characteristic of camp as unplugged from home; they also tend to make the experience less participatory.

The Value of Participation

The participatory characteristic of camp has two essential elements. First is experiential learning. Camp is a place of full-body learning. Campers do not take in information passively. They learn through doing. When people learn through experience, the knowledge tends to stick with them much longer. The second element is that campers have real agency in the experience. Campers participate in the planning and leading at camp, and they are able to take ownership of their actions and learning experience. Camper participation means that they are given meaningful decision-making roles, which helps them understand leadership and collaboration, rather than having adults plan and lead everything for them. One camper summed it up, "At camp, I get treated like a person, not like a little kid."[1] For this camper and many others, the agency that they find at camp affirms their personhood. The best camps always ask the question, "Can a camper do this?" The game is more fun when they help create it. The food tastes better when they help cook it. Worship is more engaging when they help plan and lead. Even the simple act of going to the bathroom can be an adventure at camp. This is where overreliance on technology and modern luxuries can diminish a camper's ability to participate and learn through doing.

I learned how to scramble eggs at camp. It was the morning after our harrowing canoe adventure, and we were camped out on a sandbar. It was raining a bit, so Ben and I grabbed a tarp from the beach and stretched it

1. Camp Wapo Girls.

over the cooking fire. Unfortunately, every time the wind blew, it shook sand from the tarp into the eggs. "That's a bit more pepper in the eggs!" we called out. You could say it was both trial by fire and an experience with grit, which brings us to some key theories of experiential education.

John Dewey (d. 1952) was the most influential proponent of experiential education in the twentieth century, directly influencing the summer camp movement (through L. B. Sharp and others) and countless researchers after him. He and others, such as Outward Bound founder Kurt Hahn, recognized that reliance on the passive reception of knowledge in school systems was insufficient for child learning. They advocated for value-laden experiences that led to deeper curiosity and a desire to learn or experience more. Importantly, these direct (or primary) experiences were not sufficient on their own. Equally important was the reflective (or secondary) experience that involved systematic thinking. Scott Barnett uses Dewey's theory of primary and secondary experiences to explain that camp experiences, when intentionally processed in the moment, lead to "the cognitive and affective mutually reinforcing each other to produce higher order learning."[2] Barnett also relies heavily on David Kolb and Hahn's adventure education theory, highlighting the importance of disequilibrium created by immersion in the new setting of camp and presentation of new challenges. He argues that this atmosphere of disequilibrium, when combined with caring community and intentional learning, provides space for transformational experiences in adventure education and challenge education, which he uses as subcategories of experiential learning.

Multiple researchers have confirmed that when experiential learning is combined with Christian practices and theological reflection, there is potential for deep theological learning. Outward Bound programs are camplike in their use of small groups of learners engaged in challenging activities in novel outdoor settings, usually involving multi-week wilderness excursions. Brad Daniel's examination of these experiences using retrospective accounts demonstrates that participants in Outward Bound-type wilderness expeditions that included explicit Christian components overwhelmingly regard them as significant life experiences up to twenty-five years later.[3] Another study of incoming college students who participated in a wilderness orientation program with explicit Christian components found that participants exhibited growth in multiple constructs, one of the most prevalent being "personal spiritual development," which included such specifics as "increased trust in God" and "increased awareness of

2. Barnett, "Aspects of Camp Ministry," 21–22.
3. Daniel, "Life Significance," 386–87.

one's personal faith."[4] Jimmy Griffin concludes his study on adventure-based learning thusly, "It was discovered that Christian spiritual beliefs could be strengthened through a combination of explicit spiritual teaching and the 'real world' settings of group and personal challenges in the out-of-doors."[5] These studies link Christian outdoor recreational experiences with faith formation, and they demonstrate the effectiveness of camplike programs in intentional Christian formation.

This is something that practical theologians have argued for decades. Not only does experience shape faith formation, but it also shapes theology itself. This happens through encountering the ongoing work of Jesus Christ in the world in communities of what Ray Anderson calls *Christopraxis*. Anderson writes, "Christopraxis is the continuing ministry of Christ through the power and presence of the Holy Spirit."[6] As we participate in ministry to and with one another, we are encountering the living Christ and joining his ongoing ministry to the world. Camps are effective not simply because they involve bodily movement and multiple learning styles but also because they empower young people as ministers to one another. As they come alongside one another and support one another through challenges and adversity in the camp setting, they are ministering to them, something that becomes explicit as the actions for the other are connected to the normative tradition of Scripture. In these communities, they are forming theology through the praxis-theory-praxis loop of practical theology, turning camp into a theological playground where they can test and refine their understandings of God and their role in God's ongoing creation and ministry in the world.[7]

Created to Move

The human body was created to be active and learn through interaction with the surrounding world. The very stuff with which God created the first human (*adam*) was the dust of the earth (Hebrew *adamah*), linking us inextricably to the land (Gen 2:7). Notice that one of the first things God did for the human was give him something to do. God planted a garden and put the *adam* there to till and keep it (Gen 2:15). Thus, humanity was invited into the ongoing work of creation from the very beginning. After providing work, the second thing God did for the human was create companionship,

4. Bobilya et al., "Outcomes," 314.
5. Griffin, "Effects of an Adventure-Based Program," 351.
6. Anderson, *Shape of Practical Theology*, 29.
7. For an explanation of the praxis-theory-praxis loop, see Browning, *Fundamental Practical Theology*, 7.

first with a variety of animals before finally culminating in the fellow human that provided the ideal companion (Gen 2:18–23). We are part of the created world and imbued with the Spirit of the Creator God that gives us life, making us, in a very deep theological sense, co-creators with God. The observation that "the human spirit is inherently creative" is a key part of Loder's understanding of the *analogia spiritus*.[8] Importantly from the Christomorphic perspective, this inherent creativity is a sort of "loose cannon" until it is grounded in connection to the Creator Spirit. When this happens, "All [the human spirit's] transformations are themselves transformed so that all of its creativity in its many variations throughout the whole field of human action points toward the same origin and destiny as the Holy Spirit: God became human in Jesus Christ."[9]

Name a scientific field—sociology, psychology, biology, chemistry, neurology, physics—and you will find confirmation for what theology has affirmed for millennia: the human spirit longs to participate and creatively interact rather than stay passive and sedentary. Physical activity reduces stress, boosts mood, alleviates anxiety, heightens awareness, lowers blood pressure, improves memory, reduces risk for nearly every major disease, aids knowledge retention, and the list goes on. Camps are inherently interactive spaces that engage all of the senses and help connect young people with the power of the natural world. Florence Williams explains, "Nature appears to act directly upon our autonomic systems, calming us, but it also works indirectly, through facilitating social contact and through encouraging exercise and physical movement."[10] Camp participants get out of breath and sweaty. They get scratched by thorn bushes, bitten by bugs, and sunburned. They stare in wonder at the night sky and interact with wildlife. These simple experiences are decreasingly common in our increasingly sanitized and indoor society.

Our larger society has sought to make life more streamlined and easy. In so doing, we have taken away some of the fundamental characteristics that make life worth living. There are many things that we never learn to do because they are always done for us. A big part of camping is taking away some of the automated amenities of life. This causes us to slow down because things take longer. When we slow down, we consider how things work and where they come from. We are also pushed to learn new hard skills, like paddling a canoe, starting a fire, or riding a horse. As humans, we need challenges, goals, and causes to strive for. We need daily interaction

---

8. See Loder, *Logic of the Spirit*, 35.
9. Loder, *Logic of the Spirit*, 36.
10. Williams, *Nature Fix*, 166.

with nature. Going back to the wisdom of Genesis 2, we need people to engage and gardens to tend.

Taking the Leap

Few camp experiences are more viscerally participatory than our zipline example. Place yourself again on the top of the zipline platform, where you got a new perspective on life. Now take the leap. All of the senses are engaged: the sight of the ground zooming by forty feet below, the distinctive taste of adrenaline or dry mouth, the smell of your own sweat mingled with the intensity of your outdoor surroundings, the sound of your friends cheering you on muffled by the air rushing past your ears, and the reassuring discomfort of the safety harness counterbalanced by the intensity of the wind in your face. Not every experience at camp is as physically and emotionally intense as riding a zipline, but most experiences are designed to be highly tactile and experiential. The camp environment itself facilitates a level of hyperawareness, meaning participants are attuned to their surroundings and rapidly absorbing information. This alertness means they are primed for learning.

At first glance, an activity like a zipline is little more than a thrill ride, but there is more than fun and games going on. The thrill of the zipline, which we will see has tremendous value as a pedagogical tool, is only part of the experience. In many ways, this thrill is the culmination of a challenge activity. In order to make it to the zipline platform, participants have to scale a climbing post. Besides being a physically demanding activity, most participants also have at least some fear of heights. Participants build confidence through learning a physical skill and also are challenged to step outside their comfort zones and conquer their fears.

During my camp visits and camper interviews, I have seen many campers impacted through high-ropes and challenge course activities. Several campers at Camp All Saints in Texas recounted feeling scared on the high-ropes course, and they reported the accomplishment they felt when they either completed an element or moved beyond their goal. One of the female campers explained her experience this way, "When you're about to quit, they tell you, 'Just a little bit more.' And then you get to the top and you just feel exhilarated, like you've done something that you felt you were never able to do."[11] Staff members reported that they intentionally challenge the campers through numerous activities and new experiences to help them step outside their comfort zones. "Camp is hard!" the director told me with

11. Camp All Saints Girls.

a laugh. He explained how people so often characterize camp as fun without acknowledging how difficult it is for campers to be away from home, be embedded in a new community, and try things that are very challenging physically, emotionally, and spiritually. Two of the male campers told me that they were so scared on the high ropes that they cried. What struck me was that the campers connected these challenges, new experiences, and feelings of discomfort (even crying) with their *enjoyment* of the camp experience. Clearly, this was more than fun and games. They connected the new experiences of camp to personal growth that stays with them in their lives after camp. "It'll help me do more," one girl said of overcoming her fears on high ropes. "Like when I'm afraid to do something, I'll just do it anyway. Because I pushed my limits here, so why can't I do it anywhere else?"[12]

Growth Mindsets and Grit

These highly participatory, challenging camp activities help campers move toward a growth mindset. Young people often have the impression that learning is fixed or innate, meaning some people are naturally gifted at certain activities. If they struggle at something, they might have the notion that they are simply not gifted, which can prevent them from trying and, thereby, improving.[13] Brain researchers have demonstrated that the brain works like a muscle that can be strengthened and taught to accomplish new tasks through training and repetition. This means that young people who have a fixed mindset of themselves as failures or socially incompetent can, through experience and training, develop an understanding that they can change their abilities and characteristics. David Yeager, one of the leading researchers examining mindsets, is a strong proponent of the camp environment as a place of participatory learning leading to growth mindsets. He argues, "The supportive environment of camp and the opportunity to try new challenges is mind training. You start out not knowing archery, and by the end you know how to shoot. You start out not knowing how to navigate the ropes course, and by the end you know how to make it across. It is an intensified experience overcoming fears and learning challenges with the support of others."[14] Like the camper at All Saints, the participatory camp experiences prepare campers for success in their lives as they understand that they are capable of learning a new skill or pushing beyond their perceived limits.

12. Camp All Saints Girls.
13. See Dweck, *Mindset*, 32–34.
14. Yeager, "Mindsets Matter," para. 8.

Angela Duckworth, a key collaborator with Yeager and Dweck on research into mindsets, identifies a single personality trait that is most correlated with success in life. She sums it up as *grit*, which she defines as a combination of passion and perseverance. People who have grit are resilient, hardworking, and have a clear understanding of their goals in life. Like Yeager, she prioritizes effort over innate talent, persuasively demonstrating that talent can often lead to complacency that, in effect, squanders the talent through lack of effort. The most effective ways of becoming *more gritty*, as she puts it, involve facing challenges, adversity, and things that are inherently difficult. She writes, "A growth mindset leads to optimistic ways of explaining adversity, and that, in turn, leads to perseverance and seeking out new challenges that will ultimately make you even stronger."[15]

The camp experience thrives on challenges and trying new things. In the Effective Camp Project, more than 90 percent of campers have agreed that they tried something new at camp. Novel experiences like hiking above a tree line in the Rocky Mountains, riding a horse, cooking over the open fire, climbing a high-ropes course, or canoeing on the Mississippi River can teach new skills and help build confidence and grit. Many of these activities take practice, and they often involve failure. Duckworth writes, "To be gritty is to keep putting one foot in front of the other. To be gritty is to hold fast to an interesting and purposeful goal. To be gritty is to invest, day after week after year, in challenging practice. To be gritty is to fall down seven times, and rise eight."[16] The caring community at camp and the distance from home make it a safe space to try new things and fail at them. The supportive community ministers to the individual camper, empowering them to try again and leading them to accomplish things that they previously thought impossible. Together, they celebrate success and come alongside one another in times of perceived failure.

The Value of Fun

When my research team surveys summer campers and their parents, we consistently see 97 percent of them agreeing that they had a lot of fun at camp. We also ask them to describe camp in two or three words, and the most common word they use is always "fun." Some camp directors sigh when they see these results, hoping that words like community, friendship, or faith might be the most common. But one of the hallmarks of the camp experience is that it is fun, and camp supporters should be pleased about this. First of all, it is what

---

15. Duckworth, *Grit*, 192.
16. Duckworth, *Grit*, 275.

campers and their parents want. The primary reason they come to camp is to have fun, with things like meeting people, trying new things, and growing in their faith showing up as additional motivators. More importantly, however, fun adds tremendous value to the overall experience and serves as a gateway to community, friendship, and faith.

The reason fun is so important has to do with the brain, particularly how emotion impacts memory. When we first encounter a situation, our brains activate an evaluative response based on previous experiences. Essentially, our brains tell us whether the situation is worth our attention or not. Things previously experienced as boring or unimportant do not arouse the full attention of the brain and body. Daniel Siegel writes, "Experiences that involve little emotional intensity seem to do little to arouse focal attention, and have a higher likelihood of being registered as 'unimportant' and therefore of not being easily recalled later on."[17] In contrast, unexpected experiences, those perceived to involve risk, or other experiences perceived as significant give what Siegel describes as a "jolt to the system," in which "the primary emotional experience is one of increased energy and alertness."[18] The brain then quickly evaluates whether the experience is good or bad. When an emotionally arousing experience is perceived as negative, it may trigger the body's *fight-or-flight* response. However, when the experience is perceived as positive, it creates "a primary emotional state of eager anticipation."[19] These positive, emotionally arousing experiences are deeply encoded into the brain as they are marked as significant, or value-laden.[20] This means that positive, emotionally arousing experiences, which are typically summed up with the simple word "fun," are very likely to be encoded into long-term memory and recalled later on as part of what Siegel calls "the permanent explicit autobiographical memory system."[21] That is, they have the potential to become part of the way we see ourselves and tell our stories.

When the camp experience is perceived as fun, the individual components are also given positive, value-laden assessments. You will recall from our discussion of *habitus* in the previous chapter that these value-laden assessments can affect campers' internal working models of specific circumstances, such as worship or Bible study. These arenas that may previously have been assessed as unimportant are now given strong

---

17. Siegel, *Developing Mind*, 71.
18. Siegel, *Developing Mind*, 151.
19. Siegel, *Developing Mind*, 151.
20. Siegel's use of the term "value-laden memory" is taken from LaBar and Cabeza, "Cognitive Neuroscience," 54–64.
21. Siegel, *Developing Mind*, 74.

positive meaning to the campers. Faith in God is reimagined as something important to their daily lives. One boy from the Effective Camp Project articulated it this way: "I feel as though praising God isn't a thing that I hate doing anymore. It's a lot more fun. I haven't been doing it, really going to church. I see why we do it now."[22] Notice how his evaluation of worship and church attendance change based on his emotional experience. Before camp, he had a negative appraisal of these faith practices. Camp transformed his appraisal in a way that connected his understanding to his experiences outside of the camp environment. These faith practices are now perceived positively, or, as he puts it, "fun."

Fun also keeps us coming back. Young people are not going to dedicate their time to something unless they find it enjoyable. Duckworth says, "Before hard work comes play. Before those who've yet to fix on a passion are ready to spend hours a day diligently honing skills, they must goof around, triggering and retriggering interest."[23] Camp is a playground that helps foster curiosity and deep interest in faith, religious practices, outdoor engagement, and trying new things. The thrill ride of camp becomes one of its most important pedagogical tools.

A couple summers ago, my family took a trip to Glacier National Park in Montana. We decided to hike the beautiful Highline Trail, which features amazing panoramic views of the mountains, waterfalls, and glaciers. One section of the trail traverses a narrow ledge only six feet wide, with a sheer rock wall on one side and on the other a steep drop-off of more than a hundred feet. A steel cable attached to the rock face offers some reassurance, but there is nothing but empty air on the other side. It was a dizzying experience for me, but I was most concerned for my son Elijah, who had an agonizing fear of heights. On previous family vacations to state and national parks, he was not able to climb the lookout towers, which always featured well-built staircases and railings, and he even had trouble approaching windows in tall buildings. I was worried that he might freeze up in the middle of this ledge, causing a truly dangerous situation. It was not helpful that on the way to the trailhead my wife had been reading to us from a book she purchased entitled *Death in Glacier National Park*, recounting all the horrible ways people had died in the park (including falling from the Highline Trail). I gripped the steel cable with both hands and cautiously looked behind me to check his status. I was shocked. He was walking confidently and talking with our hiking companions, even peering over the edge of the cliff. As we continued the hike on a less death-defying portion of the trail, I asked him

22. Sugar Creek Boys.
23. Duckworth, *Grit*, 106.

about the experience and his fear of heights. He admitted that he was a little scared, but he knew he could do it. He reminded me that he attended Luther Park Bible Camp earlier in the summer, where he participated in high ropes for the first time. He was scared then, too, but his counselor and cabinmates encouraged him and supported him, giving him confidence to traverse the course. The experience helped him accomplish something he thought he could never do, and in those frightening moments on the Highline Trail, he drew on this camp experience to give him strength.

An essential piece of the experience for Elijah and the campers at All Saints was that they were given agency. Success on high ropes does not mean traversing the element or even making it to the top of the climbing post. The experience is about pushing yourself and stretching your perceived limits in a controlled environment. A crucial element to any challenge activity at camp is the principle of *challenge by choice*. This means that each participant decides how much they want to challenge themselves in a particular circumstance. For many, the goal is not to complete a certain element but, rather, to climb part way up the climbing post or get farther than they did the last time they traversed the element. The community then rallies to support them in accomplishing their personal goals. This interaction between personal goals and community support helps many campers move beyond their goals and challenge themselves in new ways. In the Effective Camp Project, one of the items showing the most consistent growth from the first day to the last day of camp is agreement with the idea that, "I like going out of my comfort zone and trying new things." It is important to note that this is one of many survey items where the growth experienced at camp is maintained in the months following camp. This is compelling evidence that effective camp experiences foster a growth mindset, which continues long after the campers return home.

Building Community through Experience

I must confess, I am a low-ropes guy. I certainly see the value in high ropes, particularly after my own son was impacted so dramatically, but I love working with groups on initiatives or challenge courses designed to facilitate community building. While high ropes require elaborate safety harnesses and belay systems, low ropes are generally no more than a step above the ground. The major difference, aside from the height, is that high ropes tend to focus on individual goals and achievements, while low ropes are usually group obstacles that can only be completed by working together. Maybe the group has to traverse a series of cables from one point to another, something only a tightrope walker could accomplish alone, or all balance on a tiny wooden platform without anyone touching the ground.

These challenge courses become laboratories for group dynamics because they are effective at stripping off the veneer of general niceties that guard the self from the abrasiveness of genuine human interaction. They almost always involve close physical contact, which can quickly break down social barriers, and they require groups to strategize with one another to find novel solutions to complicated problems. People get frustrated when a seemingly simple task becomes a lengthy endeavor. Some blame themselves for letting the group down, while others deflect responsibility onto others, actions that reflect in microcosm their tendencies in daily life. What appears to be a simple game often reveals raw emotions. Because the activity is a simulation, a skilled group processor is able to pause the activity and guide the group in reflection on specific dynamics. I have worked on challenge activities with countless youth groups, summer campers, church councils, college classes, and corporate co-workers. Some know each other fairly well before the activities and others come in as near strangers. There is almost always a breakthrough of some kind, as participants learn more about themselves and gain greater appreciation for those in their group. This new knowledge, learned in the highly controlled environment of the challenge course, then benefits their group in everything else they do together, whether it is the rest of the camp week, ongoing relationships at work, or lifelong friendships.

Engaging Multiple Intelligences

I oftentimes lead group-challenge activities with college classes I teach or workshops I lead for adults. I still have people roll their eyes or opt out altogether when I explain that we will be doing a group-challenge activity. I have had more than one person walk out of my workshops when they discover participating will involve physical movement and interaction. "I hate these things," is a response that I often get. Of course they hate them. As the director at All Saints put it, they are *hard*.[24] We have been conditioned to think that learning takes place in controlled environments where someone with more knowledge about a topic imparts a portion of that knowledge to us. It is easier to sit still and either listen to the presentation or casually opt

---

24. Of course, difficulty is not the only reason that people opt out. Some have had negative or even harmful experiences in group settings that they do not want to rehash. Others have had experiences that seemed trivial or offered no opportunity for growth because they were perfunctory. These are reasons that adventure activities are best suited to camp and camp-like settings that provide time and space to build trust and adequately reflect on the experiences.

out of portions as we discreetly check in on social media or play a round of our favorite mobile game. However, learning is most effective when it involves what some educators call multiple intelligences.

Howard Gardner has developed a theory comprising eight modalities of learning, or intelligences.[25] While certain individuals seem to learn best using a specific modality (such as visual-spatial learners), the best learning happens when multiple intelligences are combined. Those wanting to sit still and absorb information from a verbal presentation are primarily learning in what Gardner calls the verbal-linguistic (and, possibly, logical) modality. Professional educators know that these are not the only ways that people learn, so they work to incorporate things like group projects (interpersonal modality) and lab work (spatial and logical modalities). Camp is one of the few places that incorporates all of Gardner's intelligences.

Whether on the high-ropes course, low-ropes course, or participating in some other group activity, the role of the facilitator is essential. Experiential learning works most effectively when the knowledge is generalized to other aspects of life, through what Dewey calls the secondary experience of reflection. This is where the counselor or group leader serves as an interpretive guide (or "spiritual facilitator") to help process the experience.[26] The process helps connect the highly kinesthetic learning of the challenge course to verbal-linguistic learning, allowing participants to put words to their experiences and feelings. The entire process is highly collaborative, as the group together reflects on what they did and more deeply analyzes specific moments. For example, in group-challenge activities, there is oftentimes a moment of perceived failure, such as when a group member falls off a low-ropes element, causing the entire group to start over. A skilled spiritual facilitator can recognize how people react in these moments and how the group works through them. Participants may be able to verbalize how they felt at certain junctures, and these reflections can sometimes be revelatory to group members who did not realize how their words or actions affected others.

Alongside this analysis, the spiritual facilitator guides the group in reflecting how experiences on the challenge course or high-ropes course are illustrative of their lives. I always encourage group facilitators to have a Bible handy because challenge activities are great times to demonstrate how Scripture applies to daily life, and reflecting on a Scripture passage

25. See Gardner, *Frames of Mind*.

26. Greg Robinson calls this role the "spiritual facilitator." He emphasizes the need for this person to be patient with participants and to help them reflect on their own experiences. As he puts it, "Most of the work of the spiritual facilitator involves waiting" (Robinson, *Adventure and the Way of Jesus*, 14).

alongside a visceral experience can offer much-needed wisdom to the group as they process an activity. Rob Ribbe envisions the truth revealed in Scripture as the third point of a triangle that, along with kinesthetic experience and intentional reflection, comprise the educational environment of Christian camping. He writes, "It is the interactive dynamic of experience, reflection, and truth that makes up the unique education potential of the camp setting."[27] There are many ways of facilitating group processing, but I tend to follow the D.R.A.G. Bi.G. model because of its explicit incorporation of biblical truth.[28]

> **D**o the activity
>
> **R**eflect on what you did
>
> **A**nalyze specific moments and feelings
>
> **G**eneralize what happened to daily life
>
> **Bi**blicize by reading a related Scripture passage
>
> **G**eneralize again, in light of Scripture and experience

Learning through Music, Art, and Drama

One of the best examples of camp's use of multiple intelligences is the role of music. The arts are oftentimes relegated to afterthoughts in public school education, if they are available at all, in spite of an abundance of research demonstrating the importance of music, art, and drama to a learning environment. At camp, the arts, particularly music, are used to full effect. Campers oftentimes learn Scripture by heart not through rote memorization but, rather, through song. There are a few things that make music an effective learning tool at camp. First, the songs are usually short, catchy, and repeated many times throughout the week, allowing campers to learn them by heart. Second, because they are able to sing along, campers sing together as a group, providing a tremendous benefit to the feeling of community. In his research on the human brain, John Medina notes that music can be incredibly powerful in forming community because it promotes the secretion of a molecule called oxytocin, which stimulates feelings of trust, intimacy, and acceptance.[29] Third, camp music is often accompanied by hand motions

---

27. Ribbe, "Redefining Camp Ministry," 151.

28. For this model, I am indebted to my friend and mentor, Paul Hill, and his work at the Center for Youth Ministry at Wartburg Theological Seminary.

29. Medina, *Brain Rules*, 217.

or actions. Camp critics sometimes point to this as evidence that camp is schmaltzy or farcical, but the bodily movement has important pedagogical functions. Actions or hand motions aid memory retention by engaging multiple intelligences through words, music, and actions combined. They also get the heart rate up, increasing blood and oxygen flow to the brain and heightening alertness, which primes the brain for learning.

I still know Prov 3:5–6 by heart because of a catchy tune, complete with actions, that I learned in my first summer at camp more than twenty-five years ago. Music at camp is an effective learning tool because it is a highly engaging, participatory activity. I love observing young people, usually middle-school boys, who come to camp with little interest in singing. They roll their eyes at the goofy camp songs and determinedly refuse to sing or participate in the actions. By the middle or end of the week, these same young people are singing their hearts out with the community of believers that has supported them and given them personal agency throughout the week.

Alongside music, campers are encouraged to participate in various forms of art and drama. They learn Bible stories by acting them out or drawing their impressions of what happened. Art or craft projects can help campers engage with nature and express the creative spirit that enlivens them and invites them into the process of ongoing creation. These activities are camper-centered, allowing them to experiment and express themselves in new ways. Drama has the ability to draw campers into story as they envision themselves in certain roles. They can act out and then reflect on what it felt like to be the good Samaritan that helps the injured person or the priest that passes by on the other side of the road.

One of the most common drama activities in the camp setting is portraying portions of Jesus' life through a passion play or Christ walk. These are most effective for camper learning when they incorporate the campers into the experience. A Christ walk, for example, involves movement as the camp community follows Jesus and the disciples from place to place.[30] Different areas of camp become key locations in Jesus' life, such as the Jordan River, Sea of Galilee, and Golgotha. Campers can then participate in the story, as they become the crowd that Jesus teaches, the ones who wave branches and shout, "Hosanna!" as he enters Jerusalem, and the ones whom

---

30. This same activity is modifiable for reenacting other important biblical time periods. In addition to Christ walks, I have participated in interactive reenactments of the exodus story (complete with camp maintenance staff chasing the campers across the Red Sea, using tractors in lieu of chariots) and the camp favorite Romans and Christians, in which campers take the role of persecuted Christians in the first or second century.

Pilate asks, "What then shall I do with Jesus?" One of my most vivid memories from my first camp experience was during the Christ walk. We had followed Jesus from his baptism by John through his miracles, teachings, and eventual betrayal. Pontius Pilate asked us, the crowd, what should be done with Jesus. My counselor, Brian, was portraying a Pharisee that week, and he was riling up the crowd, encouraging us to shout, "Crucify him!" I will never forget the look on his face: my trusted counselor, who had shared with us his passion for Jesus all week. I knew he was just acting, but that moment caused me to think and to wonder about my role in the suffering innocents of the world and under what circumstances I might deny Christ. Our group processed the experience late into the evening, as Brian helped us take advantage of the teachable moment at camp. It has stuck with me ever since, and I get chills when I hear this passage read on Good Friday, as my memory transports me back into the crowd.

The Teachable Moment: All Life Is a Challenge Course

The group-challenge course, high-ropes course, music, and drama are programmatic areas of camp that clearly demonstrate the participatory characteristic. I use group challenges and camp songs in classrooms and workshops because they are easy ways to incorporate the logic of camp in other settings. However, the camp environment facilitates full-body learning throughout the experience, not simply on the challenge course. What we cannot replicate in the classroom or a workshop is the extended time of the camp experience that allows for situational and serendipitous learning. At camp, as in daily life, every situation is an opportunity to learn. We call this the teachable moment. It might happen on a nature hike, during a field game, or sitting around the campfire. The essential component is that the group leader recognizes the moment and helps the group interpret it through the lens of faith, while applying it to daily life. As one camper remarked, "They're teaching us things without us really knowing that we're being taught."[31]

Ribbe likens camp to an "experiential laboratory" that facilitates spiritual formation and leadership development through intentional reflection on experience in the outdoor setting. He critiques camps that revert to didactic teaching, what he calls "pulpit-centered ministry," as trading in the experiential nature of camp for a "cognitive-centered philosophy of learning," and he notes that intentional reflection on experiences "is often

---

31. Sugar Creek Girls.

done poorly or is disregarded altogether."[32] He advocates for a strong focus on educating the summer staff members who are responsible for facilitating situational learning. If they are trained to recognize the teachable moment and are nurtured in their personal faith, then processing group experiences becomes almost second nature to them. Because of the immersive nature of the camp experience, "the leader/teacher/guide in the camp setting is ever-present and can facilitate learning on the spot. It looks very similar to Jesus' ministry to the disciples."[33]

Ribbe's biblical connection to Jesus' teaching style is spot-on. Jesus used the mundane, everyday experiences of common people as illustrations for his parables: a mustard seed (Matt 13:31–32), a lamp (Mark 4:21–22), and a lost sheep (Luke 15:1–7). Most of his parables were about agriculture or fishing, two of the most common occupations of the people he taught. He also used specific situations and experiences to help people reflect on their faith and his role in the world. His famous teaching, "I am the bread of life" comes immediately after he feeds 5,000 people with five loaves of bread and two fish (John 6). Imagine the hunger and even desperation of those who followed him into the wilderness just to hear him speak. He satisfies their literal hunger and uses this as an opportunity to reflect on life and faith. There are many other examples. Jesus declares that he is the resurrection and the life as he stands with those who grieve the loss of his friend Lazarus, whom he is about to raise from the dead (John 11). He declares to his disciples that they are to be servants of one another as he is at table with them, performing the incredibly experiential and intimate task of washing their feet (John 13). The disciples on the road to Emmaus only recognize the resurrected Jesus when they are at table with him and he breaks bread, recalling the deeply immersive experience of the last meal with his disciples (Luke 24).

The sacraments of communion and baptism are incredible gifts to believers because they allow us to touch, taste, and smell the forgiving grace of God. Sacramental theology offers a rich theological claim that God shows up in the mundane substances of everyday life. Camp theology is sacramental in that there is a recognition that God is present and active in some mysterious way in the normal everyday things of this world: around a campfire, at the waterfront, or on the hiking trail. While these are not to be confused with the sacraments commanded by Christ, they are *sacramental*. In intentional Christian community and through active engagement with the word of God and the practices of faith, campers are awakened to the possibility,

32. Ribbe, "Redefining Camp Ministry," 151–52.
33. Ribbe, "Redefining Camp Ministry," 151.

or even the probability, that they will see God in some unique, unexpected way. The group leader has the opportunity to connect the experiences to the truth of the Scriptures and facilitate deep learning.

Consider the experience of a group of confirmation-aged campers gathered together on a hillside at camp. They participated in the challenge course earlier that day and learned a lot about each other, including some vulnerabilities of their cabinmates. They all belong to creedal churches, where they recite the Apostle's Creed, affirming their faith in God the Father Almighty, creator of heaven and earth. They have even studied the meaning of this article in their catechetical training, but it never really sunk in. But gathered on that hillside at camp on a cool evening in early summer, they are captivated by a glimpse of faint starlight shining in the midst of the blazing red sunset. It is the planet Mercury, and they are seeing its light for the first time. Their trusted camp guide, who has given ear to their struggles and valued their opinions, allows them to gaze in rapt silence for several long minutes before reading from Psalm 19: "The heavens are telling the glory of God." They are given a new experience to add to their knowledge of God as creator, and some of them may hear the opening words of the Apostle's Creed for the first time as significant to their lives. Importantly, the camp guide does not offer an interpretation of the event but rather brings the normative theological tradition of Scripture into conversation with the lived experience and trusts in the power of the Holy Spirit at work in that moment. The campers are awake half the night talking about God, faith, and their role in the cosmos, participating in the community of Christopraxis by ministering to one another.

One of the most valuable teachable moments at camp is when conflict arises, something that is almost inevitable in the intense communal environment of camp. Skilled group leaders do not simply gloss over interpersonal conflict but, rather, process the experience in real time. Camp All Saints has one of the most creative and comprehensive systems I have seen for processing conflict in a way that facilitates learning. As the camp director pointed out, the necessity of conflict resolution lies in the intense and ongoing nature of the camp experience. "You can't just go home," he said. "You can't just take your ball and leave. When there's a real issue, there's a good chance you're going to have to work through it."[34] Campers told me that their experiences at home often involved various forms of corporal punishment or yelling, and they directly contrasted these means of punishment with their experience at All Saints. Staff members were trained to walk through several steps of conflict resolution with those involved, and these steps focused on

---

34. Camp All Saints Director.

empowering the young people to take ownership of their actions and come up with a solution to the problem. The counselors did not simply fix the problems. They made the process participatory by facilitating conversations in which the campers themselves worked to resolve the conflict and propose behavioral adjustments. In the most serious cases, campers would develop a written plan for resolving the conflict, and the community then helped them adhere to it. One summer staff member summed it up, "Simply put, it's a method of working through issues that respects the autonomy and dignity of the children themselves."[35] Importantly, this process teaches the campers how to work through problems on their own and practice the essential Christian values of forgiveness and reconciliation. After the resolution of the conflict, the campers then had to live with each other for the remaining days of the camp experience, allowing them further opportunities to negotiate the strained relationship and minister to one another.

The conflict resolution model at All Saints demonstrates how camps can take full advantage of the participatory learning environment. Notice the inclusion of the two hallmarks of the participatory characteristic: it is highly experiential and the campers are given tremendous agency rather than simply being told what to do. Whether it is conflict resolution, serendipitous sightings of Mercury, or a sacramental experience around the campfire, effective camp experiences take advantage of the teachable moment. We are reminded that we learn best through experience, whether at camp or in daily life. The day-to-day learning at camp demonstrates that all life is a challenge course and every encounter with another is an opportunity for ministry.

---

35. Camp All Saints Staff.

6

Faith at the Center: Camp Is Church, Too

We waded into the choppy waters of Lake Tahoe under a threatening sky. It had been at least fifteen minutes since the last thunder clap, but it still felt like a risky endeavor. My mind flashed to scenes of the Israelites approaching too closely the mountain of God (Exod 20). As it turned out, the awesome power of the Creator added richly to what we were all experiencing. I have never been more viscerally aware of the risky calling to discipleship in the waters of baptism. I stood there in the knee-deep water with eight United Methodist confirmation students, their two pastors, and several volunteers from their congregations.

In response to challenges getting young people and their families to commit to regular confirmation class sessions, the pastors had decided to plan an eight-day camp experience, during which they would cover the bulk of the confirmation curriculum and develop deeper relationships with the students. They frankly told me that they wanted to get the young people away from their overbearing parents and hectic life schedules. During the camp experience, the confirmands forged strong relational bonds with one another and were opened to the value of ongoing congregational involvement through the near-peer mentorship of recently confirmed high school students who volunteered to help plan and lead the camp activities. Additionally, they had deep discussions on some of the key tenets of the Christian faith and the work of the United Methodist Church. They even spent time serving at a local outreach ministry to the poor, demonstrating the importance of putting faith into action.

The group was from the Sacramento area, where barely a third of the population was religiously affiliated. Several of the confirmation students had very little faith background and were only peripherally involved in church life before coming to camp. It is not surprising, therefore, that three of them were not baptized. What surprised the pastors, however, was their insistence on being baptized there among the camp community. The usual practice would be to simply baptize them on the same day of their confirmation, in the presence of their parents and congregational community. Unplugged from their home environment and embedded in a community in which they found relational belonging, stimulating conversations, and opportunities to serve others, these confirmands discovered a faith that was meaningful to their lives. They were asking, in effect, a question akin to that of the Ethiopian eunuch in Acts 8: "Here is water (Lake Tahoe!), what is to prevent me from being baptized?"

The earnestness of their request (along with a flurry of phone calls to family members who were not present) led us to the stormy shores of the lake that evening. The immersive, participatory nature of the experience had our senses sharpened in a state of hyperawareness. We huddled around the shivering young people as they were immersed in the crystal-clear waters of Lake Tahoe and baptized in the name of the Triune God. We laid hands on them each in turn as we first prayed and then proclaimed them, "Child of God!" When we shouted our last proclamation, as if in answer, a tremendous thunderclap shook the sky, underscoring the perils of this endeavor. The path of discipleship for these young people was marked not with clean white gowns, ordered liturgy, and picture-perfect smiles, but rather with personal determination and communal affirmation, accompanied by shivers and thunderclaps. Together, we experienced the power and presence of the living God as the thunderous voice over the mighty waters (Ps 29:3), the concrete presence in the community of believers (Matt 18:20), and the promise of Christ in the waters of baptism (Gal 3:27).

When I spoke with the baptizees the next day, they were only beginning to process the experience, but they related how important it was to them that their request was taken seriously and that their church friends were there to support them. They said they would always remember it. I certainly have vivid memories of the experience, and I can only imagine what it was like for those immersed in the waters.

Camp is, in many ways, an immersion experience in the life of faith. For many campers, like those young people from Sacramento, faith is a peripheral or ignored aspect of life. The camp experience offers the possibility for a radical recentering of faith, where everything is recognized as caught up with and dependent upon the activity of God. It is not that God is more present at camp than other places but, rather, that campers are more attuned to God's presence because it is an extended, immersive faith experience. Amanda Drury points to the importance of articulation and agency of young participants, allowing them to tell the story of how

God is at work. Drury explains, "We do not cause God's inbreaking; we call attention to God's in-breaking."[1]

The faith-centered characteristic is not simply an appendage to the secular camp model. Rather, it is intertwined in all other characteristics. All camps are relational, but only Christian camps are formed around intentional Christian community. All camps are participatory, but only Christian camps structure all activities as living out the Christian faith. Camp is, first and foremost, a place of encounter. When faith is at the center, camp is a place that facilitates experiences of or encounters with God. This explains why there are so many stories of divine encounter in the camp experience. The environment is radically different from the society from which the campers are unplugged, a society that dwells in a new age of secularity.

A Secular Age

When the camp movement began in the late 1800s, faith was in many ways woven into the fabric of American society. As we saw in chapter 2, all of the early camps included religious practices, some as simply part of a well-rounded education and some with intentional evangelical fervor. It is misleading to claim that America was a Christian nation, since the reality was far more complex, with a great deal of religious diversity and many nonadherents or, at best, nonpracticing Christians. However, the rising tide of secularity was held at bay with the religious revivals and renewals of the Great Awakenings. Faith retained a privileged place at the center of public dialogue, and religious beliefs were embedded in the social imaginary. Secularity existed in certain areas of life that were considered profane or separated from the religious aspects of life, what Charles Taylor refers to in his book *A Secular Age* as just one of several definitions of secularity.[2] We can think of this as a siloing movement, effectively compartmentalizing religious life from the nonreligious aspects of life (think of the oft-referenced separation of church and state). However, religion continued to permeate society, and most people lived in what Taylor calls an *enchanted* reality, where the supernatural broke into the temporal world.

1. Drury, *Saying Is Believing*, 131.
2. Taylor offers three different understandings of secularity. Secular 1 is the most ancient understanding, with a perceived separation of secular spaces from sacred spaces, which were in some way mystically inhabited by the holy. Secular 2 is the understanding that sacred and secular are at odds in the public sphere, such as when people speak of the secularization of ethics or the need for prayer in public schools. Secular 3, in contrast, is Taylor's understanding of the present age, in which religion is seen as one option among many to find meaning in life (Taylor, *Secular Age*).

Taylor argues that society is quite different in the twenty-first century. The present secular age is one in which living a religious life is simply one option among many. He writes, "We have moved from a world in which the place of fullness was understood as unproblematically outside of or 'beyond' human life, to a conflicted age in which this construal is challenged by others which place it 'within' human life."[3] In contrast to earlier eras, we live in a *disenchanted* world, in which people are conditioned to make sense of the world through reason and reflection more than by explanations related to spirits, demons, and the supernatural. Belief in God and participating in faith practices continues to be a way to live a meaningful life for some, but people are aware that there are many other ways to find fulfillment and meaning. What is more, these alternative options appear increasingly attractive as religion becomes associated with ultra-conservative viewpoints, rancorous division, and hatred. This new type of secularity allows people to simply opt out of religion altogether, something previously inconceivable except for the most elite of society.

It is important for us to understand this new reality because the faith-centered aspect of camp is not meant to serve as a breakwater to keep back a rising tide of secularity. As Taylor points out, this is the old definition of secularity. Camps, congregations, and other faith-formation experiences cannot serve as training grounds to shield young people from the flaming arrows of the Evil One (Eph 6:16) if the need for such protection itself comes into question.

Andrew Root, drawing from Taylor's work, asserts that understanding this new reality of secularity can help change the paradigm of ministry in our churches. He admonishes ministry leaders to stop struggling against secularity as if it were a strategic battle for space or time commitments (think of the struggle of those Sacramento pastors trying in vain to carve out time for confirmation instruction). His point is not that this new secularity is bad or good but simply that it is the environment in which we live, so pastors should stop trying to fight it. Instead, he focuses attention on experiences of and encounters with the holy, most especially through the praxis of ministry. He writes, "To help people have faith is to help them experience divine action through the act of being ministered to and ministering to others."[4] In this new secular age, people do not simply take the value of religion for granted. They value authenticity above all other things, which means that individual experience is paramount. Faith formation, then, becomes a path of personal encounter with the living Christ and continually engaging in the praxis of

---

3. Taylor, *Secular Age*, 15.
4. Root, *Faith Formation*, 150.

ministry. As we seek to guide young people in the path of discipleship, we need places of encounter. We need places like camp.

As we noted in chapter 3, Root is one of many youth ministry writers who is casually dismissive, if not overtly critical, of the summer camp experience. Like so many ministry leaders, however, camp is part of his faith story. The one camp story he tells in his book on faith formation in a secular age is a negative example of a camp speaker who emphasized the substitutionary atonement theory of justification in a way that did not sit well with young Andy and his cabinmates. He reflects, "Afterwards, we sat in our cabin with our counselor, unpacking what the words of the speaker meant in our lives."[5] He ultimately left feeling dissatisfied with the explanations they reached, longing for a faith that asked something of him and invited him to participate in something beyond himself. The story is used as an example of poor (or at least, incomplete) theology, feeding into the narrative that camp is a place of bad theology.

The thing is, Root's account is spot-on and fits with what I have seen and experienced at dozens of camps across the country. I have sat through more than my share of cringeworthy testimonies and sermonettes given by mostly earnest (and maybe slightly unprepared) nineteen and twenty-year-olds. Camps are generally not bastions of theological orthodoxy. However, that is not their function. Camps are places of faith in action, of ortho*praxy*. Root's description of the postrally conversation in the intimacy of the cabin group is one of the hallmarks of camp, where experiences and concepts are related to everyday life in the context of trusted community. This involves deep relational encounter and ministering to each other in times of doubt or uncertainty. This is also where the breakdown can happen, as it did for young Andy. He found his theological musings and voice stifled in favor of an interpretation that he did not find satisfactory. This is reminiscent of my own camp experience, in which two tentmates and I stayed up into the wee hours of the morning discussing faith and life after our harrowing experience on the Mississippi River.[6] Heresies surely abounded in the tent that night, and, like young Andy's cabin group, we did not solve or satisfy our theological musings. It was the act of voluntarily sharing the faith with people my own age that had such a profound impact on me. The major difference in my experience was that our counselor did not interrupt to correct our theology or tell us how to believe. He let the Spirit dance in a way that young Andy did not experience.

---

5. Root, *Faith Formation*, 181.
6. See introduction for this story.

This is where we come across an essential component of the faith-centered environment: it must also be participatory and relational. Camp counselors and group leaders serve as role models and facilitators, though some are tempted to take a more prescriptive approach. They may want to elicit a certain spiritual response or convince campers of a specific theological viewpoint. However, camp counselors are not doctrinal specialists, and most know just enough theology to be dangerous. Well-intentioned counselors who tend toward over-instruction may unwittingly suppress the seeds of faith that are actively germinating in the hearts and minds of their young charges. Their role is not to correct bad theology but, rather, to facilitate playful interaction and active imagination. The trusted small group at camp must be a safe space to ask questions about the faith, express doubt, and play with new understandings of how God is at work in the world. At their best, counselors are active participants in this process, willing to share their own doubts and theological musings alongside of their campers.

Summer camp is a profoundly *unsafe* environment for theological doctrine because the professionals and theologians are not in control. Pastoral care and theology are placed into the hands of young, unqualified people who are engaging in a dynamic theological exchange that is best characterized in terms of play. The Christian summer camp becomes a sort of theological playground in which rigid doctrine suddenly becomes malleable. The untouchable truth claims that are safely protected behind the display case or stained glass of the church building and curated by the professional minister are suddenly accessible to young people, who have little training in their care or proper use. In carefree, youthful exuberance, they smell them, shake them, rub their faces in them, and do all manner of unspeakable things to them. The professional ministers with the stomach to endure this defilement stoop to pick up the detritus only to realize that the truth claim has not been destroyed but rather made alive again.

When young people are given agency and space to play around with truth claims, they have the opportunity to test them for authenticity. This creates space for the types of encounter and experiences of God that Root argues we need to offer in this secular age. The young confirmands at Lake Tahoe were taken seriously when they asked to be baptized, and this agency led to a powerful experience of encounter with the holy. These personal encounters with God are remarkably common at summer camp. The length and novel setting of the camp experience provides the time and space for these encounters to happen. More common than mystical experiences and theophanies are encounters with one another in the praxis of ministry, something Root highlights as essential for faith formation.

A Zipline through the Sanctuary

My experience of the zipline in the outdoor sanctuary at Lutherlyn was surprising not simply because it startled me out of my prayerful reverie but also because it irrupted the notion of secularity that seeks to separate the sacred from the profane. Faith-centered camps do not separate the fun, highly participatory camp programs from the faith activities. Rather, the entire experience is framed in the context of faith formation. The campers do not ride the zipline and then go to chapel or Bible study later. The zipline goes *through* the sanctuary. One young camper explained, "No matter what we're doing, they intertwine the Christian stuff into it. When we were canoeing, it was about God's water. When we're doing the high ropes, it's our trust that God won't let us fall and our teammates won't let us fall. Wherever we go, we try to see God in whatever we're doing."[7] In a survey of Mainline Christian camp directors, nearly 90 percent agreed that at their camp, faith formation and practices should be incorporated into all aspects of camp life.[8]

The camp experience illustrates the truth that the kingdom of God is an inbreaking reality, not something to be studied as much as experienced and striven towards in all aspects of life. This recalls Moltmann's understanding of the eschatological horizon that is the basis for his theology of hope.[9] The Christian life of discipleship is a calling to participate in the work of God's ongoing creative work in the world. Moltmann writes, "The kingdom of God ahead of us that is going to change the world becomes more important than the religious heaven above us."[10] When the entire camp experience is framed as faith-centered, the bounds of God's dwelling place are moved beyond the eternal heavenly realms to include our earthly existence and expanded beyond the walls of the sanctuary.

A sanctuary is generally set apart as a sacred space, and people often act in these spaces as if they are somehow closer to God than elsewhere. Sanctuaries act as thin places between the earthly realm and heavenly realm, where God is imagined to dwell. There are certainly positive aspects of this. For example, I have found that even the most foul-mouthed person usually refrains from swearing in church. However, acting differently in the sanctuary can also carry hints of superstition, as if God is listening a little more closely or cares more about how you act in that space. I remember one morning at church when I was leading an intergenerational

---

7. Lutherdale Girls.

8. The figure for agreement was 88 percent in the 2016 survey and 87 percent in the 2018 survey (Sorenson, "Outdoor Ministries Connection," 10).

9. Moltmann, *Theology of Hope*.

10. Moltmann, *Spirit of Life*, 111.

activity during the Christian education time on Sunday morning. Drawing from my bag of camp tricks, I set up a scavenger hunt all over the church building, with biblical clues that led the groups to various places around church, like the communion rail, bell tower, library, and baptismal font. As people were arriving for our mid-morning worship service, children were running all over the church building in search of their goals, laughing as they went. Said one disgruntled church member gruffly, "Is this how you teach children to be respectful in God's house?" He was operating from an old understanding (or *habitus*, going back to Bourdieu's terminology) of secularity, in which the church stood as a holy place and bastion against the powers of the world. In this understanding, we necessarily act differently in church than we do in profane spaces. Children running and laughing in the sanctuary were clearly not part of his understanding of appropriate behavior in God's presence. Unfortunately, this attitude is oftentimes counterproductive, teaching young people that the church building is not for them. If church is understood as the place where God dwells, these actions have serious consequences, unintentionally teaching people that they are not welcome in God's presence.

Camp is a place that can help break through the boundaries, or at least blur the lines, between sacred and secular, thus rupturing confidence in the old notion of secularity. We accomplish this by intertwining faith with the other fundamental characteristics of camp. In their home lives, most campers experience faith as siloed from the rest of their lives, and recent studies demonstrate that churches are losing the battle for space and time. Regular church attendance used to mean every Sunday, but now we count those who attend once or twice a month as regular attendees. Prayer in the home is a rarity, even among Christian families. In the Effective Camp Project, only half of camper families in Christian homes reported praying together at meal times more than once a week, and barely a third of parents said they prayed with their children other than meal times more than monthly.[11] In a world in which living a life of faith is simply one option among many, most people, even those who are nominally Christian, are either opting out altogether or offering less and less of their time and attention to Christian reflection and practices.

Faith-centered camps immerse young people in a different way of living that can help recenter their lives on God. We noted earlier that Kenda

---

11. There was no statistical difference between Mainline Protestant families and Evangelical families in the frequency of prayer with family at mealtimes. Evangelical families, however, prayed together other than mealtimes more frequently, with about half of Evangelical parents reporting they prayed with their children more than monthly, compared with 39 percent of Mainline parents.

Dean has described camp as a faith immersion experience, analogous to a language immersion.[12] Those who have studied multiple languages can relate to this. We might take a language class that meets a couple times per week or participate in a program that has us study a few minutes each day. This helps teach vocabulary and syntax, but in order to become fluent in a new language, we must be immersed in a community of native speakers for days and weeks at a time. During these immersion experiences, it is important to speak only the new language because this teaches the brain to think in the language rather than switching back and forth. By the third or fourth day of true language immersion, a person generally stops translating things in their head and simply starts listening and responding in the new language. By the end of a week or two, the person begins dreaming in the language. Young Christians often struggle to consistently live a life of faith because they are constantly switching from the Christian way of being to a worldly or secular way of being. They learn some Christian vocabulary, but they do not practice it with enough frequency to have fluency, so the incredible gifts of God and the mundane miracles of everyday life may go unrecognized because they are lost in translation. Faith-centered camps teach faith fluency. By the third or fourth day, participants no longer need to stop and translate. They think and respond in the language of faith, and their walk with Christ becomes part of their hopes and dreams. The expectation that faith is siloed from other aspects of life is upended in this immersive environment. God is here and there and all around us.

It is notable that some Christian camps have begun to struggle with keeping faith at the center of all that they do. In chapter 3, we defined these as *compartmentalized* camps, noting that they comprise up to a quarter of all Christian camps. They separate faith activities like Bible study and worship from other camp activities, effectively keeping faith practices contained in certain areas or times of the day. Compartmentalized camps reinforce the lived experience of campers, who may go to church several Sundays each month but otherwise do not have many faith practices or conversations in other spaces. Faith is something that these young people travel to do and then are able to set aside for the remainder of the week or month. It was this disconnect that Yust observed at certain faith-based camps, leading her to conclude that they were not much different from secular activities, with little more than "a spiritual gloss."[13] These practices negate the model of camp as an immersion experience, allowing the

---

12. Dean, *Almost Christian*, 154–55.
13. Yust, "Creating an Idyllic World," 187.

campers' native language of secularity to take precedence over the language of faith, which remains foreign to them.

There are several reasons that some camps compartmentalize faith from other camp activities. One reason is the difficulty of hiring quality summer staff members who are people of faith. Another reason is cultural pressure. In this new age of secularity, there is fear among some camps of being perceived as overbearing or even manipulative when it comes to faith teaching. Since some campers are unaccustomed to faith practices and camp may serve as an introduction to the Christian faith, many in camp leadership are careful not to beat them over the head with it. There is a great deal of legitimacy to this concern, since camps have tremendous power to influence young people and can easily drift toward indoctrination or manipulation, violating the safe space of camp (see chapter 8). However, the solution is not to compromise on the faith-centered characteristic of camp. Camps can provide faith immersion experiences without being manipulative or off-putting to Christianity. We also have to move beyond the zipline so that camp is not limited to a thrill ride of faith.

Communities of Christopraxis

What we mean by "faith-centered" is a space where people live and breathe the faith. It is not a program, per se, but a state of being, a *habitus*. There are certain practices that help structure a faith-centered way of living, but these practices are understood more properly as the scaffolding than the thing itself. The goal is to recognize our active participation in the ongoing work of Christ's ministry. We are not learning about something that is dead on the page or that happened thousands of years ago. Life at camp is normed in a way that identifies God's action in the present world through the mundane and the extraordinary. God is not distant and unapproachable for everyone except the most holy among us. God is here, working in us, among us, and through us, driving us toward the eschatological horizon where God's will is done on Earth, as it is in heaven.

Regular faith practices provide ritual and rhythm, keeping us grounded in our daily walk with Christ and keeping our faith lens focused. The rhythm of daily Christian living at camp is framed with morning and evening devotional practices, which serve as intentional times to pray together and to reflect on the day in light of Scripture. Each day also includes a time set aside for worship and a time for a deeper dive into a certain passage or topic in Scripture. These practices are touchpoints that are transferrable to life away from camp, so that even when campers are not immersed in a faith-centered environment, they can still structure their day with devotional practices and connect with fellow Christians in weekly worship.

Some of the best practices of camps include equipping campers and their families with devotional practices and resources that they can take home to continue the daily rhythm of Christian practices in their homes. This is one of many ways to ensure that we are not leaving the campers dangling on the end of the zip line. Dozens of studies make clear that the home is the primary place of faith formation for young people and always takes precedence over spaces like church, youth group, or camp.[14] If we want to impact campers long-term, we have to impact their homes and their families. Camps are uniquely situated to do this because of their direct communication with parents and extended time to teach regular family devotional practices that are transferrable to the home.

What makes faith practices in the camp setting so powerful and accessible is that they depend on camper participation. The young people are actively engaging in theological dialogue and biblical interpretation. I generally discourage worship bands and well-regarded speakers in the camp setting because these types of events tend to take place on a stage with the campers as spectators. This reinforces the *habitus* of faith formation as conveying correct doctrine, and it provides an uncomfortable dissonance with the relational, participatory camp environment. Campers and their trusted counselors should be the ones up front, working to articulate their understandings of God. Drury elaborates on the power of testimony when she writes, "Though human language does not make God's converting work a reality, it may help adolescents recognize where God is present and lay claim to it in their life, thereby enriching their faith."[15] Testimony featured prominently in the evening campfires at Lutherlyn, and it was clear that everyone's faith story was valued, from the visiting pastors to the summer staff members to the campers themselves. One Lutherlyn cabin group made it a goal for every one of the members to pray aloud at least once during a community worship service. One of the group members explained, "It kind of makes you come out of your comfort zone and actually admit to yourself that you believe in God. And saying it out loud helps."[16] Camp experiences offer important opportunities for young people to plan and lead worship services, to offer testimonies, and to participate in song or dance. As the Lutherlyn case highlights, camp is also a tremendous opportunity

---

14. For example, this is one of the major findings of the National Study of Youth and Religion (Smith, *Souls in Transition*, 283–86).

15. Drury, *Saying Is Believing*, 44.

16. Camp Lutherlyn Girls.

for participants to become comfortable with prayer, both privately and in a group. Campers should always have the opportunity to lead prayers. Again, this is a skill that is transferrable to the home and church environments.

One of the faith practices at camp that deserves special attention is Bible study, particularly because I have oftentimes seen it done poorly. If we take the theological playground of camp seriously, we must allow campers the opportunity to learn to navigate the Scriptures. Some camps lead Bible study in a large group, usually with an adult expert guiding the lesson and turning the Bible study into a glorified sermon. However, the most effective Bible studies at camp take place in small groups, with the cabin guide (or counselor) leading. This helps build trust among group members and offers a safe space for campers to ask questions or express doubts. It is not a time for experts. It is a time for exploration. The Bible can be an incredibly intimidating book, and many young people who have been exposed to certain passages of Scripture—or closed interpretations of biblical passages—are put off by the Bible. So many have been exposed to a weaponized version of scriptural interpretation, in which passages are often taken out of context and used to exclude or condemn others.[17] Because of these influences, young people may see the Bible as irrelevant, hopelessly confusing, or even hate-filled. Drawing from our understanding of mindsets in the previous chapter, the faith immersion of camp can help young people move from a fixed understanding of what the Bible is and does, to a growth mindset in which they understand that God's word is living and active (Heb 4:12) and are open to God's voice speaking to them in new ways through the biblical texts. If Scripture is indeed God-breathed (2 Tim 3:16), then it cannot be dead on the page, for the Spirit and breath of God (*ruach*) is alive and active in the world.

Biblical theologian Don Juel describes the Bible's worth in terms of what it does, the effect it has on real people in their contexts. He asserts that interpretation of the Bible is not a process of discovering a static truth but rather a process of deriving *meaning* that makes a difference in the world. He characterizes scriptural interpretation metaphorically, "Living with the Scriptures is more like sailing than like building cathedrals."[18] The truth certainly exists, but interpretation is a never-ending journey of discovery that may lead closer to or farther away from the truth. Arriving at the truth is only an eschatological reality. Interpretation, then, "is conceived as

---

17. David Kinnaman notes that many young people who opt out of religion view religious beliefs as anti-science, repressive, and exclusive, many of them because of personal experiences. Kinnaman, *You Lost Me*.

18. Juel, "'Your Word Is Truth,'" 30.

conversation with another person who has something important to say."[19] The text itself may be the conversation partner, but this often takes place with someone else who offers a new interpretation of the text. For Juel, this is the most exciting thing about biblical interpretation and what makes his hermeneutic most complimentary to the camp environment. Juel is not concerned with someone blaspheming the sacred text. On the contrary, the Scriptures are meant to be played with. Biblical interpretation "leads not to unity but to extraordinary diversity."[20] The conversation partner in a novel context can offer a different interpretation that can deepen and enhance a person's own interpretation. Bible study at camp, therefore, can be seen as navigational training. The goal is not to learn specific texts or make it through a Bible study curriculum (no matter how well-written and theologically sound). The goal is to engage campers in intentional discussion and reflection on the written word of God. In so doing, campers may develop a better appreciation, familiarity, and even a love for the biblical texts, and they may discover that the Bible is a resource that connects to their daily lives. This is faith immersion that leads to a certain level of competency, or even fluency, not necessarily regarding specific biblical texts but, rather, in the application of biblical texts to our lives and listening for how God's word speaks anew to our present reality.

As important as the practices of devotions, worship, prayer, and Bible study are, there is more at work at camp than learning faith language and practices. In his description of *Christopraxis*, Anderson distinguishes between practice and praxis, arguing that *practice* refers predominantly to applied theory or the carrying out of a plan. *Praxis*, on the other hand, involves discovering meaning in the tasks themselves.[21] We have observed in the previous chapter that camp takes experience and camper participation seriously, but there is more going on at camp than experience-based learning. The campers and staff members are ministering to one another. Anderson's contention is that in the very act of ministering to one another is where we encounter the living Christ and develop theological understanding.

Root draws from and expands upon Anderson's understanding of Christopraxis, anchoring his Christology to a theology of the cross that recognizes God's very being (ontology) as a minister to humankind. Throughout biblical history, but most especially in the cross of Christ, God is revealed as the one who ministers to humanity through concrete, historical encounters. What this means is that the only way to learn about

---

19. Juel, "'Your Word Is Truth,'" 21.
20. Juel, "'Your Word Is Truth,'" 17.
21. Anderson, *Shape of Practical Theology*, 48–51.

God (epistemology) is to experience the living presence of God, which we do through the praxis of ministry to one another. He writes, "Union with God comes to us through the act of ministry itself that takes us into divine encounter."[22] In particular, Root highlights the ministry of being present with the other through suffering and personal trial, something that is lived out in each small group of campers during every session of summer camp. A ministry that stops at surface-level relationships and glosses over human suffering is not a place of Christopraxis. Similarly, a ministry that overemphasizes human actions (even when these are important faith practices) tends to deny divine agency. Camps can take note of this. The worst caricatures of camp feature gimmicky activities and forced smiles, but at their best, Christian camps are places of Christopraxis that take seriously the activity of God in the world. Regular Christian practices do not serve to actualize divine presence but, rather, to provide a normative framework that supports theological reflection and ministry.

Camp works because the campers are involved in the praxis of ministry, some of them for the first time in their lives. They lead the prayers, actively interpret Scripture, and participate in communal singing so that when one fellow camper reveals his greatest existential fear under the moonless sky or another divulges for the first time the challenges of her home life, the body of Christ is present to minister to them. It is in this act of ministering to one another that campers and their counselors encounter the concrete reality of the living Christ. This was my experience as a preteen camper in that tent with my fellow campers all those years ago, as we struggled with our own mortality and the question of the existence of God. We ministered to one another, and my life has never been the same. Over five years as a camp counselor/guide and another five years as a director, I witnessed and participated in similar encounters each week of the summer, and I am now privileged periodically to walk alongside small groups at camp, as they invite me into their community and recount similar stories of ministry and encounter. One camper summed it up, "I love being at [camp] sometimes more than home because of just how much I can feel God there and truly believe in him without any judgment on me."[23] At their best, camps are places of Christopraxis.

---

22. Root, *Christopraxis*, 102.

23. This quote comes directly from a camper survey response from the Power of Camp Study, 2019.

Faith Is Caught More Than It Is Taught

Christian camps are no longer appendages to traditional church structures. In a very real sense, camp is church, too. For some participants, camp is their primary space of religious connection and belonging. They return year after year and even multiple times throughout the year for retreats, worship, and family events. It used to be that camps existed as set-apart spaces to reinforce and deepen the faith formation that was happening in the home and congregational setting. Camps still retain this role, in part, but they are also centers for reimagining faith and, for many campers and staff, an introduction to the faith or reinterpretation of faith as meaningful in their lives. This does not mean that they are standalone ministries, as is the tendency with what we have defined as *disconnected* camps. Outdoor ministries that serve as the entry point for a life of faith must work to connect participants to ongoing ministries, particularly those of congregations. When camps operate with the *integrated* model that I am advocating, they can more effectively partner with congregations in the faith formation of participants and help other ministries learn from the logic of camp. In particular, consider the emerging adult staff members who serve at Christian camps for a whole summer or multiple summers. These staff members are emerging leaders in the church with incredible ability to powerfully impact the campers in their care, as well as experience personal impact. Many of these staff members go on to serve as pastors, youth ministers, and church volunteers. This is an important way that integrated camps can impact the church.

A big part of facilitating the faith-centered characteristic of camp is hiring staff members who are people of faith and then nurturing their faith growth. This is increasingly difficult as fewer emerging adults actively practice their Christian faith. Even when camps hire people who are Christians, they have a wide variety of faith backgrounds and levels of commitment. This makes staff formation an essential piece of camper formation. In our surveys of camp directors, more than 80 percent agreed that their camp emphasizes summer staff formation as much as camper formation. These efforts include intensive staff training, along with encouraging summer staff members to engage in regular Christian practices throughout the summer, such as worship, prayer partners, and personal Christian practices that go beyond what they already do with campers. These emerging adults are still forming their own faith ideas, and it is tempting for camps to hire staff from their limited pool of candidates who were raised in their own faith tradition, reasoning that these staff might have more palatable theology. However, I believe faith commitment is more important than theological tradition. I would much rather have a staff person with questionable theology who is on fire for Jesus and wants to learn more, than a staff person who identifies with my Christian tradition but does not read the Bible, pray, or attend church regularly. We can fix the bad theology. What we want are people of faith.

Here is where we stumble upon a secret of faith formation at camp. It is really an oft-quoted truth of ministry with young people, but it is one that professional ministers seem to constantly forget. As my colleagues David Anderson and Paul Hill have put it, "Faith is caught more than it is taught."[24] Let me just say for all of us in camping: Thank God that this is how it works! Summer staff members often have poor theology. There is a reason for this. Most have never gone to seminary, and they have picked up a panoply of Christian sayings from a wide variety of sources, many of them highly questionable. So they stand up in front of the camp group and stumble through a testimony that stinks of works-righteousness or pantheism or both. All of the professional ministers in attendance cringe and worry that camp is ruining the theology of their young charges. Meanwhile, the campers are transfixed at this mature near-peer mentor, whom they have gotten to know personally throughout the week. The theological faux pas are not even absorbed. What they see is a trusted young adult who is passionately proclaiming the faith, and they are able to imagine what life might look like if they were to grow up to be people of faith.

I do not mean to suggest that theology is unimportant. A camp's core values and theology should permeate every program developed, every resource provided, and every way that staff interact with guests and each other. But we do not need to worry so much about teaching theology to summer campers. Instead, teach faith. Tell the stories of faith. Interact with Scripture. Surround them with people of faith. Ask campers what they think. Let staff members fumble through what they think (with strong theological guidance, of course). This is how faith becomes intertwined in everything at camp, from the silliest game to the most serious conversation. At faith-centered camps, campers cannot even identify aspects of camp that do not have something to do with faith and God because it is in the very air that they breathe. This is how faith is passed on. It is caught more than it is taught.

One of the great practical and theological gifts that camp can offer the church is the chance to experience the holy. This is more than just the setting, since God is not more present at camp than other places. The camp experience provides the time and space for encountering God in unique ways. There are at least five factors that facilitate these encounters. First, being unplugged and away from life's normal routine primes participants to adopt new perspectives and attitudes. Second is slowing down. While

---

24. Anderson and Hill, *Frogs without Legs Can't Hear*, 71.

it is tempting to cram the daily schedule full of activities, the most effective camps structure each day with intentional periods of down time and reflection. Like Elijah on the mountaintop, these times of relaxed solitude and sacred silence can help campers listen for the still, small voice of God (1 Kgs 19:11–13). Third, the daily routine is structured and normed with faith practices and reflections, as we have discussed. Fourth, the highly relational environment and face-to-face interactions provide opportunities for genuine encounter and ministry. We have already discussed the importance of this above, and we will dive more deeply into the nature of relationships at camp in the next chapter. Finally, a large majority of camps situate their programs and activities in the natural world, allowing most campers far greater and more intentional connection with God's creation than they enjoy in their home environments. The immersion in God's creation is a special gift to participants, as they experience everything from the awe of a sunset to the industriousness of an ant colony. They have the chance to marvel at the intricacies of God's creation, as well as its vastness. Together, these factors facilitate encounters with God.

7

The Face of the Other:
Camp Is Relational

The six boys in the ten-day junior high program at Camp Stronghold (Illinois) were an unlikely grouping. Three were school friends that came together, so they naturally gravitated to one another. To make the dynamics even more challenging, these three friends were the most athletic. As the group moved from activity to activity in the first days of the camp experience, these three were always walking together, seldom mixing voluntarily with their other three cabinmates, who each arrived without knowing anyone in the cabin group. One of these boys (we will call him Joshua) admitted to his cabinmates that he had a tough time trusting people and making friends because people at school often picked on him. He was a self-described loner and was ambivalent about the camp experience, there because his parents made him come. He much preferred being at home and playing video games. As I sat with them during a focus group, Joshua lamented, "At camp, you have to *deal* with people" (his cabinmates responded jokingly, "We're sitting right here, you know").[1] Another boy, Peter, had cerebral palsy, which made it very difficult for him to walk. He had crutches to help him get around. A staff member usually drove him around camp on a golf cart, though he walked as much as he could because he desperately wanted to be part of the group. He did not want the others to feel sorry for him or treat him differently. Camp provided an opportunity for him to mix with able-bodied peers in a way that he was seldom afforded at home and school. His favorite part of the camp day was swimming because the buoyancy allowed him to keep up with the other boys more than most activities. After several days of getting to know one another, it was clear that this eclectic group of boys was starting to bond and care for each other.

1. Camp Stronghold Boys.

During unstructured free time on the seventh day of camp, the campers were allowed to choose any activity on their own, but this group of boys chose to stick together. Five of them wanted to play gaga ball, a competitive sport that requires a high amount of mobility. Peter decided to join them rather than swim with campers from another group. He played determinedly and even inspiringly, earning cheers from his cabinmates. Then he stumbled and took a nasty fall against the side of the gaga ball pit. His cabinmates rushed to help, but he waved them off and sat out for the rest of the session, clearly in pain. When it was time to walk to the next activity, he waved off the golf cart. The group set off together, walking almost imperceptibly slower. One of the three boys who came to camp together fell in on one side of Peter, and Joshua, the self-described loner, walked closely on the other side. They did not take hold of him; they simply walked beside him. They walked in silence for a few minutes. Then Peter reached out a hand to either side, and his companions took hold and helped him to the next destination.

The relational characteristic of camp is the one that campers and staff members most frequently identify as indispensable. When describing their camp experiences, some talk about the things they did, but they almost always focus most on the people. Venable and Joy write, "The glue that holds religious camping together, that explains why it changes lives and promotes meaningful discipleship, is the power of community."[2] Camp involves living in community for extended periods of time. The camp experience at Stronghold and other Christian camps can be described in terms that participants consistently use: *intentional Christian community*. It is *intentional* because community-building is a stated goal and programmatic priority, shown most clearly in group-building activities like the low-ropes challenge courses we examined in chapter 5. It is *Christian* because it is framed by Christian faith practices, as we reviewed at length in the previous chapter. It is *community* because that is how the participants themselves describe it.

Participants at camps I have visited across the country use familial language to describe the community they form, with several saying that camp feels like a second home or their fellow campers feel like siblings. "We've only known each other for a couple days, but I feel like we're family," one boy at Camp Lutherlyn said, as his cabinmates nodded in agreement.[3] Those without stable familial situations even describe the experience as a discovery of what a family might be like. Trevor was a boy in the Lake Tahoe UMC group who spoke honestly and seriously about his family life and the importance he

---

2. Venable and Joy, *How to Use Camping Experiences*, 13.
3. Camp Lutherlyn Boys.

found in his church group, especially the group he was bonding with at camp. He quietly summed up the camp experience as "almost having siblings," adding, "I know that everyone says, 'Oh yeah, it's like a second family,' but to me it's something more because I never had that."[4]

Community is the center of camp life and is connected to all of the other major characteristics. The experience of the boys at Stronghold demonstrates a community forged out of shared experiences and deep care for one another. This created a safe space for a boy like Joshua to risk social intimacy while unplugged from his devices, and a safe space for Peter to share his personal struggles without fear of ridicule or surface-level pity. As they opened up to their cabinmates about deep personal experiences, the others were confronted with the reality of their humanity, and they responded as ministers. Peter's cabinmates chose to walk beside him rather than grab hold of him because they understood his needs in that time and place. They understood at an intimate level what he was experiencing, and they did not try for a quick fix. Camp provided the time and space for them to develop this mutual understanding and to respond appropriately. They did not have more important things to run off to or other distractions vying for their attention. They had the time to be there with and for the other.

Thinking back to our zipline analogy, we can see how camp embeds the individual experience in the context of trusted community. A small group does not start the week on the high-ropes course. The camps that I have visited or worked with required several hours of group-building initiatives or low-ropes activities before participating in high ropes. They had to do more than just learn each other's names. By the time they put on the harnesses for high ropes, they had been through a lot together to build trust and mutual respect. Though the zipline itself looks like an individual activity, the community is there through the whole experience. First, they encourage their group members in the midst of the activity and celebrate their accomplishments, whatever that might mean for the individual (from climbing partway up the pole to completing a difficult element). Second, they keep each other safe physically and emotionally by participating in a belay team. This means that a rope secured to the participant's safety harness passes through a pulley at the top of the ropes course and back down to a second person who controls a belay device. This allows them to control the slack in the rope and stop the rope from passing through altogether. If the participant falls, the belayer applies the breaking mechanism, and the participant dangles from the harness, their safety literally in the hands of the belayer. Third, the community comes together to process the experience

---

4. UMC Lake Tahoe Focus Group A.

and relate it to their daily lives. While each person has a unique experience on the zipline, like at camp in general, the experience is highly relational, centering on a trusted small group.

Centralized and Decentralized Camping Models

In a relatively short period of time, campers and staff form intentional Christian communities that are remarkably cohesive and trusting. The centerpiece of the camp community is not the large-group worship or dynamic guest speaker but, rather, the small group of five to eight campers and their counselor working to figure things out together. Starting with my very first summer camp experience with Ben, Brian, and the rest of our group, I have witnessed this special camp community form countless times in my work at Christian camps across the country. One young participant put it to me this way, "We're all so different, but we all came together and it was a puzzle that fit perfectly together. Like a 500-piece puzzle you just put together for the first time."[5]

Quantitative research corroborates these observations. An extensive 2006 study of more than 7,500 campers from eighty camps determined that camp's greatest asset is "supportive relationships."[6] In the ongoing Effective Camp Project, camps are consistently strong at developing relationships that impact camp participants. On the last day of camp, 92 percent of campers said they got along really well with their cabin group and counselor often or always. This was one of four key factors directly correlating with significant growth in outcomes related to increases in personal belief, the understanding that faith is relevant in daily life, and social skills. The other three factors were increased frequency of conversations with cabinmates about God/faith, increased agreement of enjoying the cabin counselor, and increased agreement of trying something new at camp. The last of these is most clearly related to the characteristics unplugged from home and participatory, but the other three are directly related to relationships formed in the small group. The strength of the small-group community had direct impacts on camper outcomes. When there was evidence that the relational characteristic of camp broke down for individual campers, it had serious consequences for the camper experience and outcomes.

Though relational breakdowns were measured for less than 5 percent of campers, it is notable that the breakdown rate was uneven across the camps we studied. We expect that group dynamics will occasionally break down,

---

5. Lutherdale Girls.
6. Thurber et al., "Inspirations," 9.

even at the very best camps. In our measurements, most camps had 2–4 percent of their campers show some evidence for a breakdown, but some camps had a much higher breakdown rate of 7–10 percent. These breakdowns dramatically impacted camper outcomes, with campers far less likely to report growth in faith or a desire to return to camp in the future and many campers actually showing a *decrease* in self-confidence.[7] In general, camps that were more decentralized fared better than centralized camps.

You will recall the spirited debate in the early days of the camping movement when many denominational bodies opted for the large-group conference model and others focused more on small-group ministries (see chapter 2). The strong influence of people like L. B. Sharp led to the widespread adoption of decentralized camping models that focused on the small group. However, the conference model has persisted, and most camps have a hybrid model that includes both large-group gatherings and small-group ministries. The key is where on the spectrum the camp programs lie. Centralized camps tend to have most or all of their meals together in a large dining hall, while decentralized programs have campers eating in smaller groups, oftentimes cooking over the fire. Centralized camps tend to allow cabin groups to split up at some point during the day so that campers can choose their activity areas, while decentralized programs have cabin groups participate in activities together. Centralized camps tend to have large all-camp rallies, featuring dynamic speakers, while decentralized camps have Bible study, campfires, and even worship services in small groups. In our research, camps favoring the small-group experience for as many activities as possible had greater success fostering relationships than camps that relied more heavily on the large group.

In one sense, this finding seems counterintuitive. We tend to think that giving campers a break from one another is a good thing. We might reason that allowing them to mix with the larger camp community might help them tolerate campers in their own group that they do not get along with. But the data are clear that campers tend to get along better with their fellow campers and their counselor in a decentralized camp setting. This becomes even more clear when we consider the wilderness camp programs that were involved in the study. This finding is no surprise to practitioners in the field like Ashley Denton, who richly describes the benefits and best practices of Christian wilderness programs. He notes, "The wilderness is truly a school

---

7. Of the campers who showed a breakdown in the relational characteristic, only 49 percent strongly agreed on the last day of camp that they were strengthened in their faith, compared with 72 percent of those who did not experience this breakdown. Similarly, 67 percent of those experiencing a relational breakdown agreed that they planned to return to camp, compared with 92 percent of those without a breakdown.

for learning how to build healthy relationships."[8] These programs involve small groups of eight to twelve campers on multiday canoe or backpacking trips, making them the most decentralized of all camping models. Group members slept in tents and cooked meals over a fire or cook stove. They spent large portions of each day either hiking or paddling together, and they had to work together to set up camp each day. Their time was generally not jammed full of other activities, like many on-camp programs tend to be, so campers had the chance to walk or paddle in silence. This provided time and space for them to engage one another in informal conversation about God and faith (one of the key factors we identified above that leads to camper growth). It is great to program time for Bible study in order to dive deeply into God's word, but camps also need to offer time for campers to open up about what they are curious about. This oftentimes happens in the cabin after lights out or around the campfire, as long as every second is not filled with programming or counselors talking. Wilderness adventure programs are so effective at fostering community because they are radically decentralized, providing time and space for informal conversations. Importantly, they also involve shared struggle through adversity, which is an incredibly effective way of building community (more on this below). Out of more than 300 campers we surveyed from these adventure programs, only two showed evidence for a breakdown in the relational characteristic. That is less than 1 percent.

Let me be clear about something. I am not trying to suggest that centralized camping programs are ineffective. I have experienced and studied both centralized and decentralized camping programs (though usually a hybrid of some kind) and all of these programs have the potential to be effective and transformative. Consider again our small group of boys at Stronghold. Their afternoon of unstructured free time is a hallmark of the centralized camping model. It is instructive that these boys chose to stay together rather than enjoy their separate activities. When camps like Stronghold intentionally prepare campers for these decisions, it can lead to transformative experiences where individuals who are used to being left out get included. However, this does not always happen, and this is one of the inherent challenges of centralized camps. Every time we let campers choose who to hang out with, we put them in a difficult social situation. What tends to happen, of course, is that campers gravitate towards those who are like them and away from those who might be considered the Other. The results are predictable, and we have found this over and over in the Effective Camp Project surveys. The campers who tend to feel left out in their

---

8. Denton, *Christian Outdoor Leadership*, 189.

home or school environments also feel left out at camp. Their cabinmates, who they thought they were really connecting with, choose to do something without them. Even when this is only for an hour-long activity, it can strongly reinforce insecurities among those who are accustomed to being picked on or left out. The athletic boys at Stronghold got their first choice of activities (gaga ball) and it was Peter, the boy with cerebral palsy, who had to go out of his comfort zone (and put his own safety at risk) in order to remain part of the group. The task of those in more centralized camping programs becomes to stack the deck in such a way that campers choose to be inclusive. The power of the camp community is in the small group.

The Power of the Small Group

The small-group community at camp reflects Dietrich Bonhoeffer's vision of Christian community in his classic *Life Together*. Participants experience the rhythm of daily Christian living through devotions, regular prayer, Bible study, song, worship, and the day's work.[9] Together, they negotiate challenges (often through adventure-based learning) and the conflict that arises in community. Each participant has an important role in this model of community living, and their opinions are valued. When conflicts arise, campers cannot simply walk away, hang up the phone, ignore text messages, or stay off social media to avoid another person because they have to sleep in the same room (or tent!) and participate in activities together. They face the reality of cooperation, compromise, and forgiveness on a daily basis for days on end.

This model of community living is in sharp contrast to what campers and staff normally experience at home and school. Theresa Latini identifies a "crisis of community" in Western society, where adolescents and young adults form what she refers to as "faceless relationships."[10] In conversation with sociologists Robert Putnam and Anthony Giddons, her research indicates that, while young people may be connected electronically with people throughout the world, they oftentimes lack intimate face-to-face relationships of mutual vulnerability. Latini identifies Christian small-group ministry as a place of *koinonia*, which she understands as "mutual indwelling"[11] analogous to the perichoretic relationship of God in Trinity. She argues that God is active in the intentional Christian communities of small groups formed in dynamic relationship with congregations. Picking

9. Bonhoeffer, *Life Together*.
10. Latini, *Church and the Crisis*, 5.
11. Latini, *Church and the Crisis*, 76.

up from James Loder's model of transformation, she says, "In the midst of faceless relationships, small groups can point us to the one face that never goes away, the face of God in Jesus Christ."[12] Small groups at camp differ from other small-group ministries in terms of frequency and intensity. While most Christian small groups meet weekly or even monthly, camper groups are together throughout the day for a week or more, and they do everything together.

This consistent interaction and working through challenges facilitates a community of care for one another. Cooperative games, silly songs, joyful play, and adventure activities like high ropes or canoeing are not ends in themselves. They serve the purposes of affirming life and building community. Canoeing in a circle around an island seems like a colossal waste of time until we realize that the shared activity provides space for community and encounter with the Other. Campers not only learn to work together, get along with others, and develop new skills; they form a community that worships together, prays together, and reads Scripture together. The openness of community and attentiveness to individual experience creates space for a camper to explore personal suffering and existential longing. This is why campers feel safe, often for the first time, to express the suffering they have experienced through divorce, the death of a loved one, the betrayal of a friend, or peer ridicule. I witnessed this at Stronghold as Peter and Joshua shared their personal stories with tears in their eyes and the cabin group of unlikely friends supported them. They were participating in a model of pastoral care that Charles Gerkin describes. Gerkin asserts that pastoral care happens when the "particularity of life stories" are grounded in the "story of the Christian community and its tradition."[13] Young people at camp become the recipients and the providers of pastoral care, with more direct attention to the reality of their suffering than most, if not all, other communities to which they belong. As we noted in the previous chapter, it is in this ministry to one another that Christ is revealed.

Recognition by a trusted community is empowering and life affirming. The reality of the camp experience is that the truth is not simply proclaimed didactically; it is lived out. It is participatory. A young person at camp may hear for the first time in his life that he is a beloved child of God (1 John 3:1), but it is not the mere hearing that is life affirming. The person who speaks these words to the child is a trusted member of the community who has loved, honored, and forgiven the child in daily human interaction in which the child was not able to present an idealized social media profile. The child

12. Latini, *Church and the Crisis*, 180.
13. Gerkin, *Introduction to Pastoral Care*, 110–13.

is encountered in the messiness of all his complexities and imperfections, and yet he is affirmed as a child of God. He is also given space to recognize the Other as beloved. This experience may feel *decentering* to a person accustomed to faceless relationships, in which the answer to conflict may be *defriending* the Other on social media networks, and the most tangible form of affirmation may come in the form of a letter grade. In actuality, however, the experience is *recentering*. The camp participants are brought into unmediated encounter with the Other, an encounter that is essential to the human experience and points directly to the Divine Other, the being who, as Trinity, exists in a relationship of mutual indwelling.

The Importance of Relational Encounter

The theological conviction that humans are created to be in relationship, which finds its biblical grounding in God's declaration that it is not good for the human to be alone (Gen 2:18), is corroborated by philosophy, psychology, and neuroscience. Philosopher Emmanuel Levinas claims that an understanding of self only begins as one encounters the "Face of the Other."[14] For Levinas, the Other becomes an ethical boundary that makes demands upon us and helps us understand who we are. His notion of the self in relationship to others has deep resonance with theories in psychology which recognize that, from infancy, humans make sense of the world through the face of the primary caregiver and various human attachments that prove inconsistent or "good enough."[15] The human brain is programmed at birth to engage with the face of the Other. Similarly, the exciting field of interpersonal neurobiology argues that the human mind functions only in relation to other minds. In his highly influential and integrative book *The Developing Mind*, Daniel Siegel incorporates the latest research in neuroscience with psychological attachment theory to show that knowing is always embodied and situational, and it is dependent on relationship with other embodied minds. In terms of personhood and the self, Siegel writes, "We are not just an isolated, separate self, but an ever-emerging process of 'selfing' linked with other evolving selves over time."[16] The biblical narrative, philosophy, psychology, and neuroscience demonstrate that the human need to be in relationship is embedded in the very fabric of creation. This need for relationship leads to a spiritual longing for a relationship that is reliable, a face

14. His capitalization of "Face of the Other" is not meant to refer to God, but rather a fellow human being (Levinas, *Entre Nous*).
15. See, for example, Winnicott, *Playing and Reality*, 13–14.
16. Siegel, *Developing Mind*, 209–10.

that does not go away (Loder), which orients the human being to the source of being.[17] As psychoanalyst and theologian Ann Belford Ulanov puts it, humans "are driven to find the transcendent."[18]

Pastoral care begins with an acknowledgment of the Other's humanity. This humanity is veiled in the faceless relationships that Latini identifies as the cultural norm. Humanity is also veiled through various systems of oppression that divide people. The Christian camp community is one of the few places that honors the fundamental human need for face-to-face relationships. In ACA's 2005 "Directions" study of more than 3,000 campers at eighty camps, "93 percent of campers agreed that 'Camp helped me get to know kids who are different from me.'"[19] The camp experience intentionally tears down barriers and brings together people who would normally not choose to be together into unmediated, intimate encounter. Differences certainly include preferred social circles, which are divisive enough in youth culture, though they more often include denominational or religious backgrounds, physical or mental abilities, socioeconomic status, sexual orientation, family makeup, and race. Dwight Hopkins sheds light on this, theologically. The liberating experience of affirmation provides space to recognize the Other as beloved. Hopkins writes, "The *imago dei* unfolds outward into the *missio dei*. We are called to exhibit healthy humanity by recognizing this divine image and sharing this liberation evangelism with others."[20] A person who may be marginalized in school or at home is an integrative part of the community at camp. The assumption is that the community would be worse off if one person were absent. This remains a challenge for the camping industry as a whole, which continues to struggle with engaging people of color in the summer camp movement. We noted in chapter 2 some of the deep historical roots of this challenge, and it is important to recognize in the present discussion that the camp community is strengthened with racial diversity.[21]

17. Loder contends that humans experience what he calls a "cosmic loneliness," longing for a Face analogous to the face of the primary caregiver (usually the mother) but different in substance. In Loder's words, "A Face that will transfigure human existence, inspire worship, and not go away, even in and through the ultimate separation of death" (Loder, *Logic of the Spirit*, 119).

18. Ulanov, *Unshuttered Heart*, 78.

19. American Camp Association, "Directions," 9.

20. Hopkins, *Being Human*, 185.

21. I am indebted to my colleague on the Confirmation Project, Shonda Nicole Gladden, for helping me understand more deeply the historical trauma that continues to impact the participation of young black people in outdoor ministries. There is an important connection with the history of violence against black people in America in outdoor locations, contributing to a cultural aversion to the forest that is difficult for some people to overcome. Historically black denominations have predominantly continued with the conference model, which generally relies on indoor spaces and large-group gatherings, instead of embracing summer camp.

Mary McClintock Fulkerson provides helpful terminology to understand the dynamics at work in the Christian camp experience. She uses the word "obliviousness" to describe the complex phenomenon of "not-seeing" that results from cultural constructions that "ascribe or project all manner of fears and anxieties onto 'Othered' bodies."[22] Interestingly, these projections can be conscious or unconscious, and they may in fact constitute a *benign* obliviousness. Young people's interaction with others in their normal cultural settings can often be characterized as obliviousness. They develop specific ways of interacting with one another and accept the norms of their peer groups, even if those norms are degrading to others. They also establish specific ways of being in relation to others that begin to define their own identities (e.g., the athletic one, the loner, or the cripple). Fulkerson insists, "What is needed to counter the diminishment and harm associated with obliviousness is a *place to appear*, a place to be seen, to be recognized and to recognize the other."[23] Camp provided that place for Peter and Joshua, as the other boys in their group encountered their humanity. The three athletic cabinmates who came to camp together began with the sort of benign obliviousness that Fulkerson describes, but their encounters with otherness led to gradual understanding and then deep care for people that a few days before would not have attracted more than passive curiosity. Even more significant, the camp experience can act as what Fulkerson describes as a transformative community, which goes beyond cognitive recognition of the other to include actual practices. We return again to Bourdieu's concept of *habitus* (or bodily wisdom) that we examined in chapter 4, noting that the practices of caring for one another in the camp community can help develop a "situational competence" that impacts interaction with others in an ongoing way.[24] Both ACA's "Directions" study and the ongoing Effective Camp Project demonstrate that much of the increases in developmental outcomes observed from the first day of camp to the last day are maintained months after camp. As one Effective Camp Project parent noted about her child in the weeks following camp, "She came back more respectful and thoughtful. Before she left, she was getting more sassy and rude. She honestly was kinder when she came back."[25] Other parents confirmed that their children were simply nicer, more respectful, and more forgiving of others.[26]

22. Fulkerson, *Places of Redemption*, 19.
23. Fulkerson, *Places of Redemption*, 21 (italics original).
24. Fulkerson, *Places of Redemption*, 46.
25. Camp Wapo Parent Survey.
26. In the Effective Camp Project, parents were asked if they observed certain changes in their children in the weeks following the camp experience. Of more than 1,000 parents, 47 percent indicated their child had been nicer or more pleasant to

Shared Adversity

The many cabin groups I have observed and interacted with over the years have not settled for surface interaction or maintained some idyllic form of community. They were messy, complete with all of the difficulties, frustrations, and joys that accompany making space for the Other. The Stronghold boys are one example among many. They were an unlikely grouping that got on each other's nerves as often as they showed tremendous care for one another. In the UMC confirmation camp at Lake Tahoe, four teenage boys and three adults were crammed into a space the size of a walk-in closet. Besides being fertile ground to discover smells heretofore unimagined, this confined space led to the awkwardness of underwear left on someone else's pillow, people tripping over other's things, and individuals losing patience with one another. Two campers in particular had an escalating personality conflict. They sat down, face-to-face, to discuss their differences, with an adult mentor acting as mediator and helping them interpret the process of reconciliation through a Christian lens. Forgiveness and reconciliation in these camp environments went far beyond intellectual concepts to embodied, emotionally-laden experiences.

The best camps do not settle for surface-level happiness. They intentionally problematize group interaction by presenting cabin groups with challenges and unsettling circumstances, like the challenge courses we discussed at length in chapter 5. These activities give small groups some controlled adversity to overcome together, and effectively processing these experiences can help campers apply the learning to their group at camp and their daily lives away from camp.

One of the reasons that outdoor adventure programs are so effective at building community is that the small group is consistently facing adversity together. I distinctly remember being in a thirty-five-foot canoe on Lake Superior with my youth group and two guides from Camp Amnicon (WI). The wind and the waves picked up, and all sixteen of us had to work together, paddling as one, in order to stay on course and make it to shore. If you are ever interested in an intense group-building experience, try paddling one of these behemoths in calm conditions, much less on the choppy waters of the largest lake in the world. On my first week as a backpacking guide at Sky Ranch Lutheran Camp (CO), an afternoon thunderstorm surprised our group high on a mountain pass just below tree line. We gathered in the shelter of some trees at the edge of a clearing while the hail beat down

---

family members since returning from camp, and 43 percent said that their child had been more helpful around the house.

on us, and we watched lightning strike the clearing a few minutes later. As the storm passed, we worked together to set up camp and get those who were wet into sleeping bags to keep them warm. Adventure programs like these often involve real risks to life and limb, requiring the group to work together in difficult circumstances. In both of these instances, the group bonded through the shared adversity, opening space for deep connections and emotional vulnerability. Even when adventure programs are less eventful, the shared struggle is part of the bodily experience. There is a sense of vulnerability in being exposed to the natural elements in wilderness areas, and this is combined with the physical exhaustion that results from days of paddling or hiking. Together, the group endures these challenges and works to support one another's physical needs by setting up camp, cooking meals, and massaging sore muscles. It is no wonder that so many groups come through adventure programs with deep emotional bonds that open the space for life-long friendships and faith breakthroughs.

Shared adversity is not limited to adventure camps and challenge courses. The unexpected can often provide opportunities for particularly powerful group experiences. Two examples from programmatically centralized camps illuminate this reality. One of the first camps to participate in the Effective Camp Project was Imago Dei Village (WI). Out of several sessions that participated in the camper survey, one in particular stood out as having exceptionally high levels of camper satisfaction, relational bonding, and faith outcomes. Though this camp tended towards centralized programs, they had a hybrid model that included many decentralized elements, including a river canoe trip that each group went on during a certain day of the week. On the last full day of camp one week, the group encountered some windy conditions, and about half of the canoes capsized. The group lifeguard worked against the current to help floundering campers back into their canoes and ensure that the gear was not lost downstream. When they arrived to shore, the lifeguard collapsed in exhaustion and spent the rest of the day recovering in the camp's medical station, while the camp community prayed for her. That evening during the closing worship service, the lifeguard was able to rejoin the group, and it was powerfully emotional for the campers and staff whom she worked to keep safe. The shared experience led to deep reflection, an increased willingness to be emotionally vulnerable, and a strong sense of God's presence in community. The results included significant increases in camper outcomes.

On the other side of the state, the same rains that kept the river at Imago Dei Village rushing so swiftly that summer soaked the only large playing field at Camp Wapo. The rains were so bad one week that most of the regular camp activities had to be canceled. That is when the summer staff got creative. They gathered the camp community in their large gathering space and provided each small group with cardboard boxes from the recent food service delivery. They proceeded to have a massive fort-building contest that provided a novel experience for campers young and old. The unusually rainy weather forced the summer staff out of their normal routine, making them more attentive to the camper experience. The results were clear in the camper surveys. Most weeks of the summer showed positive camper experiences and modest camper growth in outcomes, but the week with the rainy weather and creative fort construction showed significantly higher camper satisfaction, relational connection, and faith outcomes. In both of these examples, unforeseen adversity led to shared action that promoted community bonding, leading to increased camper outcomes.

It is clear that experiencing some level of shared adversity positively impacts the relational characteristic of camp. This does not mean that we should send campers out in lightning storms or intentionally capsize their canoes. However, it means that all camp staff should be equipped to respond creatively in unexpected circumstances. If every program is consistent and planned, like at many centralized camps, then camp staff may not be able to exercise the sort of creativity and spontaneity that Camp Wapo staff exhibited when they were blessed with the disruption of multiple rainy days. These examples also teach us that camps should provide the space for groups to experience challenges and controlled risks. If there are opportunities available, there is no better substitute than shared experiences in the wilderness. Even highly centralized camps can structure time for river excursions or overnight campouts, complete with meals over the open fire.

The high-ropes course and low-ropes challenge course are also great tools for teachable moments involving shared adversity. What I oftentimes see among ropes facilitators at camp is a lack of patience. The counselor wants the group to succeed, and they also want to get on to the next element or activity. It is frustrating to watch as a camper group struggles with a challenge. Here is the secret: success is not the goal. Group process is the goal. Struggle and frustration are the means to that goal. This means that the best group-building activities or ropes elements take a group 30 minutes or even an hour to complete. The key moments often come when someone accidentally steps off an element and the facilitator makes the whole group start over again. I love it when a group gets more than halfway through an element and then has to start over. This causes frustration. It sometimes causes guilt or vulnerability as someone claims that they are not good enough or have let the group down. These are oftentimes key moments that allow the group to become stronger. Participants have the chance to reassure one another, forgive one another, and receive grace from their teammates. When it comes right down to it, the facilitator can remind them that it is just a game. It teaches us about life and how to work through challenges, but it does not really matter if we complete the element. This is just like hiking or canoeing. The point is not making it to the top of the mountain or paddling around the island. The shared journey is more important than the destination.

The Counselor as Interpretive Guide

The researchers of the Confirmation Project dedicated a chapter of our book to mentoring because we discovered that it was one of the most consistently effective practices of forming faith in young people across multiple denominations and in varied contexts. Countless youth ministry projects have noted that relationships are essential to forming faith in young people, so this is not a new insight. However, there is a difference between peer-to-peer relationships and mentor relationships. My colleagues note, "The best way to learn how to live is by the example of others in the context of a community living a distinctive way of life."[27] The camp setting was one of the key spaces that our research identified for its power to form community but also its distinctive mentorship model.

Through the frustrations, shared adversity, and difficulty navigating relationships with a diverse group, the constant presence accompanying the camper is the trusted group guide, oftentimes called the camp counselor. The camper-counselor relationship is one of the most impactful elements of the camp experience (one of the four key factors related to camper growth that we identified above). Though counselors and other camp guides are sometimes older adults, including pastors or youth ministers accompanying their church groups, counselors are usually college-age young people. These emerging adults are close enough in age to the campers, particularly high school campers, that they serve as near-peer mentors. This gives them a slightly different role compared with other faith mentors. To a certain extent, the counselors are learning alongside their campers, even as they are guiding them in activities and faith reflection. In this role, they can be both friend and mentor, coming alongside the campers as an integral part of the group. The shared experiences and extended period of interaction facilitate powerful connections between counselors and campers. ACA's "Inspirations" study concluded that relationships between youth and adults "are stronger at camp

---

27. Lisa Kimball and Kate Siberine, in Osmer and Douglass, *Cultivating Teen Faith*, 45.

than in any other arena outside the family system" that the study examined (including schools and community-based organizations).[28]

The counselor oftentimes becomes for the campers a key role model that they desire to emulate. As they get to know their counselor, campers are watching their every move and discovering what life might look like in the near future. It may be difficult for an adolescent to imagine themselves as an adult with a full-time job, family, and mortgage payments, but the college-age, emerging adult is a life stage to which they can more easily aspire. The counselor becomes a powerful force for emulation, a mentorship role that is referred to as modeling. Oman and Thoresen explain: "Central to spiritual modeling phenomena is what we term observational spiritual learning, that is, the learning of spiritually relevant skills or behaviors through observing other persons."[29] This is why hiring people of faith is so important for camps. The young campers have the chance to see and build relationships with emerging adults who are committed Christians. They observe these young people living lives of faith and are able to imagine themselves as faithful emerging adults. They return home aspiring to emulate their counselors, which can help lead to acts of service to others and more consistent religious practices.

Each camp counselor leads a small group of five to ten campers through the messiness of living together and working together over the course of the camp session. The camp guide is seldom a professional pastor, yet is in a pastoral role remarkably similar to Gerkin's vision of the pastor as "interpretive guide."[30] Gerkin identifies four axes of what he calls the quadrilateral of pastoral care. Applying this to the camp community, we see how the counselor holds in tension (1) care for the individual camper, (2) care for the small-group community, (3) care for the tradition that shapes Christian identity (most explicitly through the Bible, but also with concern for the denominational confessions or core teachings), and (4) care for the cultural context (at camp, this axis of care attends to the traditions and programmatic priorities of the specific camp).[31] Gerkin says that, in the context of a local congregation, the tension among these dynamics of care is enacted in "local theology."[32] At camp, each group develops a unique way of constructing theology that is dependent on the individuals gathered in community in God's name in that time and place. The counselor as

28. Thurber et al., "Inspirations," 9.
29. Oman and Thoresen, "Spiritual Modeling," 149.
30. Gerkin, *Introduction to Pastoral Care*, 113.
31. Gerkin, *Introduction to Pastoral Care*, 35.
32. Gerkin, *Introduction to Pastoral Care*, 118.

interpretive guide participates in and facilitates this community, providing pastoral care and empowering the campers themselves to offer care for one another in the praxis of ministry. As we noted in the previous chapter, this role is not prescriptive and must allow space for the campers to express questions and doubts without fear of judgment or contradiction. In the process, the staff members themselves are dramatically impacted.

At most summer camps, the individual cabin communities are expressions of the larger community formed among the summer staff members. One staff member explained, "It's a true Christian community here. We all care about each other and we all love each other, and we truly care about these kids that come here."[33] The emerging adults on summer staff are seasonal workers that usually live together at camp for the whole summer. During their initial days and weeks of intensive staff training, they learn the camp safety protocols and activity specifics, but even more importantly, they begin forging strong communal bonds. A strong staff community is the basis for strong cabin communities that form each week throughout the summer, and it also has the power to be incredibly impactful on the lives of the staff members. Many go on to careers in professional ministry or education. In one recent study that my research team conducted among camps in the Midwest that included more than 600 summer staff members, 98 percent agreed that they grew in their leadership abilities and 78 percent agreed that their experiences at camp have helped determine their life direction and career. Similar to camper experiences, the factors most associated with growth among the staff members included personal agency, community support, and effective conflict resolution.[34] Camp staff communities are often eclectic, full of broken people struggling to find their place in the world as they minister with and to one another. These are places of encounter, an opportunity to play.

Theological anthropology modeled in the Christian camp experience affirms a transcendent God who is present and active in interpersonal relationships as they bear witness to the relationality of God revealed in Jesus Christ. Knowledge of any kind, including knowledge of God, is contingent on interaction with the other. This reality is embedded in the very fabric of the created order, as demonstrated by psychology and neuroscience, and as revealed by the God, who is Trinity. A robust understanding of God's transcendence in immanence includes a serious look at Christian summer camp as a locus of theological creativity and human thriving. Theologians

---

33. Lutherdale Summer Staff.
34. Sorenson and Anderson, "Camp 2 Congregation."

and church leaders can learn a great deal from observing the theological playground of camp.

By attending to the significance of the Christian camp experience, other Christian communities can learn to emphasize relationship over individualism, openness over rigidity, and experimentation over stagnation. At camp, living in the Spirit becomes a way of life, not a sermon point. Relationships are built not in order to influence one another, but because that is what Jesus commanded. Questioning is not only encouraged, but the deep longings and wonderings of each individual are held in a trusted community that explores new possibilities together. Camps certainly do not always practice these virtues, and even the camps that do are far from idyllic worlds. The reality is that relationships, experimentation, and openness to questioning make for a very messy environment. Genuine encounter precipitates a mess of discomfort and vulnerability. The Spirit is at work in these messy encounters, gathering the pieces into the crucible and transforming perceived realities. Perhaps the most important thing that camp can teach the larger church is to be more comfortable with the mess.

8

On Belay: Camp Is a Safe Space

"Would you like to take one more step for me?"

Twenty feet above, Rhonda looked down at her counselor and cabinmates. "No," she replied, her voice shaky. "Can I come down now?"

Following the counselor's calm instructions, Rhonda carefully let go of the climbing pole and dangled in place momentarily, her safety rope securely held by the belay team on the ground. They slowly fed slack through the belay device, and Rhonda made a gentle landing on solid ground. She exhaled the breath she did not realize she was holding, but did not speak. Two of her cabinmates had already done the element. They had climbed all the way to the top of the high-ropes course and traversed a wobbly cable, balanced only by grasping successive ropes that dangled from above them like vines. Rhonda had not even made it to the top of the climbing pole. She looked at the ground, disappointed in herself.

"Hey," her counselor said, tapping her on the shoulder and holding up an open hand. "Good job. You made it over halfway up. That was your goal, and you did it. I'm proud of you."

Rhonda smiled tentatively and high-fived the open hand. Her cabinmates came in close and showered her with supportive words. "Great job, Rhonda!" "You did awesome, girl! No way am I going that high. Unh-uh." Rhonda took her place as the back-up belayer, as one of her cabinmates had the safety rope clipped to her harness.

"Come on," Rhonda said. "You got this!"

I watched this scene play out from a short distance outside the high-ropes course at Lutherdale Bible Camp. Rhonda was never in any physical danger. She and all her cabinmates were wearing helmets and safety harnesses, with the straps doubled-back for extra safety. The belay device that the well-trained counselor was using could stop a person from falling with the pressure from a single finger. As a further redundancy, there were two campers serving as backup belayers, able to stop a fall in case some totally unforeseen and catastrophic accident occurred. I knew from the camp director that the ropes course had been professionally inspected earlier that year and that all of the climbing ropes were retired from service after a certain number of uses. Each rope was capable of supporting more than 4,000 pounds.

Rhonda's physical safety was never in question, but there was much more at stake for her. The question was not whether it was safe for her to dangle on a cable forty feet off the ground. The question was whether it was safe for her to opt out of the activity and come down without being ridiculed or judged. Safe space at camp goes beyond physical safety to include emotional and spiritual safety. There are layers to safety in the camp environment, and each layer must be attended to, beginning with physical safety. The most effective camp experiences foster a deep sense of safety that opens the space for profound growth.

Camp Safety and Parent Expectations

Safety is the number one concern of camp directors and the most anxiety-producing element of the experience for parents. In our surveys of Christian camp directors across the United States and Canada, participant safety was rated very or extremely important by every respondent, more important than all other aspects of camp, including fun, community-building, and faith formation. Camp directors understand that camper safety is their most sacred responsibility, but not all fully understand the primal fear of parenthood.

Parents are bombarded daily with news and warnings that scare the heck out of them. They have only to flip on the news or click an online story. It appears that kids are constantly being molested, trafficked, pushed into drugs, murdered by terrorists, kidnapped, drowned in a natural disaster, dying of an infectious disease, falling behind on educational standards, or having their brains irreparably damaged with overexposure to screens. Even as a parent who understands a bit about statistics and knows that catastrophes are astronomically unlikely, I still worry about my kids. It turns out that this is an evolutionary adaptation of our species. I remember the challenge of dropping my son off at a weeklong overnight camp for the first time. I kept telling myself that he would be fine, and I was determined not to be the overprotective parent who exacerbated homesickness by refusing to go away. The crazy thing is that I had recently served as program director at that very camp. I knew the safety protocols and even wrote some of them myself. I hired some of the staff members who would be caring for my son that week. But it was still a challenge to leave him. What if he needed me? What if safety measures had grown lax in my short absence? I kept all of this inside and forced myself to go away. I was surprised at how relieved I felt when I returned on Friday afternoon and saw him from a distance, not only alive and well but also smiling from ear-to-ear.

The truth is that camps are incredibly good at keeping young people physically safe, in spite of the inherently risky activities so common at camp. Summer camp is a highly regulated industry, subject to a wide variety of safety checks, from fire safety to food service to aquatics activities to sleeping arrangements. On top of all of the strict safety standards set by state and local governments, many camps go several steps further by seeking accreditation through the American Camp Association (ACA), which sets a high bar for safety and excellence.[1] The accreditation standards are updated regularly and include such important things as staff training guidelines, minimum camper supervision ratios, risk management documentation, and safety protocols for all manner of camp activities.[2] I have been through the accreditation process as a director at two different camps, and I can attest that the standards forced me to consider many important things to which I otherwise would have remained ignorant. I have visited and observed camps across the country, some of which were accredited and others that were not. There is no better way to quickly verify the safety and excellence of a camp program than to ensure it is ACA-accredited.

We have surveyed thousands of camper parents through the Effective Camp Project, and their responses make clear that when they pick their children up on the last day of camp, the only things that really concern them are that their child is 1) safe and 2) happy. If the camp shows them that their child is alive and well, the parent will not rate the experience less than a five or six on a scale of one to ten. If the child has a smile on their face, the camp cannot get less than an eight. It is interesting to me that many camps market the experience as life-changing or transformative. From a parent's perspective, this might sound pretty dangerous; I do not want camp to change my kids because I like them as they are. I certainly do not want a camp experience that is manipulative. What I want is a safe space for them to grow and develop.

It is important to remember that defining camp as a safe space does not mean that it is free from risk or injury-proof. Every camp should be up-front about this with parents. We have spent the last few chapters discussing how

---

1. In our 2018–19 surveys of Christian camp directors, over half of Mainline Protestant camps and almost a quarter of Evangelical camps (members of CCCA) were ACA accredited.

2. American Camp Association, "Accreditation Standards."

camps build grit and community through challenging activities and help campers go outside their comfort zones by taking appropriate risks. Canoeing the Mississippi River, hiking the Rocky Mountains, riding a horse, and climbing the high-ropes course are all risky activities that have the potential for serious injury, or even death. Camps work to prevent injuries, but they also prepare for responding to accidents, injuries, lost campers, and hazardous weather. As a camp director, I made my share of trips to the emergency room with campers and staff who had broken bones, cuts that required stitches, and (in one case) a fishing hook embedded in two fingers. I am thankful that I never had to respond to life-threatening injuries or death, but I know camp directors who have. For the most part, parents understand and accept the possibility that their child could get hurt, trusting that the camp has trained medical personnel on site and emergency protocols in place. In the Effective Camp Project, we surveyed several parents whose children were injured at camp, and they reflected very positively about the experience (nine or ten out of our scale of one to ten) because of how the camp responded when their child had a broken bone or other injury. Parents also tend to agree overwhelmingly (90 percent) that it is good when campers encounter challenges and frustrations at camp because these experiences help them grow. Even so, the potential for injury makes parents justifiably nervous, and camps can work to respond with compassion.

Kidsick Parents

Beginning in the mid-2000s, I began to hear from camp directors that parents were hiding cell phones in their campers' luggage. Remember from chapter 4 that this is not because parents want their children to have cell phones at camp. In fact, they overwhelmingly want them unplugged from technology. The reason that a small number of parents go to these lengths is simple: they want to know that their child is safe. They have a primal fear that their child got lost in the woods and is being devoured by coyotes. While some writers have chosen to demean these parental tendencies as overprotective, labeling them with pejorative terms like "helicopter parents," I can understand where they are coming from.[3] When I was serving as a youth minister in eastern Pennsylvania, I was promoting a youth retreat to a local camp. One father pulled me aside and told me that he

---

3. The term *helicopter parent*, coined in 1990 by Foster Cline and Jim Fay, has become a favorite in popular culture to describe parents who are overprotective of their children to the point of smothering their personal growth and autonomy. See Cline and Fay, *Parenting with Love and Logic*, 23–25.

had signed the permission form but had crossed out the part about not bringing cell phones. He explained that earlier that week he had seen a news story about a young girl who had been kidnapped and held for days until she was able to get ahold of her assailant's cell phone and send a text message to get help.[4] He said that his daughter could go on the retreat, as long as she had a cell phone in her luggage, which would be turned off except for the most dire emergency. I was tempted to explain to this father the importance of being away in God's creation without access to our cell phones and reason with him about how astronomically unlikely that news story was to repeat itself.[5] But I didn't. I realized that he was not being particularly paranoid or even unreasonable. He was seeking some shred of control and assurance. His daughter came on the retreat, and I never saw the cell phone. She is a pastor now.

Parents need reassurance because we have been conditioned to believe that this world has become exponentially more dangerous since when we were children and we have become accustomed to receiving constant updates. The archetypal parent of teenagers in the eighties or nineties was up past midnight worried sick about their children, who were repeatedly out past curfew. By 2020, the vast majority of parents knew where their children were at all times and had constant access to them via the extra appendage called a cell phone, which also served as a geopositioning device. If I am ever concerned about where my children are, I turn on a phone app that shows me their precise location.

The answer to this safety conundrum is not to give children cell phones at camp. For a variety of reasons, this would make camp considerably less safe. Some of the dangers include campers opting out of the important face-to-face interactions in favor of the lure of screen time and the very dangerous possibility of young people taking inappropriate pictures of fellow campers and posting them online. Even the ease of communication with home poses unnecessary risks. I remember being in the camp office one Tuesday morning, just getting ready to head across camp for a morning worship service, when a camper parent arrived looking rather flustered. He had come to get his son. Apparently, the boy had sent a text message at 11:00 the night before from a phone he had hidden in his luggage. He said he was miserable and wanted his dad to pick him up right away, but the father had not seen the message until that morning. He had cancelled a morning appointment and driven more than an hour to camp. Not sure exactly how to respond to this

---

4. For this remarkable story, see Associated Press, "Kidnapped Girl."

5. In fact, the story was so unique and remarkable that it was later turned into a movie called *Girl in the Bunker* in 2018.

news, I set off to morning worship with the father in tow. As we approached, we identified the man's son among his cabin group, jumping and laughing hysterically while singing an old camp favorite. I discreetly called the boy over, and his eyes widened in surprise when he saw his father.

"What are you doing here?" he asked.

It turned out that he had trouble getting to sleep the night before and had become very homesick, so he sent a quick text to his dad. He felt much better now and explained that no, of course he did not want to go home. He was having the time of his life and was scheduled to go on a horse ride that morning. The boy stayed for the rest of the week. I like to think that he became a pastor, too, but I honestly have no idea.

Every camp has strategies to care for homesick campers, but they also need to develop strategies for working with parents who are *kidsick*. Camps have begun responding creatively and compassionately to the parental need for constant updates about their children. Social media is a resource that allows camps to post status updates about how things are going throughout the day and week. Parents concerned about a weather system moving through camp can see a reassuring post letting them know that all campers are safe and accounted for in the storm shelter, passing the time with a fun game. Many camps go beyond this general status update by employing full-time media personnel to document the camp day in words, pictures, and videos. Parents can go to a secure website and view pictures or videos of their children taken that day. They also might read a brief update about what their child's camper group has been up to. For the parents who are most concerned about their children being away from their watchful eye, seeing a picture of them smiling can be a tremendous reassurance. The promise of daily updates can help convince uncertain parents that it is okay to send their children to camp, even without having to conceal a cell phone. This is an important ministry to parents. They know how important it is to empower their children to develop independence, but that does not mean it is easy to send them away. Camps are one of the safest places for young people to develop this independence, and they are equipped to help parents with this transition.

Challenges Facing Young People

There is much more than unlikely catastrophe and parental worry threatening the safety of young people today. The odd thing is that the statistics that most frightened parents in the 1990s have been declining for decades. Teen alcohol consumption is way down, and teen partying has steadily declined.[6] Gang membership has plummeted.[7] Tobacco use dropped off a cliff before resurging with the popularity of vaping, but regulations finally came in place to get this under control.[8] Teenage sex is way down, accompanied by huge drops in teen pregnancy and abortions.[9] You would think that everyone would be celebrating in the streets because of these tremendous achievements in teen safety. Instead, they are all inside on their devices. You have probably noticed some common themes among the above health indicators. They are all social activities.

We need to face the reality that all of these health risks have fallen so sharply not only because of heroic interventions (of course, there have been those, as well), but also because young people are spending less time together and more time in virtual community. There are serious consequences to these societal shifts. They have to do with isolation and loneliness. Twenge identifies an increasing number of teens who feel left out or frequently lonely. She notes, "With teens spending less time on activities that assuage loneliness, and more time on those that don't, it is not surprising that loneliness has increased."[10] The steady stream of notifications from social media apps combine with the need to manage an online presence and the continued demands of daily activities to create a climate of constant pressure for young people. Their mental health is at stake. In UCLA's annual survey of incoming college freshmen across the US, the percentage of young people indicating that in the past year they frequently felt overwhelmed by all they had to do rose sharply from 28 percent in 2008 to 39 percent in 2018. In the same time, incoming freshmen who indicated they frequently felt depressed doubled from 7 percent to 14 percent.[11] Most

---

6. Desilver, "Concerns and Challenges."

7. Desilver, "Concerns and Challenges."

8. A resurgence of teenage smoking in the mid-nineties peaked at 25 percent of twelfth-graders and 18 percent of tenth-graders smoking cigarettes daily. These numbers fell to less than 4 percent of twelfth-graders and less than 2 percent of tenth-graders by 2018. This year also saw a sharp increase in teenage vaping (Johnston et al., "Monitoring the Future," 39, 44).

9. Livingston and Thomas, "Why Is the Teen Birth Rate Falling?," paras. 9, 2, 13.

10. Twenge, iGen, 98.

11. These figures come from the 2008 and 2018 reports of the Higher Education Research Institute at UCLA, which annually surveys more than 100,000 incoming college freshmen at two- and four-year colleges and universities across the United States. Pryor et al., "American Freshman National Norms for Fall 2008"; Stolzenberg et al., "American Freshman."

troubling, the teen suicide rate has been steadily increasing since the mid-2000s, after years of decline from its high in the mid-nineties.[12]

Chap Clark observed in the early 2000s that young people were facing "systematic abandonment."[13] He traced the well-documented story of how adolescence emerged as a distinct life stage in Western culture, with things like compulsory education and the rising ubiquity of high school education through the mid-twentieth century creating a distinct adolescent culture. Clark noted that, as adolescent culture became progressively more distinct, strange, and even frightening to the majority of adults, systems emerged to support adolescent development. These systems—including schools, youth sports, youth societies, and even summer camps—served to emphasize the distinctiveness of adolescence and thereby justify their own existence. Most people now take it for granted that adolescence is so complicated that youth work is best left to the professionals, like teachers, coaches, youth ministers, and camp directors. I would not be writing this book if this were not the case! This abandonment led to the risky behavior that was so common among adolescents in the 1980s and 1990s, and Clark already observed rising feelings of isolation and loneliness in the early 2000s, just before the smartphone hit the market.

Mobile technology and virtual connectivity rapidly complexified this adolescent abandonment shortly after Clark published his book. Clark called us to task for shunting the children of our communities on professional youth workers rather than surrounding them with mentors and adult guarantors, but now this tendency has graver consequences. Online media are progressively eclipsing the youth experts in terms of time and influence. Communities that have become accustomed over the past few decades to systematically abandoning their young people to trusted professionals are ill-equipped to regain influence from online media, which are incredibly adept at captivating and retaining youth engagement.[14] The results have included further isolation of young people (from one another and from adult mentors), along with increases in anxiety and depression.

---

12. Curtin and Heron, "Death Rates," 1.

13. Clark, *Hurt 2.0*, 21.

14. In the spring of 2020, the COVID-19 pandemic closed schools across the country, forcing young people to participate in online learning and isolate from their friends, adult mentors, and family members. This experience only exacerbated the dominance of online media in the lives of young people, particularly as churches and summer camps were forced to close.

Identity Grounded in Ultimacy

Through these rapid societal shifts, the needs of the adolescent life stage have remained constant. Following developmental psychologist Erik Erikson, James Loder identifies the key task of adolescence as identity formation, which he defines as "a consistent sense of oneself."[15] He contends that there are five principal axes on which identity is built, one of which he calls the "ideological axis."[16] This axis has to do with the quest for ultimate meaning and purpose in life, which often motivates young people to adopt causes to believe in and seek out sources of truth that are trustworthy. Loder argues that each of the axes tends to become distorted when it is devoid of the transformational logic of the Spirit. Young people feel pressured to be authentic and true to themselves without connection to the spiritual resources to help them navigate their identity. Even those with positive adult mentors, like coaches, teachers, and youth ministers, face the competing ideologies of online personalities, celebrities, and YouTubers. They want something that feels right to them, and online media give them practically limitless sources of truth to explore. Some of these are positive influences and others are mostly benign, but many are deeply unhealthy, with some even designed to manipulate or radicalize young people. The abandonment of young people to online influencers creates a profoundly unsafe environment for identity formation.

Moreover, young people are compelled to establish and maintain their identity in multiple arenas, both virtual and in-person. This adds anxiety and pressure to live up to the sanitized and idealized online profiles of their peers. Many young people worry that they are failures simply because they have not yet developed a consistent sense of oneself. Their online profiles may project a veneer of confidence and authenticity that they do not feel, which serves both to veil their own hurt and place demands on their peers who feel pressured to have it all together. They hear the slogans of authenticity loud and clear: "Be yourself!" "You be you!"[17] The problem is, most have no idea how to get there, and they feel like failures for not having arrived already, even though uncertainty about identity is developmentally appropriate for their life stage. At the same time they are feeling pressured to be

---

15. Loder, *Logic of the Spirit*, 207.

16. The other four axes he identifies include the body axis, the authority axis, the love axis, and the work axis (Loder, *Logic of the Spirit*, 207).

17. Taylor describes the present age as "the age of authenticity," which features a heightened individualism and a consumer society designed to provide unique ways for people to express themselves and constantly reinvent themselves (Taylor, *Secular Age*, 473–75).

authentic, they are also living in fear of judgment that what they truly think might be wrong or silly. Online platforms thrive on ridicule, and many people seem to think that creatively mocking others is a competitive sport. Young people are cross-pressured. On the one hand, they have to discover and wholeheartedly express their authentic self. On the other hand, they cannot risk having the wrong opinion.

The camp experience is an opportunity for young people to be unplugged from the world of constant pressure and embedded in a space of caring, support, and affirmation. A week or two of safety at camp is good in and of itself. This time and space in a safe environment can also gradually break down the calcified layers and defense mechanisms guarding the self, providing opportunities for self-discovery and healthy identity formation. As one research team concluded, "Research with adolescents suggests that young people reinvent themselves through the camp experience by escaping the negative impressions of others and revising their self-identity at camp."[18] At a Christian camp, this identity formation takes place in a faith-centered environment, providing firm grounding in the gospel message. Loder explains, "Given clarity about the object of faith, Jesus Christ, and the transformational work of his spirit, the struggle to work out *who* one is only in relation to *why* one exists at all forges an identity of theological proportions."[19] Thus, campers are not simply left to their own devices in their search for identity and ideological truth, or taken to an online store to find the consumer product that might define them. Rather, they are given guidance through embeddedness in a particular community with particular truth claims. This immersion experience affirms them in their search for personal identity, while assuring them of their unconditional identity as Child of God.

The Camp Bubble

"Camp is safe."

"Safe in what way?" I asked.

"Safe to be yourself. It allows you to be who you are."[20]

I was sitting with a group of summer staff at Camp Lutherlyn in Western Pennsylvania. They had volunteered their one-hour daily break to talk with me about their camp experiences. Some were in their first year, while others had been coming back every summer since they entered college. They all

18. Garst et al., "Youth Development," 78.
19. Loder, *Logic of the Spirit*, 248 (italics original).
20. Camp Lutherlyn Staff.

agreed, and they echoed the sentiment shared by campers and staff members at camps I visited across the country, which is confirmed in other research. One study focused specifically on camp staff members found, "The camp community contrasts most staff members' home communities, particularly the camp environment as an emotionally safe place," with many saying "they are better able to show their identity—'their true self'—at camp."[21] Camp staff members in another study described the experience as living inside "the camp bubble," where they were protected from outside influences and free to grow in new ways because of a perceived isolation from their normal lives.[22] This camp bubble is created by time and space. Participants remain in the set-apart space of camp for extended periods of time, allowing them to build trust with one another and establish a new way of being, the *habitus* we discussed in chapter 4. The heightened sense of safety among staff members is partially due to the length of their tenure at camp, which can be twelve weeks or longer. However, even campers who are only at camp for five or six days experience and express feelings of profound safety.

Looking around the circle at Lutherlyn, it was clear that the staff members felt comfortable with one another. One still had patches of dirt on his face from a mud-whomping expedition earlier that day (or, perhaps, the day before), hair was braided in ridiculously eccentric ways, and the rich smells of various body odors mixed freely in the air. These were not the sanitized profiles of social media accounts. They had not put on their makeup or checked and rechecked their reflections before stepping out in public. The masks were off and humanity was laid bare. I already had been there for a couple of days mixing with the community, so they welcomed me as a camp insider. They were honest about their experiences, and they demonstrated that they were not self-conscious about expressing their feelings or about crying in front of each other. Acceptance and affirmation were unmistakably present.

At Lutherlyn, you can feel the safety and set-apartness of the camp environment settle around you like a warm blanket as you drive down the gravel road under the tree canopy and onto the camp property, the creek known as Semiconon Run forming the boundary that lets you know you have arrived. Many camps I visit have iconic entrances that help distinguish the camp property from the outside world, adding to the feeling of protection from outside forces. However, this feeling is borne out of much more than just physical boundaries. At Camp Wapo in Western Wisconsin, for example, there is no secluded road or buffer zone to let you know that you have entered

21. Garst et al., "'Growing without Limitations,'" 7.
22. Johnson et al., "Emerging Adults' Identity Exploration," 258.

another world. In fact, you can see the neighbors across the fence and people drive past the waterfront in their powerboats. But the feeling of safety is no less palpable to the campers and staff. As one Wapo camper put it, "The whole camp is like a huge safe zone."[23] It is as if everyone at camp sets out to play a game of make-believe that they are shielded from certain dangers and are going to pretend to be nicer and more respectful than they know themselves to be. The magic of camp is that because everyone is playing this same game, it turns the make-believe into reality.

Inside these safe zones, campers and staff consistently express that they are free to explore and experiment without worrying about others excluding them or judging them. Many describe this as a time of self-discovery, as if they were encountering their true selves for the first time. In particular, summer staff members often characterize their "camp selves" in contrast to who they are away from camp, almost universally referencing the identity they discover at camp as their more authentic self. Importantly, these feelings of safety extend to faith expression. Many campers and staff feel uncomfortable or even unsafe expressing their Christian faith in their school environment. They oftentimes have the impression that they are not allowed to pray or even talk about their faith in school, either because they think it is against the rules or because they might get judged or ridiculed. They indicated that camp is a place where they feel safe to talk about God, worship God, and express their faith. An essential piece of this nonjudgmental environment is feeling safe to ask questions about the faith and express doubts. They dare to ask questions like, "Do you really believe this stuff?" In the Effective Camp surveys, 89 percent of campers agreed that their questions concerning faith were taken seriously, and 82 percent agreed that they felt like they could express their doubts about God and religion. The freedom to doubt and question is essential to the camp experience. When campers feel forced or manipulated to believe a certain way, the safe space of camp breaks down. Remember the playground analogy. A safe camp environment allows participants to play with new understandings of faith without fear of judgment or ridicule.

In addition to serving as a safe zone for self-expression and exploration, camp serves as a refuge for many campers. It may be a respite from challenging or even dangerous home lives. At Camp All Saints, I spoke with campers from inner-city Dallas who contrasted the dangers of their home neighborhood with the safety and security they felt at camp. Other campers expressed relief of being in a relaxing environment away from stressful or conflict-ridden home lives. "It's a lot more peaceful here," one boy said.

---

23. Camp Wapo Girls.

"Everyone's always happy and good, when at home, well, it's not as peaceful as here."[24] In the Effective Camp Project, about 4 percent of all camper respondents indicated that they felt supported and happy at home only rarely or not at all. At some individual camps, particularly the ones that serve large numbers of at-risk campers, this number is much higher. "I was that *one camper*. I was the loner," one Lutherlyn staff member recalled. "I didn't know how to make friends because I was usually being made fun of. And camp showed me the love that I didn't get at home."[25]

Every camp director has experiences of responding to potential domestic abuse. I have vivid memories from my time as a program director of listening to campers tell heartbreaking stories of their home lives, while their trusted counselor sat with them for support and encouragement. Some of these campers were telling their stories for the first time in their lives. Since camps are mandatory reporters of domestic abuse, they can help bring vital interventions to campers in unsafe home environments. Even in circumstances where social services are already involved or unwarranted, the act of telling their stories can be empowering to young people and a part of the healing process. In the trusted camp environment, many finally feel safe to speak out.

Some camps specialize in serving young people from troubled backgrounds. Wildwood Hills Ranch in western Iowa proclaims, "We exist to transform lives and strengthen communities by providing healing, hope and God's unconditional love to children and youth at-risk."[26] They work with community organizations and state agencies to recruit campers from the foster care and juvenile justice systems. They face tremendous challenges in providing a safe space for young people when so many of them are accustomed to emotionally or physically abusive home environments.[27] Incidents and behavioral challenges are more frequent than at other camps, but the campers report feeling much more supported and freer from being bullied than in their home and school environments. Places like Wildwood Hills Ranch are intentional refuges for children whose childhood has been taken away or rocked by forces outside their control.

---

24. Camp Lutherlyn Boys.
25. Camp Lutherlyn Staff.
26. Wildwood Hills Ranch: https://www.wildwoodhillsranch.org.
27. In surveys of Wildwood Hills campers, 30 percent indicated that they felt picked on at school often or always, and 27 percent indicated they felt supported and happy at home only sometimes, rarely, or not at all. These figures are more than triple the average percentages from other camps in the Effective Camp Project.

Signs of Safety

When I was a camp counselor, I always loved working with the middle school groups because the changes between the first day and the last day of camp were so evident. Even now, when I visit camps early in the week, I look for those groups of middle school boys during group worships or songfests. They are almost unfailingly standing off to the side or in the back, looks of determined boredom and sarcasm on their faces. They look around, constantly appraising what others are doing and who might be looking at them. They are preoccupied with what other people might think if they join in with a song or a prayer, on their guard against those who might judge or ridicule them. Usually by mid-week, these same boys are jumping up and down, participating in all of the silly songs and singing their hearts out during worship, arms draped on each other's shoulders. By the end of the week, many are bold enough to share a new talent or offer a personal testimony in front of the whole camp community.

The before-and-after seems like a switch was flipped or something in the air made these young people lose their minds. What happened was much subtler and involved the gradual relaxation of many layers of protection designed to buffer the self. Through the rhythm of being together and getting to know one another, they began to trust each other. Then they slowly felt safe being vulnerable in the small-group setting, learning that they would not be ridiculed for what they said or what they did. Gradually, they internalized a profound sense of safety, freeing them not only to dance and sing with wild abandon (a la King David in 2 Sam 6:14) but also to express doubts and play with their understandings of who they are. This progression takes time and space, making camp one of the few contexts that can achieve this level of safety.

The ability to jump and sing is simply the outward sign that these previously self-conscious boys have found a safe space at camp. The signs might be different for various groups of campers. Some groups of girls, for example, have expressed relief at being away from the constant feelings of judgment based on their appearance. The outward signs of these feelings of safety are oftentimes girls who do not feel pressured to shower every day, meticulously apply makeup, or dress in certain ways. This freedom from external pressures facilitates freedom for exploration, including faith formation and expression. As one camper said, "You can focus on God, not what you're going to wear tomorrow."[28] These are outward signs that these young people have found a place to be comfortable in their own skin. When they

---

28. Camp Wapo Girls.

no longer have to be constantly self-conscious about how others are defining them, they can begin to define themselves. They are free to consider the question, "Who am I, really?"

Apart from the songfests and crowds of ungroomed, wildly gesticulating camp friends, these young people are gathering together in the context of the trusted small group. Late at night in the cabin after lights out or on a secluded nature hike, they share things that they may have never before felt comfortable expressing. If the entire camp community is a bubble where participants are safe to more freely express themselves and be comfortable in their own skin, the trusted small group is a bubble within the bubble, an added layer of trust and safety.

Security and Exploration

Each camper arrives at camp with their own unique experiences and comfort level. Consequently, what may seem safe to one camper may seem profoundly unsafe to another, whether it is traversing a ropes course or sharing deeply personal thoughts and opinions. Attachment theory is one of many theories that help to explain this phenomenon. Attachment patterns are established in infancy as each child forms attachment to the primary caregivers. John Bowlby writes, "For a person to know that an attachment figure is available and responsive gives him a strong and pervasive feeling of security, and so encourages him to value and continue the relationship."[29] These patterns continue to develop into childhood and throughout a person's life based on subsequent relationships. As Bowlby describes it, the "pathway" that each individual follows over the course of a lifetime is "determined at every moment by the interaction of the individual as he now is with the environment in which he happens then to be."[30] This means that experiences and relationships help to shape who a person understands themselves to be. Caring relationships are important because they help a person live a healthy life based on secure attachments. However, some people develop insecure or disorganized attachment patterns, which can be detrimental to psychological health. Importantly, these attachment patterns are not fixed. They are constantly being revised throughout life, so the profound safety of the camp environment can provide a place of healing and personal growth for those who are particularly at risk.

An important concept in attachment theory is the secure base. In childhood, this manifests in the ability of an infant or toddler to venture

---

29. Bowlby, *Secure Base*, 27.
30. Bowlby, *Secure Base*, 136.

away from the primary caregiver and engage in play. A child who is insecurely attached is oftentimes unable to play because she is not sure of the consistent presence of the caregiver.[31] Professional psychotherapists work to establish trust with their patients and through a process known as transference, they establish a secure base for the patient to work towards healing and self-exploration. Other nonclinical settings can also serve as safe spaces that function in similar ways.

The safe zone of camp is an important space that can offer a secure base for campers. This is done by first taking care of their physical safety and basic physical needs and, next, providing safety from casual ridicule and prejudice that young people are accustomed to at school, online, or even in their home environments. These first layers of safety are structured and enforced by rules, policies, and supervision. They should be seen as prerequisites to deeper levels of safety. To provide the secure base needed for play, exploration, and expression in the camp environment, the camp community must next foster a culture and ethos of affirmation. This is the level of safety where young people are set free from expectations of conformity. They feel free to appear unmasked before others, knowing that the community itself is affirming and does not judge based on appearance, ability, or self-identity. For campers with avoidant or resistant attachment patterns, they may constantly test the boundaries of this community of affirmation, skeptical of whether or not they can rely on camp as a secure base. Some will never truly step outside their comfort zone because they are just becoming accustomed to what it feels like to have a comfort zone. This in itself is positive growth, and campers should never be coerced to progress farther than what feels safe to them. Other campers will latch onto the secure base of camp and feel free to express themselves in new ways, stepping far outside their comfort zones and feeling safe to express their deepest thoughts, doubts, and ideas. It is important to remember that camp is not a clinical setting and camp counselors, despite what the name implies, are not psychotherapists. Part of the safety of camp is understanding the limitations of the staff and setting, always referring particular cases to professional services.

The key is to walk with each individual camper and meet them where they are in their journey. Venable and Joy write, "Ultimate respect for each camper as a unique creation and a living representation of God's love must always be shown."[32] Not every camper is going to feel comfortable expressing their deepest thoughts with one another, and part of creating a safe

---

31. This theory is based on Mary Ainsworth's work with young children and the Strange Situation. For more on the application of this theory to psychology, see Weinfield et al., "Nature of Individual Differences," 81.

32. Venable and Joy, *How to Use Camping Experiences*, 11.

space is being okay with that. I have met some camp counselors—and even encountered entire camp programs—that feel they have somehow failed if their campers do not cry by the last night of camp. As we have discussed in earlier chapters, other camps culminate in a highly emotional event that encourages participants to publicly commit their lives to Christ. While the vast majority of these camps have positive motivations, they must tread carefully when campers are so vulnerable to suggestion and manipulation. A key question to ask is whether it is safe for individual campers to feel comfortable not crying, not sharing, and not committing or recommitting their lives to Christ. Many of my Evangelical friends have expressed feeling pressured to commit to Christ at camp, fearing in the moment that there was something wrong with them if they chose not to do so. Looking back on these experiences, they have mixed emotions about them. Some see the experiences as life-changing, even if they recognize them as emotionally manipulative, but others see them as detrimental to their faith journey because they felt pressured to be inauthentic in the moment. The key metric of success at camp is not how many kids cried on the last night, or how many gave their lives to Christ, but, rather, how many felt safe, loved, and affirmed. This is how we help young people live into their identity as children of God and learn the core truth of Christ's teaching (Mark 12:28–31; John 13:34–35).

When Safety Breaks Down

Of all the five fundamentals of the Christian camp experience, safe space is the one that breaks down most frequently.[33] This often comes as a shock to camp directors because they prioritize safety above all else. Physical safety is almost never the problem. When campers are put down, judged, or ridiculed in a place they thought was safe to let down their guard and become vulnerable, it can feel like a deep violation of safety. Everything can suddenly feel fake or inauthentic, and the participant may be unwilling to trust others or show their true self in future situations after returning home from camp. This is one of the key distinctions between safe space and the other four characteristics that we have covered. In general, when one of the other characteristics breaks

---

33. Through 2019, about 9 percent of all campers participating in the Effective Camp Project showed evidence for a breakdown in the safe space measurement, which is based on frequency of being picked on, left out, or having to hide their true selves at camp, combined with a lack of feeling supported in the camp environment. Some camps were more effective at providing a safe space than others, with some having less than 5 percent of campers show evidence for a breakdown, while others were 15 percent or higher.

down (especially unplugged from home, participatory, and faith-centered), we observe in the Effective Camp Project a lack of the growth observed in most camp experiences. With breakdowns in safe space, we oftentimes observe *declines* in outcomes, particularly those related to self-confidence and the understanding that faith is relevant in daily life. Young people return home damaged, both emotionally and spiritually.

A summer staff member I worked with many years ago had spent previous summers working at another Christian camp, where she developed strong relationships with fellow staff members and felt supported enough to share her personal stories and struggles. In confidence, she revealed that she was gay. At least one of her confidants broke her trust and told the camp leadership. She was fired. I can only begin to imagine the hurt this caused a young woman who was already struggling with her identity and who now discovered that she could not be authentic, even among those whom she most trusted. In our camp community, she found a welcoming space where she could share her love of the gospel and minister to children, but she was understandably hesitant to trust the other staff members because of her past experience.

Every Christian camp summer staff I have ever worked with has had at least one person who identified as lesbian, gay, bisexual, or transgender (LGBTQ+). Some trusted me enough to share this identity while we were working together, while others did not tell me until years later. It is a sad reality that LGBTQ+ people oftentimes feel unwelcome, judged, and unloved, particularly among fellow Christians. The camp community must be a place of welcome and affirmation or it is no longer a safe space. Even if your Christian tradition is not openly welcoming, your camp can serve as a safe space where every participant feels loved for who they are and free to explore their identity.

It is clear that those most vulnerable to breakdowns in safe space at camp are the ones who have become accustomed to being left out or picked on in their home and school environments. In the Effective Camp Project, campers who indicated they were often picked on or left out at school were more than seven times more likely to say they were picked on or left out at camp compared to their fellow campers who did not have these experiences at school. Importantly, a large majority of the campers who were often picked on at school (67 percent) said they were not picked on at camp at all, indicating that camp was safer for them in many ways. However, the data are clear that they are more susceptible to breakdowns in safe space. As we have discussed, this is because they are not accustomed to having a secure base in their home and school environments. Offhanded comments or things meant to be jokes might roll off the backs of some campers but be interpreted as deeply hurtful to others. At the very least, these comments or actions may confirm that camp is not, in fact, a safe space where participants are free to let down their barriers, step outside their comfort zones, or reveal their authentic selves.

One camp that participated in the Effective Camp Project was dismayed that 20 percent of their campers showed evidence for a breakdown in safe space. The camp ministered to a large number of at-risk young people, so it was not surprising that the number was elevated, but the camp leadership was determined to improve the camp experience. They identified the afternoon activity period as a time when campers were free to travel to different activities and had less staff supervision. They received feedback from campers and parents that this centralized time felt like school recess, a time when many of these young people were accustomed to being bullied or picked on. They decided to take the simple step of restructuring the afternoon activity time so that there was more staff supervision and it felt like less of a free-for-all. The following year saw a significant decline in the percentage of campers showing evidence for a breakdown in safe space.[34] The simple intervention, which was context-specific, made the camp experience safer for participants, resulting in more positive outcomes.

Even in the context of a trusting camp community, kids are sometimes mean to each other or say hurtful things, particularly when they are tired and sleep-deprived. They sometimes have no idea whether their words and actions are directed at a resilient camper or one who is more vulnerable to feeling hurt and excluded. We are not going to put an end to all hurtful things at camp, and I contend that should not even be our goal. What we must do as camp ministers is facilitate honesty, trust, and reconciliation. This hard work can help the most vulnerable campers come to a better understanding of social interaction and strengthen their resiliency. It can also help campers become more aware of how their actions and words affect others, leading to greater empathy and compassion. The easiest thing for a camp counselor to do is to ignore or gloss over what appear to be relatively harmless incidents of banter or poking fun. This is clearly the wrong approach. What may seem harmless on the surface can lead to a breakdown in the feeling that camp is a safe space.

A longstanding tradition at many camps across the country is to play pranks on one another. In my years of working with camps, I have heard directors and program staff staunchly defend the practice as something that builds tradition, identity, and community. I have also witnessed staff members

---

34. You can read more about this case in an article I co-wrote with the camp director (Covert and Sorenson, "Power of Data," 24–32).

going way too far with pranks, causing property damage and hurt feelings. Personally, I strongly dislike pranks and think that every camp should snuff them out of existence. The truth is that they are fine and even fun for most participants, but the most vulnerable are the ones who suffer. Naysayers who dismiss hurt feelings by saying "It was just a joke" are dismissing the humanity of the other. It is long past time to reimagine these practices.

I got a lesson on this reimagining when I was program director at Sugar Creek. I remember seeing one of my cabin counselors walking off with a roll of toilet paper and some markers. When I asked what they were for, she explained that her cabin got egged the night before by another cabin group, so they were going to retaliate by toilet papering the other cabin. I remember feeling the warmth rise up my neck as I tried to remain calm. Had I been unclear during staff training about the potential dangers of pranks at camp? How could they justify wasting food? How the heck were we going to get egg off the side of a cabin on a ninety-degree day? My head must have looked ready to explode because my staff member's eyes got wide and she quickly launched into an explanation. She pulled an egg out of her bag. But it wasn't really an egg. It was a white piece of paper cut out to look like an egg, complete with a yellow yolk in the center. On it were the words, "Jesus loves you!" The rival cabin group had taped dozens of these "eggs" on the side of her cabin, each with a special message of love, affirmation, or a Bible verse. I smiled and decided to join her cabin group as they wrote similar messages on individual squares of toilet paper. I was amazed at how creative and intentional the girls were with their words. They kept egging each other on, saying that they had to get back at the rival cabin group and be even more affirming to them. I recalled the words from Rom 12:10: "Love one another with mutual affection; outdo one another in showing honor."

Each camp community is different, but they all must be spaces of safety that go far beyond caring for physical needs. They must be places where campers and staff feel loved just as they are, for they are fearfully and wonderfully made (Ps 139:14). This provides a respite from the pressures they face in the world outside the camp bubble and a secure base from which they can explore their faith and identity. Combined in a dynamic interplay with the other fundamental characteristics of camp, this opens the space for lasting growth. With our exploration of camp nearing completion, it is time to bring us home and better understand how the transformative potential of camp is actualized.

9

Taking Us Home

I walk the dusty trails, and my mind is full of memories. I come back again and again, sometimes searching, sometimes just needing to get away. This time, it is a little of both. Describing camp suddenly seems like a monumental task. I suppose it has always been that way. We ask young people to put it into words, and they struggle to describe it. Nothing quite encapsulates the feelings and emotions, so they have to settle on generic descriptors like "fun" or "awesome." I remember hearing renowned camp author and staff training expert Michael Brandwein once say, "Camp is like an inside joke. You had to be there to get it." So, I come back to the place it all started for me to try and put this into words. It would seem disingenuous to do it anywhere but here. I can almost see the faces of my friends and mentors, summer staff and directors who have walked with me on these very trails. I write haltingly, self-consciously seeking their approval.

Everywhere I go, there are memories. Over there is where one of my campers picked up a mouse by the tail and got bitten. Here is where we spotted the wheelchair constellation during my first summer at camp. This is the cabin I stayed in with both my dad and my son during a memorable father-son camp we all did together. There is where I slipped and fell off the cross while I was portraying Jesus in the Christ Hike (don't worry, the Roman centurion caught me). The place is littered with stories. As I walk, I can almost hear the laughter and singing of children. In my mind's eye, I see a group of boys running past with towels draped over their shoulders like capes and underwear on their heads. I smile. That was a great group of kids.

None of them are here. It is the first week of summer, and the place should be bustling with activity. Dozens of college-age summer staff should be engaged in training that would prepare them for a summer of ministry and a lifetime of service to Christ. But there is a global pandemic this year, and summer camps across the country have either closed or delayed their start. I walk alone, realizing there is power in this place but that it only exists because of the people and the experiences. It feels empty, reminding me that it is just a place. Yet, the place is dripping with meaning for me, making me wonder aloud, *If God is not more present in this place, then why do I feel God's presence more tangibly when I am here?* I weep as I think about all the lost memories, the campers who will not be able to come to this place and other camps this summer. I know that God is present and at work in other places, but part of the reason I know that is because of my experiences in this place.

The church existed for centuries without summer camp, so I know in some recess of my mind that the gospel will continue to be proclaimed, with or without it. The church will continue to grow and develop ecosystems that nurture life. Summer camp developed as an integral part of this faith ecology. Certainly, times change and ecosystems adapt. Some have suggested to me that summer camp has run its course.[1] Like other Christian movements over the centuries, it may be time to prune it back or simply let it die out so that new life can take root.

The COVID-19 pandemic of 2020 provided incredible clarity on this matter. The term of the pandemic was "social distancing." People needed to stay away from each other in order to reduce the risk of spreading the virus. Businesses shuttered, schools across the country transitioned to online learning, and high school seniors were unable to gather for graduation celebrations. No gathering for funerals or weddings. Technology allowed people to stay connected, which was a tremendous gift when gathering in person was not possible. But the longer social distancing guidelines went on, the clearer it became that we needed face-to-face, person-to-person encounter. People were lonely and none more so than the children and youth. The COVID-19 pandemic served as a test-run to see if we could just move everything online. The answer was a resounding no. The experience highlighted the benefits of technology at the same time as it exposed the inadequacy of virtual connection, not to mention the ongoing disparity in access. As more things transition online and young people spend more of their time on devices, we need places of experiential learning and relational encounter more than ever. Summer camp has never been more valuable. What began as a series of tender shoots in the 1880s has grown into a thriving biome that nurtures life and offers a source of fruit for the church and the world. It has become an integral part of the ecology of faith formation.

---

1. This became most vividly clear when I was in the airport on my way home from a site visit for the Confirmation Project and heard a person at a nearby gate talking loudly about the director of the camp I had just visited. The person said it felt like the director was begging for money "to save the dinosaurs." When I introduced myself to this person, I learned that it was a local pastor who thought that the camp experiment had run its course.

Dusk settles in, and my journey takes me past the pond, where I spot the empty campfire ring where hundreds of voices have lifted their praises to God and echoed their *amens* across the hills. The ashes are cold, and there is no sound of guitar or drum, but the chorus continues. I forgot how loud the frogs are. The sound is almost deafening! I look up and see the stars beginning to twinkle, and I recall the age-old words from Psalm 19: "There is no speech, nor are there words; their voice is not heard; yet their voice goes out through all the earth, and their words to the end of the world." Here is the voice that we cannot hear through the computer screen, the pages of a book, or a virtual connection. You have to be there to get it. I know that the campfire ring will not sit idle forever. Campers will once again gather together and join their voices to the chorus that is already in progress. We need places like this.

As I journey back to my cabin, I stop by the spring that cascades down the hillside in a gentle waterfall. I fill my water bottle and take a drink, savoring the familiar sweetness of the water. Sugar Creek, we call it. I get settled into my cabin and lie awake. I realize that over a thousand campers have stayed in this cabin over the years, sharing prayer requests, songs, and stories of where they saw God at work that day. I start counting all the other cabins, covered wagons, and tents on camp, each of which has housed many hundreds or thousands of campers. Then I consider that this is only one camp among thousands across the country. Each story is unique. The breadth and depth of summer camp's impact on the church and the world seems impossible to encapsulate, especially when I struggle to put my own experience into words. This is, indeed, a daunting task.

The place holds deep meaning to me because of my past experiences and memories. My longing for connection keeps me coming back to this place to drink deeply from its sweetness so that I may be sent forth again with greater clarity and renewed vision. It is not the place itself that does this, I realize. The place is meaningful and holy because of the Holy One I have encountered here time and time again. God is not more present here than in other places of my life, just more recognizable. This is a thin space, a place where it is easier for me to recognize and experience the presence of God. Camps across the country provide these thin (or liminal) spaces for millions of participants. This same God who has encountered me in this place has accompanied me through the greatest joys and deepest struggles of my life. I take another drink and savor the sweetness of being in God's presence. It is good to be here. I sleep contentedly and dream of the apostle Peter.

Leaving the Mountaintop

"Lord, it is good for us to be here." It was the quintessential mountaintop experience. Peter was with his two best friends and Jesus, their trusted guide and teacher. There on the mountaintop, away from the crowds, Peter, James, and John saw Jesus for who he truly was. His clothes became dazzling white and his face shone (Matt 17:2). They saw him talking with Moses, the great lawgiver, and Elijah, the great prophet. To top it off, the disciples actually heard the voice of God. The text is very clear that Jesus did not change. His *appearance* changed. But it was the same Jesus, the one who had gone fishing with Peter (Luke 5:1–11), healed his mother-in-law (Mark 1:31), and taken him for a memorable swim (Matt 14:31). This same Jesus would soon accompany them down the mountain and continue to walk beside them through the mundane and the extraordinary. The Mount of Transfiguration is not where Peter, James, and John met God for the first time. It is where they saw clearly that God had been present with them the whole time. This is what camp did for me.

It is not surprising that Peter wanted to savor the moment, to linger on the mountaintop. He even suggested adding a measure of permanence to the place, by building dwellings for Jesus, Moses, and Elijah. As the text says, he did not know what to say (Mark 9:6). The disciples were never meant to stay. As with other mountaintop encounters with God in the Bible (e.g., Exod 3 and 1 Kgs 19), they were called away to a place of encounter and then sent forth with a mission. The place was never the important part.[2] What was important was the person they encountered there, the one who accompanied them back into the messiness of daily life. They got very little reprieve. The moment they got to the bottom of the mountain, they had to break up an argument and care for the sick (Mark 9:14–19). But the experience had a profound impact on the disciples, serving as a rare moment of clarity amidst the challenges of taking up their cross and following Jesus. Decades after descending the Mount of Transfiguration, the experience continued to encourage the faith community in their commitment to the gospel message (2 Pet 1:16–19).

To the extent that Christian summer camp can be considered a mountaintop experience, it follows the biblical rhythm of coming away,

---

2. As if to highlight this fact, the disciples did not even report which mountain it was, and scholars still disagree about the location. This has not stopped Christians from trying to identify the mountain and turn it into a holy pilgrimage site. It is ironic that The Church of the Transfiguration, built on one of the possible mountains, is an extravagant building complete with three chapels (for Jesus, Moses, and Elijah).

encountering God, and being sent forth with renewed vision.³ The sending forth becomes the most challenging piece for the camp community because, like Peter, many camp participants want to linger. They have been immersed in what feels like an alternate reality, a liminal space suspended between the world they know and the world as it could be. Dean connects this experience with the eschatological hope of Moltmann. She writes, "What is left when camp is over is hope—hope for a return next year, hope for a new way of life on the return home, because now we live with a glimpse of what the future holds."⁴ She views the rituals of the last day at camp as one of the few times in which young people gain a bodily understanding of Christian eschatology. Everyone is aware that camp is temporary, which provides purpose to the drama of the final campfire, the last cabin group prayer, and the closing worship service. The unplugged, participatory, faith-centered, relational, safe space of camp is provisional. As participants are sent forth, they wonder how the experience will affect them and if life will be any different when they plug back into their cycle of spiritual dwelling.

Jerry Manlove flips the script on camping ministry, which is often seen as a retreat from the real world or a bubble that serves to protect participants from the outside world. Manlove suggests that the camp community is the "real world" in that it is closer to the world as it should be, as God intended it to be. He writes, "We have seen a glimpse of the kingdom. We have seen a bit of life as it should be. Working together, we create places where people can come, learn, and go out into the world to make it as it should be."⁵ Those who are sent forth from camp oftentimes have a strong desire to experience again the same love, acceptance, community, and empowerment. This leads many of them to come back to camp to try and tap into these experiences again. It also leads them to change the world, to work towards bringing the kingdom of God near to those they encounter.

At the end of each week at Camp Lutherlyn, the campers gather with their parents in the outdoor sanctuary, the same place through which the zipline passes. They receive the closing benediction:

> *Go from here as witnesses of what you have seen and heard. Share God's love with those you meet. Bring hope to those who are in despair. Live lives of gratitude and praise. May the love of God, the peace of Jesus Christ, and the ongoing presence of the Holy*

---

3. Moltmann writes, "For the people who experience themselves in the presence of the Spirit, two movements follow which are rhythmically related to one another: 1. The *gathering* of Christians in the church. 2. The mission or *sending out* of the church to Christians in the world" (Moltmann, *Spirit of Life*, 234; italics original).

4. Dean, in Root and Dean, *Theological Turn*, 170.

5. Manlove and Kettl, *Common Book of Camping*, 138.

Spirit be within you and among you until we meet again. Go as a follower of Christ, and spread the love and grace of God.[6]

This benediction mirrors the closing songs and final prayers of many camps I have visited. The words acknowledge that the participants have experienced something special at camp, but they are sent forth with an assurance that God goes with them. Notice that they are commissioned as disciples (followers of Christ) entrusted with the gospel message. Their task is to leave the mountaintop, the place of encounter, and live as faithful people in the world. Though many seek to return to the place of the mountaintop experience, we do not live our lives as a series of mountaintops. We always must remember that it is not the place but, rather, the person we encountered in that place that matters.

God of the Tabernacle

It is a simple truth that the people of God get attached to places. This happens with church buildings, camps, and other sacred spaces. This is one reason that specific pilgrimages become so popular. People have an experience or encounter with God in a particular place, and that place becomes meaningful to them, so they return and bring others with them. They want to tap into the holy. While we might acknowledge theologically that God is everywhere, there is something about following in the footsteps of others who have had experiences of God that primes us for our own experiences. For those who have attended the same church for decades, there is something wonderfully familiar about seeking the presence of God in that place. Here is where they received their first communion or publicly professed their faith in Christ. There is where their children were baptized. This is where they were mentored by the great pillars of the faith who have now passed into glory, and they now seek to pass on this faith so that a generation yet unborn may hear of all that God has done (Ps 22:29–31).

Camp is similar. One of the measures of success is that young people want to come back. In the Effective Camp Project, over 90 percent of the campers said on the last day of camp that they planned to return in the future, and over two-thirds of the campers were returning from previous years.[7] Multiple experiences provide multiple touchpoints and opportunities for

---

6. Courtesy of Deb Brut Roberts, Executive Director of Camp Lutherlyn, 2020.

7. These numbers consider all of the more than 7,000 campers that have participated in the project, regardless of age. When considering just those age 12 and over, 70 percent had attended at least once, and 34 percent had attended four or more times. The numbers varied widely from camp to camp.

encounter. However, there is also the danger of faith becoming attached to the place of camp. In both the Effective Camp Project and the Confirmation Project, I spoke with staff members who had come to rely almost exclusively on camp experiences for their faith formation. They confessed having trouble recognizing God's presence or living out their Christian faith anywhere but camp. Most had come through the ranks as campers for eight or more summers and subsequently had served on summer staff for multiple years. One of them said alarmingly, as if realizing it for the first time, "Camp is like my God."[8] This staff person described incredibly powerful encounters at camp that were interpreted as life-changing. The camp experience had all five of the fundamental characteristics intact, but it was clearly missing a key element, leading to the substitution of the place for the person. This camp did not effectively send this particular young person forth into the world. The goal of camp is not to get people to come back. The goal is to facilitate encounter and then send forth. When they return, it is only to be sent forth again.

Mount Sinai is one of the most iconic places of God encounter. There on its slopes, Moses encountered God speaking to him from a burning bush (Exod 3). After leading the people of Israel out of slavery and across the Red Sea, Moses brought them back to Sinai, where the entire nation heard the voice of God thundering from the mountain (Exod 20:18–19). They received the Ten Commandments and all the laws of Leviticus and Numbers at Sinai. Reading the text, it is plausible to conclude that God lives on Mount Sinai. Then the text takes a new theological turn. The God of Sinai gives detailed instructions for building a mobile structure called a tabernacle. It is a glorified tent, capable of being taken down and erected again as the people journeyed. The drama of Exodus concludes with the glory of the Lord filling the tabernacle (Exod 40:34–38), the tangible sign that God traveled with the people of Israel as they wandered through the wilderness. The message is clear that God does not dwell on the mountain but, rather, in the midst of the people.

Even when the Israelites settled in the promised land, they did not build the Lord a permanent structure for hundreds of years. It was the desire to consolidate imperial power under David and Solomon that led to construction of a temple, even though the Lord was ambivalent to its construction and content with the tabernacle (2 Sam 7:6–7). Solomon's temple centralized imperial power and offered a potent symbol of divine favor centered on Jerusalem and the throne of David's house. It can be seen as a way

---

8. Staff focus group, The Confirmation Project, 2015. For the sake of anonymity, I have left out the name of this camp.

of domesticating God. The structure propagated the belief that God lived on Mount Zion, the temple mount in Jerusalem, or at least rested there (since even heaven cannot contain God—1 Kgs 8:27–29). This understanding shattered when the Babylonians destroyed the temple in 587 BCE, thinking that they could destroy the enemy god and wipe out the religious culture in the process. It was the memory of the sojourner God, the God who did not dwell on a mountain or any place constructed by human hands, that sustained the Jewish faith through exile.[9] This God accompanied the people to a faraway land and showed up among the exiles in Babylon (Ezek 1). God is not contained by temple, church, camp, or any other special place of encounter. Our God is Immanuel ("God with us"—Matt 1:23), the one who accompanies us through the darkest valley (Ps 23:4), who promised to be with us always (Matt 28:20), whose hand will hold us fast even if we settle at the farthest limits of the sea (Ps 139:9–10).

Camp experiences can remind us that God does not dwell within the walls of the church building. This is a revelation to many young people, who may have only experienced a specific style of worship in a specific place. They have been raised on temple-oriented theology among people who call the church building "God's house." Without an alternative understanding of God's activity in the world, their faith may be in jeopardy once they move away from home and find themselves in feelings of spiritual exile. This is the lament of Psalm 137, which I consider the most disturbing and theologically problematic psalm in the Bible. The writer is in exile in Babylon and cannot bear to sing the Lord's song anyplace but Jerusalem. The place itself becomes this person's highest joy (v. 6), a clear distortion of understanding that culminates in the horrifying celebration of murdering babies (v. 9). If you ever wondered why it was problematic to put too much pride in a church building, camp property, or nationalist religion, turn to Psalm 137.

We neither want to set up dwellings to linger on the mountaintops nor get stuck in a temple-centered theology. Whether it is the temple, church building, camp property, or mountaintop, the culmination is in the sending. The God who thundered from Sinai tabernacles with us. The Christ whom the disciples saw in glory accompanies us. Until the day when all the valleys are lifted up and all the mountains are made low (Isa 40:4), our work is in the valleys.

---

9. Biblical theologian Walter Brueggemann points out that the Torah was compiled while the Israelites were in exile in Babylon, making the understanding of the sojourner God crucial to their ongoing faith. He writes, "The Torah is then a normative resource, rooted in the authority of Moses, for the sustenance of a peculiar community of faith and life that is displaced and without other resources" (Brueggemann, *Introduction to the Old Testament*, 42).

What Happens at Camp Does Not Stay at Camp

The five fundamental characteristics of the camp experience function in relationship to unique individuals and their life circumstances to open the space for change. Consider this response from a Camp Wapo parent observing how the camp experience impacted a particular child:

> Her mom is going through a divorce. She was sad and anxious but wanted this camp experience. She made friends, learned how to pray, learned about faith and was uplifted and healed throughout the week. It was one of the best weeks of her life according to her: "I'm not depressed, my appetite is back, I believe I can make friends in a new school, I am closer to God." This camp experience for her was the best!

Notice the particularity of this child's life circumstances and how all five fundamental characteristics of the camp experience came alongside her life story. The *unplugged* nature of camp gave her time and space away from the challenging realities of her home life, allowing her to adopt a new perspective. The camp experience was clearly *participatory*, which we glimpse from her experience of learning how to pray. The *faith-centered* nature of camp brought her closer to God and helped her interpret her experience through the lens of faith. The *relational* characteristic was clearly present, in that she made friends and gained confidence in her social skills. All of these elements combined to make the camp environment a *safe space* for her to be "uplifted" and "healed." The outcomes of this experience are related to the five fundamental characteristics, but they are specific to her unique story and the context to which she was returning, including a new school. The changes are dramatic in this case, with clear impacts related to mental health (not depressed), physical health (appetite is back), social health (can make new friends), and spiritual health (closer to God).

Throughout the preceding chapters, we have explored the characteristics of effective camp experiences and how they come alongside the lived experiences of each individual camper, such as the young girl from Camp Wapo. We have considered some of the mechanisms by which the *habitus* of camp is incorporated into the cycle of spiritual dwelling in daily life. We must bear in mind that camp is not a magic formula or a secret sauce. It does not cause change. The presence of the five fundamental characteristics opens the space for change and provides opportunities for encounter. Dramatic conversion experiences happen at camp, and this should not be surprising, but these should also not be expected of every participant. Each camper has a story as unique as the girl from Camp Wapo, and facilitating outcomes means attending to the particular story of each unique child of God. We want camps that facilitate rather than manipulate. We want playgrounds, not factories. We prefer ministry over mountaintops. It is clear that the camp experience provides the setting for encounters between the self, the other, and the holy that some of the participants describe as life-changing, but there is no time limit on the inbreaking of God, and the dance of the Spirit does not conform to our choreography.

The data are clear that camp experiences have significant, lasting impacts on the participants and their supporting networks. However, it is also clear that not everyone has a *life-changing* experience at camp. In fact, a small minority (1 to 2 percent) have poor experiences and never want to go back. The majority, however, have something in between. They have positive experiences that continue affecting them after they return home. For some, these impacts translate into lasting change through a combination of factors and experiences. For others, most of the impacts wear off after a period of days, weeks, or months. Just because some impacts wear off, however, does not mean we should dismiss the whole experience as a *camp high* that quickly fades. We can generally classify camp outcomes into four categories: immediate, subsequent, lasting, and life-changing.

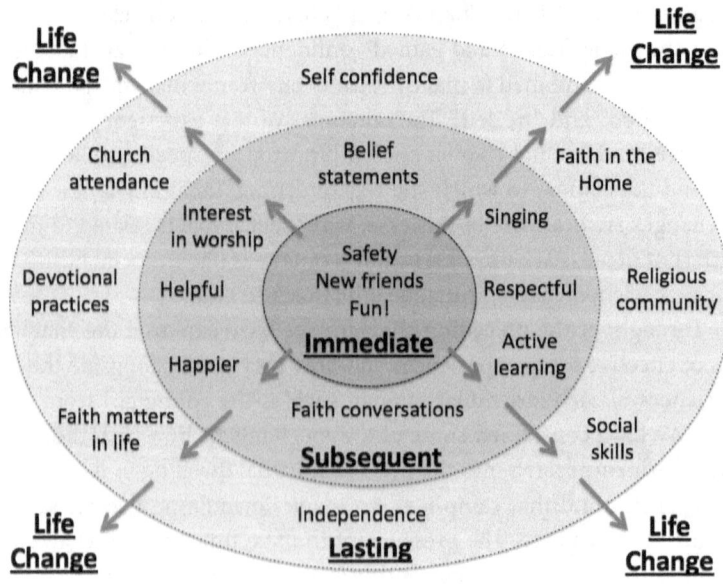

Immediate outcomes lie at the center of the camp experience and generally do not continue after a camper returns home, but that does not mean they are unimportant. Consider safety. As we noted in the previous chapter, some campers have very difficult home lives, and others are picked on or left out at school. The physical, emotional, and spiritual safety they experience at camp is good in and of itself. Fun is probably the most recognizable immediate outcome. When I was director at Cross Roads in New Jersey, we had two weeks set aside for a group of young people in residential treatment for delinquency and abuse prevention. At camp, they had two solid weeks to have fun and be kids. It was incredibly valuable for them, whether or not these outcomes lasted. A final example is new friends. Thanks to modern communication, many camp friendships continue after campers return home, but others do not. Again, that does not change or cheapen the value of these friendships, as many campers have insisted to me about the friendships they formed in previous summers.

Subsequent outcomes are the most noticeable of the camp outcomes because they impact family members and friends in the days following camp. They are also the outcomes characteristic of the so-called *camp high*. One of the first years that both of my kids went to week-long summer camp, they returned home not all that interested in playing their video games. Instead, they got out a stack of long-neglected puzzles and assembled them together. Anna and I did not expect our children to foreswear electronic devices long-term, but we were able to build some memories together, along with the puzzles. Other parents note such things as their children being more polite, more helpful around the house, nicer to other people, and generally happier. These feelings of overall positivity tend to fade over time, which does not negate their significance for the families affected. Even a few days of improved dialogue and happiness can be tremendous gifts. Other common subsequent outcomes include less dependence on electronics, an increased interest in worship services, and faith conversations. In the Effective Camp Project, young people who reported that they never or infrequently had faith conversations with their family members before camp reported having multiple conversations about God and faith in the days and weeks following camp. If these subsequent outcomes are nurtured, they can become lasting. Unfortunately, many of the young people involved in our studies went home with an increased interest in attending worship and a hope for increased agency only to find that worship services away from camp were just as boring and nonparticipatory as they remembered.

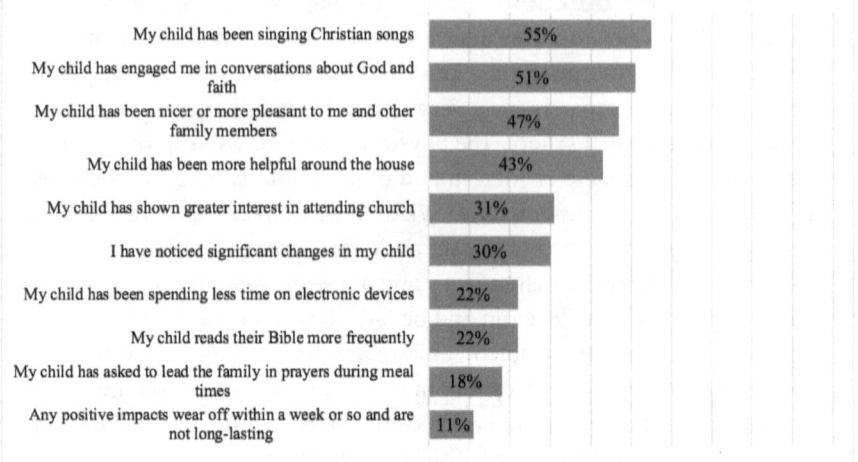

Parent respondents (N=1470) to Effective Camp and Power of Camp surveys 2015–2019 (31 camps). Percentages indicate how many identified the specified changes in their children between 1 and 4 weeks following the camp experience. 88 percent identified at least one of the specific changes, and 52 percent identified three or more.

Lasting outcomes are those still evident months after the camp experience. The euphoria and emotional boost of camp has faded into memory. Worship services may have become boring again. Learning once again involves lots of sitting still and being quiet. It is once again difficult to believe in this crazy God-story, which seemed so immediate and obvious at camp. The campers have returned to their cycle of spiritual dwelling, but they are not the same. For some, the lasting outcomes are subtle and for others, they are transformative. Self-confidence, connection with Christian community, and the conviction that faith matters in daily life are a few key examples of camp outcomes that persist months after returning home. More than two months after camp, many Effective Camp Project participants were also praying more frequently than before camp and reading their Bibles more. Their excitement about worship may have worn off, but they were attending more frequently and seeing more value in connection to Christian community.[10] They may not have been as sure or *on fire* about God as they were at camp, but they were willing to say that faith matters in their lives and that they want to know more. Discipleship,

---

10. These lasting outcomes were some of the major findings of the second phase of the Effective Camp Research Project. See Sorenson, "Fundamental Characteristics."

at its core, is not about knowing the right stuff or feeling excitement. It is about seeking the faith and following Jesus Christ. These are the lasting outcomes of the Christian camp experience.

Life-changing outcomes comprise the outer layer of camp outcomes. As we noted at the very beginning of this book, about 5 percent of camp participants characterize the experience as transformative or life-changing. Life change seldom happens all at once, and most of us only realize that an experience helped to change our lives as we look back years later. Lasting change is something we can measure and plan for. Life change and transformation is Holy Spirit territory. However, we can also recognize that the Spirit works through us to encourage and empower these young people in their lives of faith. When they are surrounded by faithful people who genuinely want to know about their camp experience, the outcomes are more likely to last. When campers come home excited about worship, they are more likely to stay excited and engaged if they are given agency and allowed to lead or actively participate. We are doing the campers a great disservice if they come home from camp and the best we as parents and Christian leaders can come up with is, "Did you have fun?" Remember, for more than 97 percent of them, the answer is a resounding yes! We can go beyond this. Surround them in Christian love, discover what they learned about God, and find out how they want to participate in God's kingdom breaking in on this earth. They are primed and ready.

Nurturing the Ecology of Faith Formation

Whether the subsequent outcomes of camp become lasting and the lasting outcomes translate into life change depends on the individual experiences of each unique camper. It strikes me that I now interpret my first summer camp experience as transformational and even life-changing, but my fellow campers may see things totally differently. We canoed the river together, sang the same songs, and had the same late-night conversations in our tent or cabin, but our experiences diverged when we left camp. We can see this in the Effective Camp Project participants, as well. In a single cabin group, there might be several campers who show clear evidence for lasting change and some that even describe the experience as transformational, while others in the group show only minor outcomes or none at all. Each individual camper is actively interpreting their experience (mostly subconsciously) in relation to their cycle of spiritual dwelling.

In chapter 4, we introduced the concept of the crucible of spiritual transformation proposed by Shults and Sandage.[11] When it comes to summer camp, we prefer the metaphor of playground to crucible, but their formulation is helpful to developing a conceptual model of Christian summer camp (see figure). The cycle of spiritual dwelling is represented at left. The young people work to make sense of their relation to the holy as they navigate relationships at home, school, church, online, and other arenas of life. The cycle of dwelling provides a degree of stability and normalcy, which are connected to feelings of comfort and safety. As Shults and Sandage point out, this cycle also leads to feelings of boredom, disappointment, and even spiritual complacency. The cycle does not assume that a person is stuck in a rut or cut off from God's presence. On the contrary, God is constantly at work in and through relationships with others. The arrows indicate that the transcendent God is breaking into temporal reality and calling the human into relationship with the holy.[12]

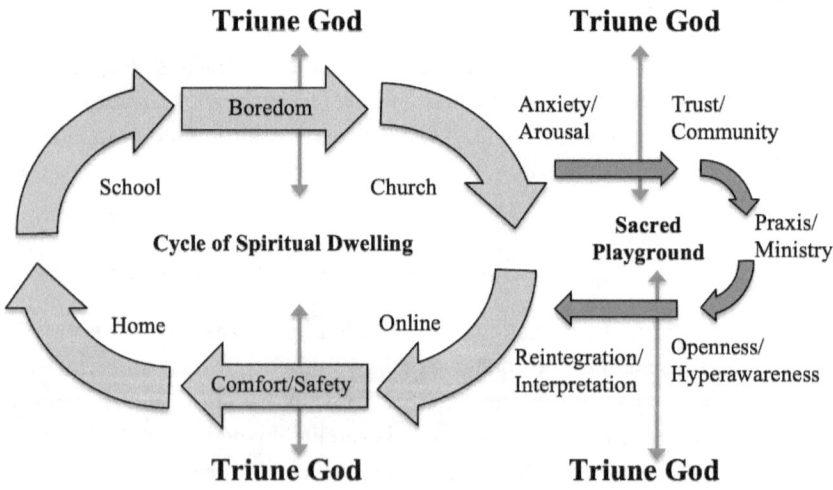

Conceptual model of camp as sacred playground

The summer camp experience is conceptualized as the sacred playground at right. Notice that the arc of the experience does not seek to

---

11. For their model, which envisions the crucible of spiritual transformation as a separate, concentric circle, see Shults and Sandage, *Transforming Spirituality*, 33.

12. This conceptual model of God's inbreaking is adapted from Anderson's understanding of God's activity in Christopraxis (Anderson, *Shape of Practical Theology*, 29).

create its own separate cycle but, rather, to lead away from and towards the ongoing cycle of spiritual dwelling. Camping experiences, pilgrimages, retreats, and other sacred playgrounds do not exist on their own but, rather, always in relationship to other embodied cultural realities. There are feelings of heightened anxiety and emotional arousal when the participant is unplugged from home and separated from the normalcy of the cycle of dwelling. These feelings of uncertainty and dislocation are held and, in many cases, soothed as the participants build trust in an intentional Christian community and discover that it is a safe space. This community is the context for shared Christian praxis and ministry to one another. The emotional arousal combined with the embeddedness in a community of Christopraxis creates openness to recognition of Christ's concrete presence and shared understandings of the holy. The God who is at work in the world is encountered in a new way in the faith-centered environment of camp, facilitating a hyperawareness through which young people not only identify but also participate in the activity of God. The young people feel safe to express themselves in ways that feel authentic, creating a sense of freedom to explore and play with their beliefs.

The trajectory of the experience leads back to the cycle of spiritual dwelling, and there is a critical period of reintegration when the participants interpret the experience in connection with their relationships away from camp. This reintegration is the locus of spiritual transformation, or more critical understanding of themselves in relation to others and the holy. This is the moment when the zipline ends and the supportive community comes with the ladder to help the participant down to solid ground and helps the participant make sense of what has happened. The empirical data make clear that camp does not end with the closing worship service or the final goodbye. Participants leave camp thinking more deeply about their faith, even calling some assumptions into question. The days and weeks immediately following the camp week are critical to the long-term interpretation of the experience as a whole.

Some congregations and families get nervous when young people explore their own theological voices. One of the great tragedies of the Christian camp experience is when an empowered young person returns to a home community hoping to have a voice and is instead stifled. The young person may be forced back into a cycle of spiritual dwelling that is no longer comfortable. Instead of acknowledging spiritual growth in the young person and their own potential for transformation in an encounter with that young person, adults demand that the young person reintegrate without change. These adults, who may be well-meaning church leaders, are operating under a theological anthropology that does not take into account an expectation for spiritual transformation. These families and faith communities are missing tremendous opportunities for spiritual growth, and they are inauthenticating genuine spiritual transformation in favor of the rigidity of the status quo. Camp participants need help making sense of the experience as they return to a home and a church that seem like different places in light of what they have learned about themselves and God. They return excited about a faith that matters and feel empowered to do something about it. They do not need a dose of *real* theology. They need opportunities to put their faith into action and through theological praxis to have an impact on other people's understandings of God and faith. They need accompaniment. They need ministry and ongoing opportunities to minister to others.

The readiness and even eagerness of campers to participate in kingdom work when they return home reminds us that Christian summer camp is not a standalone ministry. It is part of a much larger ecology of faith formation that includes congregations, homes, and other expressions of the church. Contrary to many interpretations of a mountaintop experience, the point is not to get a spiritual high. Like Peter, James, and John on the Mount of Transfiguration, the experience is about encounter and recognition. This makes camp and any other camplike or mountaintop experience (such as mission trips, conferences, and retreats) supplemental. We have already noted that Christianity got along just fine without summer camp for hundreds of years. The movement has grown into a vibrant ministry, but it is only integral as far as it nurtures and supports the larger ecology of the church. Because of this, every camp experience must have an eye toward reintegration into the participant's cycle of spiritual dwelling, particularly looking to supplement the ministry of the congregation and the home. I have characterized this as the *integrated* model of Christian camping, in which faith-centered camp experiences are intentionally connected to congregational ministries. As we seek to impact campers long-term, the integrated approach is much more effective than the *disconnected* model.

Congregational Connection

For a small number of participants, the Christian camp experience is their first introduction to living a life of faith, but this is far from the norm. Even camps that seek out unchurched young people draw participants who have some faith background in the home or a loose connection to congregational ministries. In the Effective Camp Project, only 11 percent of the more than 7,000 participants were not church attendees. Even among the more evangelical camps that sought out unchurched participants, fewer than half were almost totally disengaged from church. More than three-quarters of the Effective Camp participants attended church at least monthly, and nearly half attended almost every week. This means that for the vast majority of camp participants, the experience comes alongside a faith journey that is already in progress, though sometimes haltingly, through congregational ministry. If camps and congregations see themselves as partners in ministry, they can more intentionally come alongside one another and supplement each other's programs.

The clearest long-term impact of the Christian summer camp experience is that it promotes connection to Christian community. Campers in the Effective Camp Project and the Confirmation Project left more interested in congregational ministry and more clearly understanding that they had something important to offer the church and the world.[13] Participants in the National Study of Youth and Religion were significantly more likely to participate in communal religious practices, including increased church attendance, as young adults if they had at least one religious summer camp experience as children or youth.[14] These impacts were evident at least five years later, highlighting the role of camp as a supplemental ministry that effectively nurtures ongoing faith formation in other settings.

In order to strengthen these impacts, we can work to nurture relationships between camps and congregations. The intentional connections between these ministries have suffered in recent decades, though almost two-thirds of mainline camp directors still consider strengthening/supporting congregations as a very or extremely important part of their ministry, and more than three-quarters agree that their worship/programs are designed to get participants more excited about and engaged in their home congregations.[15] Improving camping ministries means strengthening these connections. We do not need islands of faith. We need bridges and interconnected webs of faithful interaction among ministries.

There are at least five practical steps that camps can take to nurture stronger connection to congregational ministries and adopt a more integrated approach. First, they can seek theological training for their staff members, particularly camp directors. These people are professional minsters and Christian educators, yet many of them do not have formal theological education, and data from camp director surveys show that a lack of theological education is a key predictor of a camp having a weak connection to

---

13. Osmer and Douglass, *Cultivating Teen Faith*, 76.
14. Sorenson, "Summer Camp Experience," 28.
15. These are key characteristics of *integrated* camps (Sorenson, "Outdoor Ministries Connection").

congregational ministries and denominational teachings.[16] Second, camps must be intentional about hiring people of faith, especially their summer staff members. The staff members have tremendous influence on the lives of the camp participants, and they form the core of the sacred community into which all other participants are welcomed. Third, camps should intentionally use the resources of their churches and theological traditions, including such things as common liturgical responses, prayers, and songs/hymns. This provides tremendous continuity between the camp and congregation, emphasizing the connection even in the context of difference. This is not to claim the superiority of a specific theological tradition but, rather, to acknowledge that theological traditions, liturgy, prayers, and music are faithful expressions of worship and theological interplay. Camp ministers can also strengthen this connection by providing worship resources to congregations so that they are empowered to include camp songs, prayers, and other camp traditions in weekly worship. Fourth, camps cannot settle for the *compartmentalized* model, which separates faith practices from fun and games, but must intentionally incorporate faith practices into all aspects of camp life. Fifth, camps should seek the wisdom and input of congregational leaders. Camp is a participatory ministry, and if congregational leaders have buy-in and meaningful input, they will more willingly encourage people to go to camp and even accompany them to camp. It can be tremendously meaningful and memorable when a pastor, youth minister, or other adult member is able to be present during the camp experience. Many of the camps in the Effective Camp Project allowed or even encouraged adults from the congregation to accompany young people to camp, usually staying in a separate space or just visiting for the day and able to check in throughout the experience during meals or specific activities. Campers who had an adult from their congregation visit them at camp showed significantly higher growth in outcomes related to congregational connection.

Home Connections

The primary locus of spiritual formation is the home. This is true whether or not the home is a place of spiritual practices or faith discussions. If we want to have lasting impacts on campers, we have to impact their family and home life. In the Confirmation Project, family faith practices had a stronger correlation with increased faith of young people than any other factor, including religious service attendance. The most significantly impactful family faith practice the research identified was family prayer at bedtime.

16. Sorenson, "Theological Playground," 159.

The authors conclude, "This suggests that if we want our children to grow in faith and develop a sense of belonging to Christian community, one of the most important things we can do is pray with them every night before bed."[17] Almost three-quarters of the Effective Camp participants said they had conversations with their family about God and faith at least sometimes.[18] Interestingly, barely half (54 percent) of campers indicated that they prayed with their family more than once a week before coming to camp, and a third did not pray with their family at all. I consider this low-hanging fruit for camp impact. Camps that take seriously their place in the ecology of faith formation should consider how their ministries can directly impact the congregation and the home. Perhaps the most basic step that camps can take is empowering campers for family prayer. This begins with the simplicity of mealtime prayers. Every Christian camp I have visited prays before meals. Unfortunately, these do not always translate into increased family prayer. Notice above that only 18 percent of parents said that their children offered to lead the family in prayer following the camp experience.

I remember when my oldest brother came home from his first camp experience. He was laughing about the funny stories and recounting some of the adventurous things his group did together. I also remember him leading the family in a camp grace. It was silly, and we all had fun with it. If memory serves, it was a grace sung to the tune of the *Superman* theme song (still a favorite at many camps after all these years). I think that was the only time we did a camp grace together. Seeing my older brother's joy upon returning home certainly primed me for my own camp experience a few years later. It strikes me, though, that not every young person is going to feel comfortable leading their family in the Superman grace. Maybe the disconnect is the sheer level of silliness, which may be appropriate at camp but not in other venues. When they understand their role in the larger ecology of faith formation, camps can adjust their programming more intentionally to bridge the gap between camp and home.

Camp Judson in Pennsylvania offers an important example. They participated in the Effective Camp Project for two years in a row.[19] Looking at the first year of survey data, they were surprised at the number of their campers who had little or no faith support in the home, including some who did not attend church at all. They decided to modify their programming for the subsequent summer in order to better minister to campers

---

17. Osmer and Douglass, *Cultivating Teen Faith*, 97.

18. Similar to the church attendance numbers, 10 percent of respondents said they did not have faith conversations with their family at all.

19. This project is known as the Power of Camp Project among CCCA member camps, and Camp Judson participated in both 2018 and 2019.

who did not have the basics of faith language. They had always prayed before meals, but they added a component on the first evening of camp that invited campers to consider the purpose and significance of prayer. It was a subtle but intentional shift that sparked conversations about prayer and increased camper participation in prayer, particularly at mealtimes. The programmatic change was very minor in the grand scheme of things, but it produced incredible results. The percentage of campers reporting that they prayed with their family four or more times per week nearly doubled from 38 percent before camp to 68 percent in the months after camp, a larger increase than any other camp in the study. These results were confirmed in the parent survey, in which the number reporting that their children asked to lead the family in prayer increased significantly from the first year to the second year of the study.

Mealtime prayers might be the low-hanging fruit, but there is opportunity for even greater impact through nightly devotions. I have been privileged to sit in for evening devotions with groups of campers across the country. It is a holy time when they share stories from the day, read a passage from the Bible, and pray together. As my friend, colleague, and mentor Rich Melheim has pointed out, if we could get what happens every night at camp to happen every night in every home, we could change the world. The camp experience makes nightly devotions part of the daily rhythm of Christian living for the cabin group, and camps can greatly enhance the ministry of the home by intentionally empowering campers to bring this practice home. In addition to songs, stories, and memories, camps can send young people forth with a plan that applies the logic of camp to their daily home rituals. This is what Melheim has done with his simple devotional method called the Faith5, which is drawn from his camp experiences and faith practices with his own family. He is another former camp counselor who became a pastor and met his wife at camp. His simple model includes sharing highs and lows, reading from the Bible, talking about how it relates to their lives, praying for one another, and blessing one another.[20] Many camps I have worked with use Melheim's model in their cabin devotions because it is easy to remember and translates easily into the home. There are other simple devotional models that can work just as well. The key is to make it systematic enough so that every camper can learn the ritual and easily teach their family.

What happens at camp should not stay at camp. It should infuse every home and congregation with new life.

20. Melheim has outlined the logic of his plan—summarized as share, read, talk, pray, bless—in detail on the website, www.faithink.com, and in his book, *Holding Your Family Together*.

The Ride Home

Another camp experience comes to an end. I pack up my things and sweep out my cabin, wondering when I will return. It was a nice trip back to Sugar Creek. I got to hike a few of the old familiar trails and see some good friends. I got caught in the rain, slipped and fell in the mud, and got to see a bobcat walk right past my cabin (a first in all my years coming here)![21] I am looking forward to getting home, telling my family about my adventures, and putting on some dry socks. My family always shares our highs and lows virtually when I am away, but it is so much better to share with them and bless them in person. The ride home is always a special time. I remember my first trip home from this place. My parents were working, so my pastor came down to drive me and my brother home. I remember it being meaningful to see my pastor validate the camp experience and take the time to be present there with us. I suspect that this validation helped me bridge the divide between camp and congregational ministry.

As a camper parent, I have really come to appreciate the experience of picking my kids up from camp. The musk of camp is so familiar by now that I do not even have to roll down the windows anymore. The ride home is the transition point, when a person has left camp but is not yet home. I love when my children talk to me about their camp experiences on the ride home. I ask them about their counselor, the new friends they made, the part that was most fun, whether they encountered something new or challenging, and where they saw God. If they get going on a story, the conversation might go on for quite a while, but they are usually not up to talking for more than a few minutes. For most of the trip, they ride in silence, looking out the window as the distance between camp and home grows shorter and shorter. They are processing, almost dreamlike. Sometimes they even fall asleep. I know they have had some great, impactful experiences at summer camp. Whether these might be considered life-changing is an open question that they will answer themselves in the coming years, but that is not really the point. They have had opportunities for encounter, and their camp experiences have come alongside and impacted their personal stories. Like every camper, they are unique children of God, and I am confident that the Holy Spirit is at work in their lives.

Camp is a set-apart space that facilitates relational encounter between the self, the other, and God. It has developed as an indispensable part of the ecology of faith formation in the Christian church, and it is worth taking seriously. There are so many miles to go on this journey. I thank you for

---

21. Note to parents: bobcats eat rabbits, not people.

accompanying me this far. Maybe this encounter has helped lead to deeper thoughts, grander visions, and new opportunities for connection. At the very least, I hope you had fun.

God be with you until we meet again.

APPENDIX A

Self-Evaluation for Camp Directors and Full-Time Staff

This resource is designed as a discussion and evaluation guide for camp directors, boards of directors, and year-round staff as they consider how they can make their ministries more effective. This is designed as a discussion guide to accompany chapters 4–8 based on the five fundamentals of Christian summer camp.

Chapter 4: Unplugged from Home

Questions for Discussion

1. What stood out to you as the most important takeaway from this chapter?

2. What specific elements of your camp are intentionally different from home?

3. Where does your camp use plugged-in technology?

4. Campers make decisions about their camp counselor, fellow campers, and sometimes their feelings about the camp experience, in general, in the first thirty to sixty seconds of interaction. How do you set up your registration process and train your staff to help campers navigate this important time of anxiety and hyperawareness?

5. How do you ensure that camp experiences vary (in specific and recognizable ways) for campers when they return year after year?

6. What is your camp doing to help with the important transition from camp to home?

7. How do you empower parents and church leaders to engage campers in conversation about camp and bring camp experiences home and to congregational environments?

Assignment

Remember that camp is an in-between space. Parents send their children to camp and receive them home again. Create a plan for resourcing campers and their parents to better prepare them for camp departure and reintegration into their home life/reimagined cycle of dwelling.

Chapter 5: Participatory

Questions for Discussion

1. What stood out to you as the most important takeaway from this chapter?
2. What are the *hard skills* that you teach at your camp?
3. Consider three important areas of the camp experience: food preparation and clean-up, activity time, and worship. With respect to each of these areas, consider as a group and record in a matrix: a) the camper's primary role in this area; b) how campers participate in the planning or leading in this area; and c) how this area can be more participatory at your camp.
4. What things at your camp are done for campers that they can take a more active role in? What one or two program areas should your team focus on for more participation?
5. In what ways are your campers challenged and allowed to take appropriate risks? What new ways can you help stretch them and help them build confidence and grit?
6. What are the *sacred cows* at your camp that staff love but are probably not the healthiest for campers?
7. Two key aspects of the participatory characteristic are experiential learning and agency. Considering what you have discussed so far today, which of these two needs the most focus, and how does your team plan to proceed toward action?

Assignment

Using the matrix you developed in question 3, identify one of the three key areas (food prep/clean-up, activity time, or worship) that you can focus on to give the campers more agency and make it more experiential. Create a plan of implementation.

Chapter 6: Faith-Centered

Questions for Discussion

1. What stood out to you as the most important takeaway from this chapter?
2. What elements of your program are *siloed* or *compartmentalized* from Christian practices and reflection?
3. What camp songs do campers and staff sing the most and get most excited about? Of these, which ones are Christian and which ones are secular?
4. How are you engaging campers in the praxis of ministry to and with one another? Do they lead worship? Do they lead songs/actions? Do they give testimonies? Do they have opportunities for intentional conflict resolution, including forgiveness/reconciliation?
5. What do you think about the encouragement to hire people of faith, even when they may come from a different Christian tradition? What might this mean for staff hiring?
6. In what ways do you intentionally connect your camp programs and the campers themselves with congregational ministries? Are there ways you can improve on this?
7. What ways can your camp connect more intentionally with the faith life in the home?

Assignment

Take a walk around your camp property, carrying your notebook and doodling utensil. Pause in different areas of camp, both inside and outside, and consider how each specific space is faith-centered. Make sure to stop at your playing fields, cabins, walking trails, and other key spaces around camp. When you pause, consider and write answers for the following questions:

> How are campers reminded that this space is faith-centered?
>
> How are campers engaged in the praxis of ministry in this space?
>
> How are your staff members trained to make faith connections in this specific space?

Chapter 7: Relational

Questions for Discussion

1. What stood out to you as the most important takeaway from this chapter?

2. When do your campers and counselors have time and space for informal conversations?

3. Make a two-column list and provide the specific program elements at your camp that are *centralized* and those that are *decentralized.*

4. Look at your lists for centralized and decentralized programming. Discuss the benefits and drawbacks of these programs, specifically considering the relational characteristic of camp. How can you prepare your staff to engage campers relationally in these spaces?

5. We briefly described the D.R.A.G. Bi.G. debriefing method in this chapter. What method do you teach your staff to use when debriefing challenge course and other activities? How can you better incorporate this method of processing into other aspects of camp life?

6. Whether you are centralized or decentralized, small-group time is critical to relational engagement. How much do you focus on group dynamics during staff training and in summer programming? How can you enhance your campers' small-group experience?

7. What is your camper:counselor ratio for each age group, and why? Under what circumstances have you exceeded this ratio? Discuss the benefits and drawbacks of sticking with a specific ratio, considering the research discussed in the lesson.

Assignment

Take an audit of the camper's initial experience, from the car turning into your camp entrance, first interaction with staff, registration process, and introductions in their camper/counselor group. Imagine how you can make this experience more welcoming, reassuring, and relational.

Chapter 8: Safe Space

Questions for Discussion

1. What stood out to you as the most important takeaway from this chapter?
2. How do you ensure that your camp is a safe space for campers to explore their identity?
3. How do you assure parents of the safety of your camp? How do you reassure parents that their children are safe *while* they are at camp?
4. Physical safety always comes first. What do you do to ensure campers' physical safety? When is your annual risk management assessment? What other checks do you have on your safety policies (aside from those required by state law), such as ACA or other accreditations?
5. Identify the specific times during the day/week when your campers are most vulnerable to being picked on, left out, put down, etc. How do you plan to mitigate the emotional and psychosocial safety risks during these times?
6. How do you train your staff to handle conflict resolution and reconciliation? Is there a specific method you teach, and are you giving this enough attention in light of the importance of this characteristic?
7. Parents' number one concern is camper safety, but they also agree overwhelmingly (89 percent): "It is good when campers encounter challenges and frustrations because these experiences help them grow." How do you balance adventure, novelty, and risk-taking (all essential elements of camp associated with the characteristics *unplugged from home* and *participatory*) with ensuring camp as a safe space?

Assignment

Conduct an emotional/psychosocial safety-risk management assessment. Make a list that includes your key programs and your key program spaces. Identify potential risks in these programs and spaces, focusing on emotional/psychosocial safety. Then describe how you work to mitigate these risks. Flag two or three programs/spaces to focus on for improvement.

Bibliography

American Camp Association. "Accreditation Standards for Camp Programs and Services." 2019.

———. "Directions: Youth Development Outcomes of the Camp Experience." Martinville, IN: Author, 2005.

Anderson, David, and Paul Hill. *Frogs without Legs Can't Hear: Nurturing Discipleship in Home and Congregation*. Minneapolis: Augsburg Fortress, 2003.

Anderson, Monica, and Jingjing Jiang. "Teens, Social Media & Technology 2018." May 31, 2018. https://www.pewresearch.org/internet/2018/05/31/teens-social-media-technology-2018.

Anderson, Ray S. *The Shape of Practical Theology: Empowering Ministry with Theological Praxis*. Downers Grove, IL: InterVarsity, 2001.

Associated Press. "Kidnapped Girl Used Ingenuity and Cellphone to Arrange Rescue." *The New York Times*, September 19, 2006. https://www.nytimes.com/2006/09/19/us/kidnapped-girl-used-ingenuity-and-cellphone-to-arrange-rescue.html.

Ball, Armand. "How the American Camp Association Has Evolved through Certain Crisis." *Camping Magazine* (September/October 2010) 35–38.

Barnett, Scott. "Aspects of Camp Ministry That Facilitate Spiritual Growth: A Study of Two Single Gender Wilderness Camps." PhD diss., Trinity International University, 2010.

Barth, Karl. *Church Dogmatics II/1*. Edited by G. W. Bromiley and T. F. Torrance. Translated by T. H. L. Parker et al. London: T. & T. Clark, 1957.

Bennett, Troy. "Camper Enrollment Continued Upward Trend in 2014." *Camping Magazine* (March/April 2014) 31–36.

Bobilya, Andrew J., et al. "Outcomes of a Spiritually Focused Wilderness Orientation Program." *Journal of Experiential Education* 33 (2011) 301–22.

Bonhoeffer, Dietrich. *Life Together*. Translated by Daniel W. Bloesch and James H. Burtness. Minneapolis: Fortress, 2005.

Bourdieu, Pierre. *Language and Symbolic Power*. Edited by John B. Thompson. Translated by Gino Raymond and Matthew Adamson. Cambridge: Harvard University Press, 1991.

———. *The Logic of Practice*. Translated by Richard Nice. Stanford: Stanford University Press, 1980.

Bowlby, John. *Attachment*. New York: Basic, 1982.

———. *A Secure Base: Parent-Child Attachment and Healthy Human Development*. New York: Basic, 1988.
Bowman, Clarice M. *Spiritual Values in Camping*. New York: American Book-Stratford, 1954.
Boyd, Danah. *It's Complicated: The Social Lives of Networked Teens*. New Haven: Yale University Press, 2014.
Browne, Laurie. "Research 360: Promising Themes from Phase 1 of the 5-Year Impact Study" (2018). https://www.acacamps.org/news-publications/blogs/research-360/research-360-promising-themes-phase-1-5-year-impact-study.
Browning, Don S. *A Fundamental Practical Theology: Descriptive and Strategic Proposals*. Minneapolis: Fortress, 1991.
Brubaker, Dale L. "History of Camp Kosciusko." Unpublished manuscript. 1993.
Brueggemann, Walter. *An Introduction to the Old Testament: The Canon and Christian Imagination*. Updated ed. Louisville: Westminster John Knox, 2012.
Bugbee, Leroy E. *He Holds the Stars in His Hands: The Centennial History of the Wyoming Annual Conference of the Methodist Church*. Scranton, PA: Wyoming Annual Conference, 1952.
Burkhardt, Mark D. "A History of Lutheran Church Camping in the United States, 1919–1949." MS thesis, Pennsylvania State University, 1982.
Bushnell, Horace. *Christian Nurture*. 1861. Reprint, Cleveland: Pilgrim, 1994.
Camp All Saints Director Interview, The Confirmation Project, 2015.
Camp All Saints Girls Focus Group, The Confirmation Project, 2015.
Camp All Saints Staff Focus Group, The Confirmation Project, 2015.
Camp Lutherlyn Boys Focus Group, The Confirmation Project, 2015.
Camp Lutherlyn Girls Focus Group, The Confirmation Project, 2015.
Camp Lutherlyn Staff Focus Group, The Confirmation Project, 2015.
Camp Stronghold Boys Focus Group, The Confirmation Project, 2015.
Camp Wapo Girls Focus Group, Effective Camp Research Project, 2015.
Camp Wapo Parent Survey, Effective Camp Research Project, 2015.
Clark, Chap. *Hurt 2.0: Inside the World of Today's Teenagers*. Grand Rapids: Baker Academic, 2004.
Clark, F. E. *The Children and the Church, and the Young People's Society of Christian Endeavor as a Means of Bringing Them Together*. Boston: Congregational Sunday School and Publishing Society, 1882.
Cline, Foster, and Jim Fay. *Parenting with Love and Logic: Teaching Children Responsibility*. Colorado Springs: Pinon, 1990.
Covert, Ed, and Jacob Sorenson. "The Power of Data." *InSite Magazine* (February/March 2020) 24–32.
Curtin, Sally C., and Melonie Heron. "Death Rates Due to Suicide and Homicide among Persons Aged 10–24: United States, 2000–2017." U.S. Centers for Disease Control and Prevention National Center for Health Statistics, 2019. https://www.cdc.gov/nchs/data/databriefs/db352-h.pdf.
Dacey, Rick. "The History of Calumet." http://www.calumet.org/about/history.
Daniel, Brad. "The Life Significance of a Spiritually Oriented, Outward Bound-Type Wilderness Expedition." *Journal of Experiential Education* 29 (2007) 386–89.
Davis, Robert Pickens. *Church Camping*. Richmond, VA: John Knox, 1969.
Dean, Kenda Creasy. *Almost Christian: What the Faith of Our Teenagers Is Telling the American Church*. New York: Oxford University Press, 2010.

Denton, Ashley. *Christian Outdoor Leadership: Theology, Theory, and Practice.* Fort Collins, CO: Smooth Stone, 2011.

Desilver, Drew. "The Concerns and Challenges of Being a U.S. Teen: What the Data Show." *Pew Research Center*, February 26, 2019. https://pewrsr.ch/2N6h9q1.

Devries, Mark. *Sustainable Youth Ministry: Why Most Youth Ministry Doesn't Last and What Your Church Can Do about It.* Downers Grove, IL: InterVarsity, 2008.

Drury, Amanda. *Saying Is Believing: The Necessity of Testimony in Adolescent Spiritual Development.* Downers Grove, IL: InterVarsity, 2015.

Duckworth, Angela. *Grit: The Power of Passion and Perseverance.* New York: Scribner, 2016.

Dweck, Carol S. *Mindset: The New Psychology of Success.* New York: Ballantine, 2016.

Eells, Eleanor. *History of Organized Camping: The First 100 Years.* Martinsville, IN: American Camping Association, 1986.

Ensign, John, and Ruth Ensign. *Camping Together as Christians.* Richmond, VA: John Knox, 1958.

Ferguson, Nancy. "Camps and Spirituality." *Camping Magazine* (March/April 2007) 47–52.

Ferguson, Nancy, and Jennifer Burch. "Religious Camps: Common Roots and New Sprouts." *Camping Magazine* (November/December 2011) 49–53.

Fleming, Laura F., and Mark W. Cannister. "Assessing the Spiritual Formation Factors Most Effectual in the Renovation and Sanctification Process of Adolescents in New England." *Journal of Youth Ministry* 9 (2010) 55–91.

Freeman, John. "A Short History of Mark Freeman and Twinlow as Told by His Son John." Courtesy of Camp Twinlow.

Fulkerson, Mary McClintock. *Places of Redemption: Theology for a Worldly Church.* New York: Oxford University Press, 2007.

Gane, Barry, and Jimmy Kijai. "The Relationship between Faith Maturity, Intrinsic and Extrinsic Orientations to Religion and Youth Ministry Involvement." *Journal of Youth Ministry* 4 (2006) 49–64.

Gardner, Howard. *Frames of Mind: The Theory of Multiple Intelligences.* New York: Basic, 2011.

Garst, Barry A., et al. "'Growing without Limitations': Transformation among Youth Adult Camp Staff." *Journal of Youth Development* 4 (2009). https://doi.org/10.5195/jyd.2009.272.

———. "Youth Development and the Camp Experience." *New Directions for Youth Development* 130 (2011) 73–87.

Gerkin, Charles V. *An Introduction to Pastoral Care.* Nashville: Abingdon, 1997.

Griffin, Jimmy. "The Effects of an Adventure-Based Program with an Explicit Spiritual Component on the Spiritual Growth of Adolescents." *Journal of Experiential Education* 25 (2003) 351.

Griffiths, Mark D. "Adolescent Social Networking: How Do Social Media Operators Facilitate Habitual Use?" *Education and Health* 36 (2018) 66–69.

Henderson, Karla A., and M. Deborah Bialeschki. "Spiritual Development and Camp Experiences." *New Directions for Youth Development* 118 (2008) 107–10.

Henderson, Karla A., et al. "Development and Application of a Camper Growth Index for Youth." *Journal of Experiential Education* 29 (2006) 1–17.

———. "Questions Raised in Exploring Spiritual Growth and Camp Experiences." *Leisure/Loisir* 33 (2009) 179–95.

Hine, Thomas. *The Rise and Fall of the American Teenager.* New York: Avon, 1999.
Hopkins, C. Howard. *History of the Y.M.C.A. in North America.* New York: Association, 1951.
Hopkins, Dwight N. *Being Human: Race, Culture, and Religion.* Minneapolis: Fortress, 2005.
James, Penny A., and Karla A. Henderson. "Camps and Nature Report." American Camp Association, June 2007. http://camps.qc.ca/files/2914/2671/0036/camps_nature_report.pdf.
Johnson, Sara K., et al. "Emerging Adults' Identity Exploration: Illustrations from Inside the 'Camp Bubble.'" *Journal of Adolescent Research* 26 (2011) 258–95.
Johnston, Lloyd D., et al. "Monitoring the Future: National Survey Results on Drug Use 1975–2018." Ann Arbor: Institute for Social Research, University of Michigan, 2019.
Juel, Don. "'Your Word Is Truth': Some Reflections on a Hard Saying." In *Shaping the Scriptural Imagination: Truth, Meaning, and the Theological Interpretation of the Bible,* edited by Shane Berg and Matthew L. Skinner, 13–32. Waco, TX: Baylor University Press, 2011.
Kidwell, Clara Sue, et al. *A Native American Theology.* Maryknoll, NY: Orbis, 2001.
Kilpatrick, William H. "Foreword." In *Camping and Character: A Camp Experiment in Character Education,* by Hedley S. Dimock and Charles E. Hendry, vii–xi. New York: Association, 1929.
Kinnaman, David. *You Lost Me: Why Young Christians Are Leaving Church . . . and Rethinking Faith.* Grand Rapids: Baker, 2011.
LaBar, Kevin S., and Roberto Cabeza. "Cognitive Neuroscience of Emotional Memory." *Nature Reviews Neuroscience* 7 (2006) 54–64.
Lanker, Jason, and Klaus Issler. "The Relationship between Natural Mentoring and Spirituality in Christian Adolescents." *Journal of Youth Ministry* 9 (2010) 93–109.
Latini, Theresa F. *The Church and the Crisis of Community: A Practical Theology of Small-Group Ministry.* Grand Rapids: Eerdmans, 2011.
Levinas, Emmanuel. *Entre Nous: On Thinking-of-the-Other.* Translated by Michael B. Smith and Barbara Harshav. New York: Columbia University Press, 1998.
Livingston, Gretchen, and Deja Thomas. "Why Is the Teen Birth Rate Falling?" *Pew Research Center,* August 2, 2019. https://pewrsr.ch/31fCuD1.
Loder, James. *The Logic of the Spirit: Human Development in Theological Perspective.* San Francisco: Jossey-Bass, 1998.
Louv, Richard. *Last Child in the Woods: Saving Our Children from Nature-Deficit Disorder.* Chapel Hill, NC: Algonquin, 2008.
Lutherdale Boys Focus Group, Effective Camp Research Project, 2015.
Lutherdale Girls Focus Group, Effective Camp Research Project, 2015.
Lutherdale Summer Staff Focus Group, Effective Camp Research Project, 2015.
Manlove, Jerry, and Mary Kettl. *A Common Book of Camping: Reflections and Learnings on Outdoor Ministries.* N.p.: Jerry Manlove, 1996.
Martinson, Roland, et al. *The Spirit and Culture of Youth Ministry: Leading Congregations toward Exemplary Youth Ministry.* St. Paul: EYM, 2010.
Mattson, Lloyd. *Christian Camping Today.* Minneapolis: River City, 1998.
Medina, John. *Brain Rules: 12 Principles for Surviving and Thriving at Work, Home, and School.* Seattle: Pear Press, 2014.

Meier, Joel F., and Karla A. Henderson. *Camp Counseling: Leadership and Programming for the Organized Camp.* Long Grove, IL: Waveland, 2012.

Melheim, Rich. *Holding Your Family Together: Five Simple Steps to Help Bring Your Family Closer to God and Each Other.* Ventura, CA: Regal, 2013.

Miller, Lee Mathers. "Lutheran Camping: A Theological Perspective." EdD diss., Columbia University, 1972.

Moltmann, Jürgen. *The Spirit of Life: A Universal Affirmation.* Translated by Margaret Kohl. Minneapolis: Fortress, 2001.

———. *Theology of Hope.* Translated by James W. Leitch. Minneapolis: Fortress, 1993.

———. *Theology of Play.* Translated by Reinhard Ulrich. New York: Harper & Row, 1972.

Niemelä, Kati. *Does Confirmation Training Really Matter? A Longitudinal Study of the Quality and Effectiveness of Confirmation Training in Finland.* Tampere, Finland: Church Research Institute, 2008.

Oman, Doug, and Carl E. Thoresen. "Spiritual Modeling: A Key to Spiritual and Religious Growth?" *International Journal for the Psychology of Religion* 13 (2003) 149–65.

Osmer, Richard, and Katherine Douglass. *Cultivating Teen Faith: Insights from the Confirmation Project.* Grand Rapids: Eerdmans, 2018.

Ozier, Lance. "Camp as Educator: Lessons Learned from History." *Camping Magazine* (September/October 2010) 24–27.

Paris, Leslie. *Children's Nature: The Rise of the American Summer Camp.* New York: New York University Press, 2008.

Penner, James, et al. "Hemorrhaging Faith: Why and When Canadian Young Adults Are Leaving, Staying, and Returning to Church." EFC Youth and Young Adult Ministry Roundtable, 2013.

Powell, Kara, and Chap Clark. *Sticky Faith: Everyday Ideas to Build Lasting Faith in Your Kids.* Grand Rapids: Zondervan, 2011.

Pryor, John H., et al. "The American Freshman National Norms for Fall 2008." Los Angeles: UCLA Higher Education Research Institute, 2008. https://www.heri.ucla.edu/PDFs/pubs/TFS/Norms/Monographs/TheAmericanFreshman2008.pdf.

Ribbe, Rob. "Redefining Camp Ministry as Experiential Laboratory for Spiritual Formation and Leadership Development." *Christian Education Journal* 9 (2010) 144–61.

Rieser, Andrew C. *The Chautauqua Moment: Protestants, Progressives, and the Culture of Modern Liberalism.* New York: Columbia University Press, 2003.

Robbins, Duffy. *Building a Youth Ministry That Builds Disciples: A Small Book about a Big Idea.* Grand Rapids: Zondervan, 2011.

Robinson, Greg. *Adventure and the Way of Jesus: An Experiential Approach to Spiritual Formation.* Bethany, OK: Wood 'N' Barnes, 2009.

Roehlkepartain, Eugene C. "Loose Bonds, Emerging Commitments: The Lives and Faith of Lutheran Youth." *Journal of Youth Ministry* 5 (2006) 93–114.

Root, Andrew. *Bonhoeffer as Youth Worker: A Theological Vision for Discipleship and Life Together.* Grand Rapids: Baker Academic, 2014.

———. *Christopraxis: A Practical Theology of the Cross.* Minneapolis: Fortress, 2014.

———. *Faith Formation in a Secular Age.* Grand Rapids: Baker Academic, 2017.

Root, Andrew, and Kenda Creasy Dean. *The Theological Turn in Youth Ministry.* Downers Grove, IL: InterVarsity, 2011.

Sales, Amy L., and Leonard Saxe. *"How Goodly Are Thy Tents": Summer Camps as Jewish Socializing Experiences*. Lebanon, NH: University of New England Press, 2004.

Schleiermacher, Friedrich. *Brief Outline of Theology as a Field of Study*. Translated by Terrence N. Tice. 3rd ed. Louisville: Westminster John Knox, 2011.

Schnitker, Sarah A., et al. "Virtue Development Following Spiritual Transformation in Adolescents Attending Evangelistic Summer Camp." *Journal of Psychology and Christianity* 33 (2014) 22–35.

Senter, Mark H. *When God Shows Up: A History of Protestant Youth Ministry in America*. Grand Rapids: Baker Academic, 2010.

Setran, David P., and Chris A. Kiesling. *Spiritual Formation in Emerging Adulthood: A Practical Theology for College and Young Adult Ministry*. Grand Rapids: Baker Academic, 2013.

Shults, F. LeRon, and Steven J. Sandage. *Transforming Spirituality: Integrating Theology and Psychology*. Grand Rapids: Baker Academic, 2006.

Siegel, Daniel J. *The Developing Mind: How Relationships and the Brain Interact to Shape Who We Are*. 2nd ed. New York: Guilford, 2012.

Smith, Christian. *Souls in Transition: The Religious and Spiritual Lives of Emerging Adults*. New York: Oxford University Press, 2009.

Smith, Christian, and Melinda Lundquist Denton. *Soul Searching: The Religious and Spiritual Lives of American Teenagers*. New York: Oxford University Press, 2005.

Sorenson, Jacob. "The Fundamental Characteristics and Unique Outcomes of Christian Summer Camp Experiences." *Journal of Youth Development* 13 (2018) 183–200.

———. "Outdoor Ministries Connection 2018 Director Survey." Lutheran Outdoor Ministries, LOM Data Report, Summer 2019.

———. "The Summer Camp Experience and Faith Formation of Emerging Adults." *Journal of Youth Ministry* 13 (2014) 17–40.

———. "A Theological Playground: Christian Summer Camp in Theological Perspective." PhD diss., Luther Seminary, 2016.

———. "Transforming the Spiritual Storehouse: A Portrait of Confirmation Camp in Finland." *Journal of Youth and Theology* 14 (2015) 172–90.

Sorenson, Jacob, and Amber Hill Anderson. "The Camp 2 Congregation Project: Summer Staff Survey Report." 2020.

Sorenson, Jacob, et al. "Effective Camp Research Project, Phase 1: Narrative Summary." May 2016. https://vibrantfaith.org/wp-content/uploads/2016/05/ECRP1-Narrative-Summary.pdf.

Stolzenberg, Ellen Bara, et al. "The American Freshman: National Norms Fall 2018." Los Angeles: UCLA Higher Education Research Institute, 2018. https://www.heri.ucla.edu/monographs/TheAmericanFreshman2018.pdf.

Sugar Creek Boys Focus Group, Effective Camp Research Project, 2015.

Sugar Creek Girls Focus Group, Effective Camp Research Project, 2015.

Sweatman, Mary M., and Paul Heintzman. "The Perceived Impact of Outdoor Residential Camp Experience on the Spirituality of Youth." *World Leisure* 1 (2004) 23–31.

Taylor, Charles. *A Secular Age*. Cambridge: Harvard University Press, 2007.

Thompson, Michael. *Homesick and Happy: How Time Away from Parents Can Help a Child Grow*. New York: Ballantine, 2012.

Thurber, Christopher, et al. "Inspirations: Developmental Supports and Opportunities of Youths' Experiences at Camp." 2006. https://www.acacamps.org/sites/default/files/resource_library/Inspirations.pdf.
Thurber, Christopher A., et al. "Youth Development Outcomes of the Camp Experience: Evidence for Multidimensional Growth." *Journal of Youth Adolescence* 36 (2007) 241–54.
Todd, Floyd, and Pauline Todd. *Camping for Christian Youth: A Guide to Methods and Principles for Evangelical Camps*. New York: Harper & Row, 1963.
Turkle, Sherry. *Alone Together: Why We Expect More from Technology and Less from Each Other*. New York: Basic, 2011.
Twenge, Jean M. *iGen: Why Today's Super-Connected Kids Are Growing Up Less Rebellious, More Tolerant, Less Happy—and Completely Unprepared for Adulthood*. New York: Atria, 2017.
Ulanov, Ann Belford. *The Unshuttered Heart: Opening Aliveness/Deadness in the Self*. Nashville: Abingdon, 2007.
UMC Lake Tahoe Camper Focus Group A, The Confirmation Project, 2015.
Van Slyck, Abigail A. *A Manufactured Wilderness: Summer Camps and the Shaping of American Youth, 1890–1960*. Minneapolis: University of Minnesota Press, 2006.
Venable, Stephen F., and Donald M. Joy. *How to Use Camping Experiences in Religious Education*. Birmingham, AL: Religious Education, 1998.
Ward, Carlos Edgar. *Organized Camping and Progressive Education*. Galax, VA: C. E. Ward, 1935.
Webb-Mitchell, Brett. *Practicing Pilgrimage: On Being and Becoming God's Pilgrim People*. Eugene, OR: Cascade, 2016.
Weinfield, Nancy S., et al. "The Nature of Individual Differences in Infant-Caregiver Attachment: Conceptual and Empirical Aspects of Security." In *Handbook of Attachment: Theory, Research, and Clinical Applications*, edited by Jude Cassidy and Phillip R. Shaver, 78–101. 2nd ed. New York: Guilford, 2008.
Williams, Florence. *The Nature Fix: Why Nature Makes Us Happier, Healthier, and More Creative*. New York: Norton, 2017.
Winnicott, D. W. *Playing and Reality*. London: Routledge, 2005.
Wuthnow, Robert. *After Heaven: Spirituality in America Since the 1950s*. Berkeley: University of California Press, 1998.
Yaconelli, Mark. *Contemplative Youth Ministry*. Grand Rapids: Zondervan, 2006.
Yeager, David. "Mindsets Matter." *Camping Magazine* (January 2020). https://www.acacamps.org/resource-library/camping-magazine/mindsets-matter.
Yernberg, Ralph. *The Camping Movement of the American Lutheran Church, Volume 1: A History of the National Camping Movement in the American Lutheran Church*. s.l.: self-published, 2003.
———. *The Camping Movement of the American Lutheran Church. The Collected Histories of Camps Related to the American Lutheran Church*. s.l.: self-published, 2003.
Yust, Karen-Marie. "Creating an Idyllic World for Children's Spiritual Formation." *International Journal of Children's Spirituality* 11 (2006) 177–88.

Index

4-H Club, 32

adventure education. *See* experiential learning
adversity leading to growth, 88, 92, 126, 132–35
agency, importance of at camp, 65, 76, 85–86, 95, 109, 169, 171
agency camps, 25, 27, 29–30, 32, 36–37
Ainsworth, Mary, 154n31
American Camp Association (ACA), 9, 29–30, 34–35, 41, 55–56, 61, 76, 130, 135, 141
Anderson, David, 119
Anderson, Ray, 87, 116
Anthony of Egypt, 18
authenticity, 107–9, 147–48, 150, 156–57, 173

Balch, Ernest, 23–25
Baptist ministries, 22–23, 37
Barnett, Scott, 87
Barth, Karl, 13, 71
Bialeschki, M. Deborah, 56
Bible study at camp, 24, 34, 59, 61, 83, 93, 112, 115–16
bodily wisdom. *See* habitus
Bonhoeffer, Dietrich, 49, 127
Bourdieu, Pierre, 81–83, 111, 131
Bowlby, John, 153
Boy Scouts of America, 28–29, 32
Boyd, Danah, 78
Brandwein, Michael, 159

Brooks, Arthur, 23, 25–26, 29–30, 32, 34, 42
Brotherhood of St. Andrew, 22
Browne, Laurie, 56
Browning, Don, 45–46
Brueggemann, Walter, 166n9
Burkhardt, Mark, 28
Burroughs, John, 19
Bushnell, Horace, 22

Camp Algonquin (NH), 24
Camp All Saints (TX), 68, 90–91, 95–96, 102–3, 150
Camp Amhek (ON), 46
Camp Amnicon (WI), 132
Camp Asquam (NH), 24, 27, 35
Camp Calumet (NH), 36
camp counselor. *See* Summer camp staff
Camp Chocorua (NH), 23–27, 35, 38
Camp Dudley (NY), 25–26, 30
camp high, 6, 53, 59–60, 168–69
Camp Judson (PA), 84, 177–78
Camp Kosciusko (IN), 28, 33
Camp Lutherlyn (PA), 63–65, 68, 77, 110, 114, 122, 148–49, 151, 163–64
Camp Marienfeld (NH), 25
camp meetings, 20, 27, 33
Camp of the Cross (ND), 36
Camp Stronghold (IL), 121–23, 126–28, 132
Camp Twinlow (ID), 32–33
Camp Wa-ba-ne-ki (PA), 32–33

Camp Wapo (WI), 76n19, 86n1, 131n25, 133–34, 149–50, 152n28, 167
Camp Wilbur Herrlich (NY), 32
Camp2Congregation Project, 137
Campfire Girls, 25–26, 28, 32
Cane Ridge revival, 20
cell phones, 79–80, 142–43. *See also* technology and camp.
centralized camping, 12, 16, 33, 35, 124–27, 133–34, 157
challenge by choice, 16, 95
challenge course. *See* low ropes challenge course
Chautauqua, 20–21, 27–29, 33
Christ walk. *See* drama at camp
Christian Camp and Conference Association (CCCA), 35, 37, 43, 56, 141n1, 177n19
Christian Endeavor, 22–23, 26–27, 30, 32–33
Christian nurture model, 16, 22, 26, 37–38, 40, 43, 60
Christomorphic, 14–15, 89
Christopraxis, 87, 102, 113–17, 173
Clark, Chap, 47, 146
Clark, Francis, 22
comfort zones, 68–69, 76, 90, 95, 114, 142, 154, 157
compartmentalized camps, 57, 61, 112–13, 176
conferences, conference model, 12, 28, 31, 33–35, 48, 125, 130n21, 174
confirmation ministries, 41, 44, 63
Confirmation Project, 58, 63, 135, 160n1, 165, 175–77
conflict resolution, 102–3, 127, 132, 137, 157
counselors. *See* summer camp staff
COVID-19 pandemic, 43, 55, 146n14, 160
creation. *See* outdoors, importance of
crisis conversion model, 16, 37–38, 40, 43, 52–53, 60, 155
Cross Roads Outdoor Ministries (NJ), 18, 74, 169
Crystal Springs Camp (MI), 28

cycle of spiritual dwelling, 73–76, 81–82, 84, 167, 170–74

Daniel, Brad, 87
Daughters of the King, 22, 26
day camp, 12
Dean, Kenda, 50–51, 111–12, 163
decentralized camping, 12, 16, 31, 35, 39, 124–26, 133
Devries, Mark, 49
Dewey, John, 31, 87, 97
differentiation. *See* independence
Directions Study (ACA), 54–56, 76, 130, 132
disconnected camps, 61–62, 118, 174
Dooly Campground (GA), 27
D.R.A.G. Bi.G. group processing, 98
drama at camp, 2, 98–100, 159
Drury, Amanda, 51, 105–6, 114
Duckworth, Angela, 92, 94
Dudley, Sumner, 23, 25
Dweck, Carol, 76, 92

ecumenical movement, 35–37, 42–43
Eells, Eleanor, 35
Effective Camp Project, 5–6, 63, 69, 76, 92, 94–95, 111, 132, 141–42, 150–51, 156–57, 164–65, 169–70, 174–77
Eliot, Charles, 31
Episcopal Camps and Conference Centers (ECCC), 26, 34, 36
Epworth League, 22, 27, 33
Erikson, Erik, 147
Evangelical Lutheran Church in America (ELCA), 36–37
experiential learning, 31, 45, 65, 86–87, 97, 100, 160

faith-centered characteristic, 61–62, 64–65, 75, 104–20, 163, 167, 173
faith formation, 6, 24, 43, 46–48, 51, 54, 56, 62, 88, 107–10, 114, 118–19, 140, 152, 160, 171–75, 179
faith immersion experience, 51, 57–58, 105, 112, 116, 118–19
faith in the home, 7, 83, 111, 114–15, 176–78

INDEX

Faith5 devotional practice, 178
family camp, 12, 39
Fellowship of Christian Athletes (FCA), 41
Finland confirmation camp, 58–61
Finney, Charles, 37
fixed mindset. See mindsets
Flathead Lake camps (MT), 36
Fortune Lake Bible Camp (MI), 33
Francis of Assisi, 18
Freeman, Mark, 32–33
fresh air movement, 19, 27
Fulkerson, Mary McClintock, 131
Fuller Theological Seminary, 37
fun at camp, 6, 46, 50, 69, 90–94, 110, 169
fundamental characteristics of Christian camp, 17, 62, 64–65, 165, 167. See also faith-centered, participatory, relational, safe space, and unplugged from home

Gardner, Howard, 97
Gerkin, Charles, 128, 135
Girl Scouts, 30
Gladden, Shonda Nicole, 130n21
Graham, Billy, 37
Gray, George, 27, 30, 32, 41–42
Great Gathering of OMC, 43
Great Recession, 41–42
Griffin, Jimmy, 88
grit, 91–92
growth mindset. See mindsets
Gulick, Luther Halsey, 26
Gunnery School, 21

habitus, 81–84, 93, 111, 113–14, 131, 167
Hahn, Kurt, 87
Hall, G. Stanley, 28
Heartland Presbyterian Center (MO), 36
Heintzman, Paul, 56–57
helicopter parents, 142
Hemorrhaging Faith Study, 52
Henderson, Hanford, 25
Henderson, Karla A., 11n8, 42, 55–56

high ropes, 64–65, 68, 84, 90, 92, 95, 97, 100, 110, 134, 139–40
Hill, Paul, 119
Hinckley, George, 23, 26, 29–30, 32, 42
Hine, Thomas, 31
Holy Spirit, work of, 3, 11, 15, 20, 64, 71–72, 88–89, 102, 138, 171
homesickness, 68, 74–75, 140, 143–44
Hopkins, C. Howard, 32
Hopkins, Dwight, 15, 130
Howells, Paul, 39
hyperawareness, 75, 90, 105, 173

identity development, 58, 74–75, 147–50, 152–53, 156–58
Imago Dei Village (WI), 133
immediate outcomes, 168–69
Incarnation Center (CT), 23, 25
inclusion, 26, 126–27, 130, 154
independence, 56, 74–76, 144
Inspirations Study (ACA), 124n6, 135–36
integrated camps, 57, 62, 82, 84, 118, 174
intentional Christian community, 101, 106, 122–24, 127, 137, 173

Jesus Camp, 9, 53
Jewish camping, 27, 57–58
Juel, Don, 115–16

Kavanagh Life Enrichment Center (KY), 28
kidsick parents, 142–44
Kimball, Lisa, 135n27
Kinnaman, David, 48
Kolb, David, 87

Lake Geneva (WI), 28
Lake Junaluska (NC), 43
Lake Okoboji camps (IA), 36
Lake Tahoe United Methodist camp (CA), 104–5, 109, 122–23, 132
Latini, Theresa, 127, 130
Levinas, Emmanuel, 129
lasting outcomes of camp, 6–7, 54–55, 65, 82–84, 114, 168–71, 175
leadership skills, 56, 86, 100, 137

LGBTQ+ community, 156
life-changing experiences at camp, 1–3, 5–7, 45, 82, 165, 167–68, 171, 179
liminality, 50, 70, 161, 163
Loder, James, 14–15, 89, 128, 130, 147
Louv, Richard, 11, 71
low ropes challenge course, 95–98, 100, 132, 134
Luther League, 23, 33
Lutherdale Bible Camp (WI), 68n2, 77n22, 79n29, 110n7, 124n5, 137n33, 139–40
Luther Park Bible Camp (WI), 95
Lutheran Church, Missouri Synod (LCMS), 36
Lutheran Outdoor Ministries (LOM), 29, 32–33, 36, 39, 44

manipulation, dangers of at camp, 9, 50, 113, 141, 150, 155
Manlove, Jerry, 39, 44, 71–72, 163
Mattson, Lloyd, 10
Medina, John, 98
Melheim, Rich, 178
Miller, Lewis, 20
mindsets, 75–76, 91–92, 95, 115
mission trips, 48, 51–52, 54, 174
Moltmann, Jürgen, 13, 71–72, 110, 163
Montreat Conference Center (NC), 33
mountaintop experience, 52, 162–66, 174
Muir, John, 19
multiple intelligences theory, 97
muscular Christianity, 27–30
music at camp, 2, 82–83, 85, 98–100, 152, 161, 176

National Council of Churches, 35, 38
National Study of Youth and Religion (NSYR), 53–54, 59, 175
natural theology, 40, 71
Niemelä, Kati, 59
nominal camps, 60–61
nones, 54

Outdoor Ministries Connection, 43
outdoors, importance of, 11, 67–68, 70–73, 80, 85–86, 89, 102, 120, 123–24, 132–34
Outward Bound, 87

parent perspectives of camp, 5–6, 74–75, 80, 131, 139–43, 167, 169–70, 179
Paris, Leslie, 19, 24, 27, 29, 32
participatory characteristic, 64–65, 85–103, 105, 109, 128, 163, 167
partnership of camp and congregation, 40, 61–62, 174–76
pastoral care, 106, 128–30, 136–37
pilgrimage, camp as, 69–70, 83, 164, 173
play, importance of, 8, 13–14, 71, 94, 109, 150–54
Positive Youth Development (PYD), 42
practical theology, 45–46, 51, 87
pranks at camp, 157–58
prayer at camp, 2, 24, 54, 83–84, 111, 115, 127, 176–78
Presbyterian Camps, Saugatuck (MI) 27, 41
Presbyterian Church Camp and Conference Association (PCCCA), 27–28, 33, 36, 41
private camps, 9, 23–27, 29–30, 32, 34–36, 38
progressive education, 31, 37, 40–41, 46–47

racism and racial diversity at camp, 26, 29, 130–31
Rayburn, Jim, 37
relational characteristic, 10–11, 13, 64–65, 109, 120–38, 153, 163, 167
retreats, 12, 39–40, 47–48, 51, 118, 142–43, 173–74
Ribbe, Rob, 45, 98, 100–101
Richter, Frank, 33
Rieser, Andrew, 20
Robbins, Duffy, 48, 52
Robinson, Edgar M., 28
Robinson, Greg, 97n26
Root, Andrew, 49, 107–9, 116–17

sacraments, sacramental, 101, 105
safe space characteristic, 64–65, 68, 80, 113, 122, 128, 139–58, 163, 167, 173
Sandage, Steven, 73, 172
Schleiermacher, Freidrich, 45
Search Institute, 51
secularity, 10, 14–15, 29, 34, 56, 106–9, 111–13
self-confidence, 6–7, 56, 125, 156, 170
Senter, Mark, 22–23, 32–33, 47
Sharp, L. B., 31, 33, 35, 39, 46, 87
Shults, F LeRon, 73, 172
Siegel, Daniel, 93, 129
Sky Ranch Lutheran Camp (CO), 132
small groups, 12, 31, 33–35, 37, 39, 109, 115, 122–29, 132, 136, 152–53
social media, 77–79, 127–29, 144–45. *See also* technology and camp
social skills, 56, 78–80, 124, 167
spiritual seeking. *See* Cycle of spiritual dwelling
spirituality, in contrast with faith formation, 38, 40–41, 43, 50, 55–57, 60
subsequent outcomes, 169
Sugar Creek Bible Camp (WI), 3, 94n22, 100n31, 158–61, 179
summer camp staff, 7, 35, 97, 101, 103, 109, 118–19, 133–37, 148–50, 156, 165, 176
Sunday, Billy, 37
Sunday school, 22, 28, 41–42, 44, 111

Taylor, Charles, 106–7, 147n17
technology and camp, 68, 72, 76–81, 86, 142–47, 160
temple theology, 165–66
Tertullian, 14–15
testimony at camp, 51, 114, 119, 152
Thompson, Michael, 74

Thoreau, Henry David, 19
Turkle, Sherry, 78
Twenge, Jean, 78, 145

Ulanov, Ann Belford, 130
United Methodist Camp and Retreat Ministries (UMCRM), 27–28, 32–33, 36
unplugged from home characteristic, 64–65, 67–84, 86, 119, 148–49, 163, 167

Van Slyck, Abigail, 29–30
Venable and Joy, 69, 122, 154
Vincent, John Heyl, 20

Walther League, 23
Ward, Carlos, 31, 34, 46
Webb-Mitchell, Brett, 69–70, 83
wilderness. *See* outdoors, importance of
Wilderness Canoe Base (MN), 36
Wildwood Hills Ranch (IA), 151
Williams, Florence, 70, 89
Winona Lake Bible Conference, 28
Winona Lake School of Theology, 37
Woodcraft Indians, 29
worship at camp, 2, 24–25, 32, 81–84, 93–94, 112–14, 118, 124–25, 133, 152, 166, 176
Wuthnow, Robert, 73n14

Yaconelli, Mark, 47
Yeager, David, 91–92
Yernberg, Ralph, 39
YMCA, 9, 19–20, 22–23, 25, 27–30, 32, 37, 39, 57, 60
Young Life, 34, 37, 41, 52
Yust, Karen-Marie, 49–50, 52, 112
YWCA, 20, 25

zipline. *See* high ropes

www.ingramcontent.com/pod-product-compliance
Lightning Source LLC
Chambersburg PA
CBHW021731220426
43662CB00008B/802